Empathic Mastery

Empathic Mastery

A 5-Step System to Go from Emotional Hot Mess to Thriving Success

Jennifer Elizabeth Moore

Des'Tai Press

ISBN: (E-book) 978-1-950984-01-5 ISBN: (Paperback) 978-1-950984-02-2
ISBN: (Hardcover) 978-1-950984-00-8 ISBN: (Audiobook) 978-1-950984-05-3
Library of Congress Control Number: 2019909948

Some names and identifying details have been changed to protect the privacy of individuals.

Although the author and publisher have made every effort to ensure that the information in this book was correct at press time, the author and publisher do not assume and hereby disclaim any liability to any party for any loss, damage, or disruption caused by errors or omissions, whether such errors or omissions result from negligence, accident, or any other cause. Because of the dynamic nature of the Internet, any web addresses or links contained in this book may have changed since publication of this book and may no longer be valid.

This book is not intended as a substitute for the medical advice of a licensed healthcare provider. The reader should consult a qualified medical professional in matters relating to his/her mental and physical health and particularly with respect to any symptoms that may require diagnosis or medical attention. The intent of the author is to share information to support you in your pursuit of empathic, emotional and spiritual wellness. In the event that you use any of the information in this book for yourself or anyone else, the author and publisher assume no responsibility for your choices and actions.

Book Design, Cover Image, Illustrations and Graphics by Jennifer E Moore
Back Cover Photograph by Jen Dean ©2018

Printed by Jennifer Elizabeth Moore in Pownal, ME in the United States of America

First Printing Edition 2019

Des'Tai Press
attn: Modern Medicine Lady LLC
P. O. Box 93
Pownal, ME 04069
USA
EmpathicMastery.com

Praise for Empathic Mastery

Empathic Mastery is SO well-written! Sometimes books about esoteric subjects feel like you're reading a college text – not this book! It's entertaining while being informative, completely accessible, and draws you in continuously.

I believe this book will give highly sensitive empathic people a roadmap to handle the dozens of situations in which they have a uniquely difficult time. It offers a step-by-step process for handling their empathic nature effectively. With these tools, they'll feel more confident, more effective, and more in control in their lives.

I'd recommend this for anyone who thinks they might be empathic or sensitive, or anyone who deals regularly with that group, including coaches, healers, and trainers. One of the best self-help books I've read in a long time!

— PAMELA BRUNER
CEO of Attract Clients Online & Co-Author
of Tapping Into Ultimate Success with Jack Canfield

"This book uplifted my heart!

Empathic Mastery is a priceless key that empaths must grasp to unlock their magnificence. The author, Jennifer Moore shares her greatest knowledge which she obtained through self-experience in conjunction with a lifetime of education. Witnessing Jennifer's path is not the only reason I highly recommend this book as a resource to enlighten, inspire, and guide anyone who struggles to serve the world through their empathic gifts. She also offers the 'how' and 'why' in practical ways that truly allow you to harness and shine YOUR light in a glorious way.

Your struggle is over, dear empath.

This is your ultimate guidebook so you can live in splendor as you share your blessed gifts."

— ANNA PEREIRA
Founder of TheWellnessUniverse.com,
CEO of SoulVentures.

Most people do not understand that our histories of childhood trauma and the stories we tell ourselves about them can leave scars that cause lasting emotional pain. In this book, one learns of the how to's with respect to getting rid of the emotional pain and gaining an understanding of why it was there. Great read.

— MARCELLE PICK, NP Co-founder of the Women to Women Clinic & Author of *The Core Balance Diet, Is It Me or My Adrenals?* and *Is It Me or My Hormones?*

I LOVE THIS BOOK!!! *Empathic Mastery* is educational, informative, immensely relatable, not bogged down by overused extensive medical jargon, and just simply amazing. It is truly a beautiful and gentle mixture of personal stories and useful information. I love how Jen writes so openly and gently guides the reader to a place of love and acceptance and comfort. I sincerely believe this journey is meant to be shared, and as a big advocate for women's community and self-care, I really appreciate that the message "you are not alone" is gracefully intertwined throughout every chapter. I love the five steps to Empathic Health; I truly wish I had this book as a tool in my teens and twenties.

— JESSICA E. SMITH, B.S. Author of *The Seven Lessons: A Gentle Guide to Embracing Change* and *Soulshine*

"*Empathic Mastery* is the perfect book for empathic women to understand how to control emotional and psychic overwhelm. This book teaches them to develop their abilities so they can be part of the solution instead of drowning in the sea of global despair and suffering. Energizing, inspiring with the right mix of down-to-earth advice, no BS, wit and clear step-by-step directions to help sensitives claim their gifts and find their purpose."

— TERRI ANN HEIMAN, Host of The Empowered Spirit Show and Author of *Confessions of A Shower Tapper*

REALLY, REALLY, mind-blowing. I am SO amazed by this book.

I have known, loved, and learned from Jen for YEARS, and yet I still discovered new and priceless information to help me understand why I am the way I am, how to protect myself, and support my many empathic clients. When you read this book you'll feel like Jen is sitting right across from you, holding sacred space and supporting you. Jen's explanation of HOW we become so sensitive, and why we can't just "let it go" gives readers a new, deeper understanding of why and how we need to care for ourselves. This book is very digestible, clear, and offers straightforward tools for immediate relief. The information strikes a nearly impossible balance between profoundly powerful and life-changing, and yet sublimely simple and easy to comprehend and apply. If you are already struggling and overwhelmed, it's like Jen is holding your hand and revealing the explanation you've been waiting your whole life for.

Empathic Mastery is written for empaths and intuitives who identify as such AND for the deeply sensitive people who've struggled through life feeling pain but aren't really sure WHY. This book is a veritable operating manual for those of us who feel ALL the feels and have struggled and suffered because we were never given the tools to cope. This book will literally change lives as it puts simple, easily applicable but profoundly powerful tools in the hands of the staggering number of people on this planet who have been searching for relief and support their whole lives.

— BRITT BOLNICK
Mentor and Owner of In Arms Coaching,
and founder of Pittie Posse Rescue

"Empath is the new black in the spiritual world these days.

So many empaths carry a ton of guilt, grief, pain and shame... now there's *Empathic Mastery*. *Empathic Mastery* is THE go-to resource for those just discovering their highly sensitive/empathic gifts and even for the seasoned intuitive. It's unlike anything else I've ever encountered on my journey. I love its candor. This book is incredibly raw and honest. It reassures us that we're not alone or broken but actually gifted, and there are others in the world like us. I hope empaths around the world read this book and discover they can master their gifts and use them for good – especially for themselves. As an Extreme Empath myself, I'll refer to this book and its incredible teachings from now on!"

— ALTHEA BRANTON
Breakup Coach & Podcast Host of "Brokenhearted"

Empathic Mastery is an absolute gem in the world of self-help books! Jennifer Moore delivers a must-read guide for all Empaths. No longer will you feel alone, no longer will you hide, no longer will you wonder, "How can I ever thrive in this overwhelming world?"

Being an Empath can be a difficult journey to navigate. Most self-care advice doesn't resonate with Empaths because it just doesn't grasp the complexity of dealing with way more than our own personal gunk. But Jennifer definitely gets it! She knows what it's like to be a walking emotional sonar and feel utterly lost and depleted as we try to navigate this world.

So the Modern Medicine Lady went to her cauldron, poured all her wisdom and experience about Empaths, the energetic body, and EFT, and brewed a potion for self-acceptance and self-love into the leaves of *Empathic Mastery*.

Jennifer lovingly holds our hand, inspires us (and also nudges us when needed!) as we take on full responsibility and ownership of our stuff, allow true release of what isn't ours, and deeply embrace our growth and expansion process.

You'll come out of this read with a deep understanding of your empathic nature, and a down-to-earth, actionable road map to become the best version of you possible. So grab a copy and get ready to create your empowered Empath life!

— SABINE MINSKY
Founder of Empath Soul, Healer & Coach

This book will go down in history as the essential guide for conscious people living in an unconscious world – everything from self-realization to the vital subject of appropriate etiquette in helping others. I can't wait to return to these pages again and again as I travel my path in health and healing. Thank you, Modern Medicine Lady!

— DEREK LIBBY, D.O.

A lot of spiritual and self-help books have crossed my path during the 25+ years that I've been a teacher and author of holistic healing. I'm always looking for a great resource to share with my students and colleagues.

Empathic Mastery is that book.

This is a guide that teaches people how to help themselves and others on all points of the empathic spectrum. For many, the path of healer and empathic sensitivity go hand in hand. Self-protection and intuitive development are tools of a successful practice. Jennifer's five-step system lays this (and so much more) out clearly and thoroughly.

Empathic Mastery is a deep, experience-based understanding of meditation, EFT, and the human energy system. It's full of candid stories and relatable experiences. I've been inspired by Jennifer's healing work for decades. I am delighted to be able to share her work and recommend this book.

— JESSICA MILLER
Author of *Reiki's Birthplace,*
A Guide to Kurama Mountain and
Founder of Reiki Mastery Institute

Empathic Mastery shares the vital message that empaths NEED to know: There is nothing wrong with us! We are, in fact, here to heal us all. This book is so timely for what so many of us are going through. It's like a guidebook for 2019! As our world goes through a period of huge transition, I believe it's necessary that empaths realize their powerful place. We do not need to feel guilt when we can't rescue, fix, or take everyone along on this journey. This book is a guide that gives our souls permission to live creatively, freely, lovingly. It validates everything we are feeling as empaths and, most importantly, lets us know we are not alone!!

— MAGGIE KNOWLES
Founder of Sugar Bee Creative and
Author of *Smoothies Gone Raw*

"There are so many people in my life who will benefit from Jen's expertise! No matter where you identify on the empathetic spectrum – if you are looking for strategies that will help reduce stress, increase awareness, and lead to a more productive life path, this book is for you! Keep one for your bookshelf and one for your lending library – you need this and others do, too!"

— ARLY SCULLY
Writer and Intuitive Healer

In *Empathic Mastery,* Jennifer Moore uses her substantial literary gifts, wisdom, and sensitivity to invite the reader into her highly empathic world. Through personal stories, creative examples, and hard-won strategies, she offers a well-worn roadmap that highly sensitive people can use to discover and value what it takes to masterfully develop their intuitive and empathic abilities. If you love someone who is highly sensitive, this book will expertly help you understand what it's like to navigate the world as an empathic child or adult.

All in all, *Empathic Mastery* offers a rare and awesome opportunity to more fully explore intuition and empathy – one that simultaneously demystifies AND holds sacred these undervalued, but deeply human, attributes.

— JADE BARBEE
Master Trainer of Trainers for EFT International

Empathic Mastery is the most useful resource for empaths I've ever read. I spent the past several years studying this topic after discovering that I am an empath. This book filled in many holes that I still had in my understanding. I was in love with this book from the introduction because you can really see that Jennifer gets empaths. It feels so great to be understood like that. As the book went on and the content became more instructional and actionable, I loved the simplicity and practicality of the advice given. As an empath myself, I can see that Jen has a deep understanding of what it's like to grow up as an empath in today's society.

This book is a must read for anyone who identifies as an empath, or a sensitive person. The book is wonderful. I really enjoyed reading it. Every time I picked it up I learned so much.

— MELISSA DAWN BEASLEY
Coach and Founder of Love Essential Skincare

Where have you been all my life?

I now have a bigger picture of who I am, what to accept, what to change, how to love myself better. This book answered questions I didn't know I had. Plus I learned actual physical world exercises to help balance my inner and outer worlds.

An excellent user's manual for Empathic and Sensitive people. What a beautiful creation!

— LUCRETIA HATFIELD
Artist and Creator of the
Visionary Heartwork Oracle System

Engaging. Mind-blowing. Needed!

Empathic Mastery assures us that we are not broken or overly sensitive. Instead, author Jennifer Moore suggests that empaths are being given valuable information that not everyone has access to. It's in our and the world's best interest to learn to be in power with this wisdom and sensitivity rather than letting it control us. This book has the power to transform many, many lives. It provides the guidance to know how to identify what is yours and what is someone else's. It validates your experience and helps you to not feel crazy because you finally have tools that allow you to feel in control. Having used these tools for myself and my four empathic daughters (soon to be five), I believe that if you go slowly and really dig into the information and techniques in this book, you'll be able to transition from feeling like a constant hot mess and shift to a sense of calmness and strength. I have no doubt this will ripple out into all areas of your life in new and surprising ways that you might not even be able imagine as you stand in the muck today.

I can't wait for this book to sit on my bookshelf and to give copies of this valuable resource to my friends and colleagues.

— CHASE YOUNG
Founder of the Mommy Rebellion Movement
and Author of *The Mommy Rebellion*

In *Empathic Mastery,* Jen provides a wonderfully detailed portrait of the myriad possibilities of ways an empath can experience the world. She links many phenomena in ways that highly sensitive folks may not have been able to connect before. Simply reading this book will be a healing experience for a hurting empath—and doing the work that Jen describes in easy-to-understand steps will only make that healing all the more powerful.

One of my favorite aspects of this book is Jen's voice: warm, funny, matter-of-fact, compassionate, hopeful, validating, reassuring, and with a deep sense of the sacred—all the while willing and able to call the reader out on any "hot messiness" that they might be trying to hold onto!

This book needs to be in the possession of anyone who is an empath, lives with empaths, or works closely with empaths. This will be a very valuable resource for mental health counselors, life coaches, and educators; I'll be recommending it enthusiastically to those professionals in my circles—and to my own bright, intense, highly-sensitive, quirky, creative clients, as well!

— KATHY ANDERSON COURCHENE M.A., LPC
Creator of the From Mis-fit to Great Fit Program

Every day more and more people are awakening to their empathic abilities. It can come as a shock when mental, emotional and energetic sensitivities are suddenly amplified. Empathic Mastery is the perfect resource. Offering practical advice, understandable explanations and doable actions, Jennifer Moore has written a book that will help empaths to deal with being highly sensitive in all aspects of their lives. This book is priceless, and exactly what we need today!

— DAWN DELVECCHIO
Author, Priestess, Business Mentor

Dedication

For the seven generations who came before us and the seven generations yet to come.

May this book offer tools to heal our past, bring ease to this moment and open the way for a better future.

I dedicate this book to the confused & anxious twenty-year-old I once was, and to all the other highly sensitive people who've been told they are "too sensitive and over-reacting" and to "just get over it."

I dedicate this especially to K and M.

To K and your sensitive heart, I wish I could have shared this long before the world wore you down to the point that stepping off this mortal coil felt like your only choice.

To M and your courageous soul, I celebrate your tenacity and your choice to stick around despite the pain. Here's to continuing to pass the open windows and asking for help even in the darkest hours.

Foreword

Imagine:

You wake up feeling an odd sense of foreboding. It's like heaviness has engulfed you. Something feels really *off*, but you don't know what. *Must be that appointment today*, you assume, as the foreboding morphs into anxiety. There's tightness in your chest and your breathing has become shallow. Looking at the clock, the feelings are pushed aside as you start your day. Shower, breakfast. News on your phone and texts from a friend in a crisis have now intensified, but you have to go! Stuck in traffic, the blaring of engines and horns feels like you're being painfully poked. With already plummeting energy, you stop for a latte to make it through the morning, only to find that after you've gulped it down, you're now feeling wired and even more anxious.

Back in the car, guilt about that friend rules your thoughts. Meanwhile, an email comes in with yet another request from a challenging client. "Oh God. Here she comes again." You're trying to figure out how you're going to meet her needs with your already overloaded schedule. Yet, you can never seem to say, "No." By 3:00 PM, you're craving another caffeine-sugar hit; otherwise, you'll fall sleep standing up. "Here she comes again." Debbie Downer messages you to dump yet another high drama story. Now you really feel awful. By dinner, you're so overwhelmed, you numb out to a Netflix binge-watch while mindlessly stuffing popcorn and ice cream in your face. Even though you're exhausted, sleep is a struggle.

Does any of this sound familiar?

Here's an alternative scenario:

You wake up with a sense of a foreboding. Curious, you reflect, "Wonder what this is." Because you've had a restful night's sleep, you're up earlier than usual, and decide to start the day with some grounding exercises, conscious breathing, and a prayer. You tap a little on the sensations you're feeling and within a couple minutes realize this doom isn't even yours. You've picked it up from a friend in a crisis. You easily release it while sending your friend love, knowing she has everything she needs to heal from this experience. Shielding well, the commute to your first appointment is gentle as you listen to an uplifting podcast in the car.

Your assistant heads your challenging client's demand off at the pass and gives them the resources they need. You had reviewed your plans with her last week and she's got your back. So 3:00 PM comes, and while most people would take a coffee break, you take a brisk walk outside to feel your connection to the earth and the sky. You remember you're so much more than a doormat who's forced to put out fires all the time. After a nourishing meal, you work on your creative project and then spend some down time listening to music as you easily drift off to a sleep.

This. Is. Absolutely. Possible.

And not only possible, completely doable. This book is the perfect companion and path to feeling safe and enjoying life on planet earth in a way you didn't know was possible.

Please know: You're. Not. Crazy.

Your vulnerable sensitivity and capacity to love deeply, the discerning of information that defies logic, the way everyone feels better after having spent time with you.

These, my dear, are your Superpowers. And you came here, at this moment in time, to use them to help save the world.

(Overwhelmed by this? Keep reading. This book is going to help you in ways nothing else out there can!) It's the story from every superhero comic ever written. What is unique and different in us, what feels like a burden and prevents us from fitting in, is what makes us special. Our inability to understand it ultimately leads to a crisis. It could be a health, financial, or relationship crisis. We are faced with our illusions and our pain. We confront all the times we've tried to force ourselves into some cookie-cutter mold. We start to understand our traumas. And in healing, we triumph! We transform! We become more and more of who we truly are! Exactly what the world needs most now.

When I met Jennifer, I saw her across a crowded conference ballroom and immediately thought, *Oh, she's one of my people.* And sure enough, she was.

As we got to know each other, we shared such similarities: a history of anxiety and depression; a profound love of God, nature, art, music, and beauty; strikingly accurate intuition; an ability to be vessels for, and facilitators of, powerful healing transformation in others; and, a dedication to getting information about EFT (Emotional Freedom Techniques, aka Tapping) into as many minds, hearts, and hands as possible.

This isn't just a book. It's a guide. A pathway. Brilliant sun cutting through the darkness. Recipes. Instructions. A manifesto. The clear roadmap for emotional wellbeing, health, and happiness. A trusted teacher. A compassionate friend. A conscious plan for mastery indeed. Read it, contemplate it, journal about it, and use it; use every single practice and tip it has to offer.

We empaths bring passion, creativity, and light into the world. This is the call of our soul. We're just born into societies that don't get it. But Jen gets it, gets US, and expresses it more profoundly than I've ever experienced.

We are not at the mercy of the pain, the overwhelm, the fears. We are Change Agents. We are Trailblazers. We are individual pieces of Universal Love. The time is NOW to understand, heal, and shine. Allow this book to show you the way.

— Kris Ferraro
Author of the #1 Amazon bestseller,
"Energy Healing: Simple and Effective Practices
to Become Your Own Healer" from St. Martin's Press

How to Use This Book

Welcome! If you're holding this book, chances are good that you've identified as an empath. In the following pages I share principles, exercises, and tools that I've discovered, developed, and refined in my personal and professional life over the last three decades. It's my deepest hope that this book will help to bring greater ease, joy, and safety to your life.

Sadly, in my 30+ years as a healer and mentor to many highly sensitive, empathic women, I have frequently witnessed the extreme price paid by those who've not learned to harness their sensitivities. This Empathic Mastery System was created to help control the distress that comes from picking up all the thoughts, feelings, and energy surrounding you. It was also designed to support the quantum shift from empathic overwhelm to embracing the benefits that come with being a responsible empath. As empaths, we are capable of either amplifying the pain and fear we absorb from the world around us, or serving as beacons for calmness, love, and healing. I believe there is far too much at stake in the world right now for us to not do everything we can to manage these traits and transform them into powerful abilities. I feel confident that mastering my five-step system: *Recognize, Release, Protect, Connect,* and *Act* will allow you to do just that.

Coming to terms with and embracing your empathic nature is the best way to be in right relationship with all the thoughts, feelings, and energy you encounter on a daily basis. I wrote this book and developed my programs for this reason, as I believe both will allow you to make the adjustments necessary to love the life you're living.

I'm not going to lie. There's no magic pill or wave of the wand that can ease the challenge of being highly sensitive and empathic. Most of us have lived like this for a long time. Just as it usually takes far longer to lose weight than to gain it, empathic mastery involves effort and persistence. I wrote this book to serve as a comprehensive guide for you. While this is a dense book, I believe that everything in it is doable.

This book is formatted into two parts. The first is designed to give you a clear and comprehensive overview of what it means to be empathic, why we are this way, and how this affects us. This section details the theories I've formed through my experiences and discoveries over the years. It is the foundation upon which the rest of the book stands.

The second part teaches the Five Steps of Empathic Mastery: *Recognize, Release, Protect, Connect* and *Act.* This is where you'll find the tools you need to manage your sensitivity and make lasting changes.

I strongly encourage you to begin by reading through from beginning to end. Even if you suspect I'm talking about things you "already know," I write from my own perspective, so you'll have a better understanding of my approach. Every explanation is written to support the action steps, so I recommend investing some time to integrate the information prior to putting it into practice.

To dive deeper, I continue this work in my online program: "Empathic Mastery Academy." The Academy is a comprehensive program that provides additional resources to help you grasp and integrate this information more fully. In this book we'll go over the big picture concepts starting with broad strokes and then narrowing down to fine brush strokes to help you better understand and navigate your empathic nature. The Academy teaches practical action steps so you can implement this system effectively and reap greater rewards. This book is designed to give you a solid foundation. Initial readers have remarked how it helped them to shift the way they operate in the world. If you feel called to pursue this further, the Academy will be ready when you are.

While this book is not religious, it does have a spiritual orientation. This guide was written for empaths and highly sensitive people from all walks of life and cultural backgrounds. There are many places where I share about Divine Source and our connection to it, as well as how prayer, meditation, and ceremony can be used to improve our lives. I believe with every fiber of my being that your relationship with your Higher Power is exactly that: your relationship. Whomever or Whatever you invoke -- God, Goddess, Buddha, Jesus, the Angels, Ganesh, Gaia, the Force, Universal Love, Spirit, or one of countless other names or guises -- is entirely up to you. I make an effort to keep names as neutral as possible, but if you find my choice of words doesn't always fit yours, replace it with one that works for you. Regardless of your faith (or lack thereof), I believe there is a reason you are reading this book right now. I trust that your Higher Power and mine arranged this Divine appointment between us.

I share many different tools and techniques in this book, but you'll find that one has particular prominence. In all my years of working with energy healing, I've never experienced anything as simple, elegant, and efficient as Emotional Freedom Techniques (EFT). (For this reason, I chose to study and eventually become an Accredited EFT Practitioner, Master Trainer and Mentor.)

Because I find EFT to be one of the most effective ways to address and clear almost anything, I teach all the basics you'll need to start using it on your own. I share this tool with far greater depth on my social media platforms, during my EFT practitioner trainings, and in the Empathic Mastery Academy. While tapping may seem a bit odd or awkward at first, I encourage you to keep an open mind and persist. My own life has transformed significantly by practicing EFT. I've also witnessed remarkable shifts for people I work with, my colleagues, and those they serve as well.

Now, I know some of us are inclined to cut to the chase and skip the explanations, going straight for the solutions. For this reason, I put a "triage" section at the end of the introduction. This way you can find support as you study the rest of this material in greater depth.

Please be aware that while the triage is designed to bring you relief, it's no substitute for doing the deeper work this system teaches. For shifts to be sustainable, we must change the way we live. Just as a crash diet yields only a temporary outcome, working with the concepts of this system is definitely a marathon, not a sprint. If you are someone who likes to skip ahead, know that you'll only be scratching the surface. To reap the full benefits of this system, please read the material thoroughly. Every section builds on the foundation of the previous one.

Once you've established a good foundation, dig into the action items. Practice the exercises. Get comfortable with them. Find the ones that work best for you and use them to connect more deeply and effectively with your abilities.

As you read this book, you may find that you need to digest it one segment at a time. Move at the pace that works best for you. When it comes to Empathic Mastery, integration is far more important than speed.

Take your time. Give yourself a chance to pause between sections. Drink a glass of water, go for a walk, invite a friend to read along with you and check in with each other to discuss and process what you've discovered. As you become more familiar with the concepts outlined in the book, I encourage you to return to them. This book is intended to be used as a manual and a resource. This is the foundation of the system that changed my life. I hope it will serve as a cornerstone for a life that is filled with ease and abundance for you too!

Greetings!

Before you jump into the deep end of the pool with me, you might want to know a little more about who I am and what I do. As you might imagine, my road to wellness and ease has been a rather convoluted one. I grew up in the lily-white suburbs of Boston, Massachusetts in a family of intellectual professionals. My mom was a nurse and my dad a social worker. I've always gravitated towards the world of magic and imagination, and spent most of my spare time making art. I knew from a very early age that I wanted to be an artist when I grew up. I was groomed to be an artist starting around fourth grade and, despite the fact that I'd heard that artists starve, I always believed I'd somehow find a way to make it.

I also knew that I perceived the world differently than most of the kids around me. Always a sensitive, I cannot recall a time in my life when I have not "picked up" feelings and had premonitions. As a preteen, I devoured every book I could find about ESP, intuition, and working to develop my psychic abilities. Being a sensitive meant that I was often affected by this hectic and over-stimulating modern world. Therefore, I was not only led to pursue skills to help others, I was committed to finding the keys for my own well-being and recovery.

I acquired my first Tarot deck in 1981. From the moment I picked up my first cards, I was fascinated and compelled by the information I was able to receive while peering at the images and corresponding patterns each spread created. I started reading cards professionally while I was in art school at the Cleveland Institute of

Art. Later, I earned a B.F.A. in visual art from the Boston Museum School and Tufts University. I quickly discovered after I graduated that it was easier to pursue a career as a psychic than as a fresh-out-of-college, wet-behind-the-ears professional artist.

At first my ability to "predict the future" was the primary motivation for doing readings, but it did not take long for me to become curious about what causes us to make the choices we make and why we so often fall back into less-than-optimal behaviors, even though we sincerely want to change. So instead of telling people, "You're going to meet a tall dark cesspool and fall in," I started to focus on the questions, "What keeps us attracted to tall dark cesspools and why do we keep falling in?" As I began to examine these questions with my clients, it became apparent that merely understanding why we engage in certain behaviors is not enough. We also need to find tools and strategies for healing our issues, as well as ways to integrate wisdom and anchor the transformations we work towards.

As I deepened my skills as a reader and healer, I began teaching Tarot and intuitive development to others. Through my experiences aiding others in deepening their intuitive abilities, I realized that honing psychic skills had more to do with learning how to distinguish our own thoughts and feelings from those that we'd taken on from others, than about learning how to be a more open channel, since empaths are already constantly receiving tons of information.

Despite my struggles with empathic overwhelm, depression, anxiety, and sugar addiction, I managed to get keep my butt in school long enough to earn a master's degree, as well as training extensively as a healer and practitioner of positive magic and metaphysics. Here's a list of some of the things I've done:

⊛ A few years after graduating from art school, I embarked on creating a photographic, living Tarot deck. With a hiatus for graduate school, it took nearly nine years to complete and publish this deck.

- ❀ I studied and became certified as a Transformational Breath Facilitator.
- ❀ I trained and was attuned to be a Reiki Master.
- ❀ I earned my Master of Arts in Psychology and Religion from Andover Newton Theological School.
- ❀ Simultaneous to pursuing this degree in mind/body healing and pastoral care, I completed a year-long training with a focus on body-centered spiritual healing.
- ❀ I've studied and worked with flower essences for over 30 years and eventually attended a Professional Flower Essence Practitioner Training.
- ❀ Following my graduation from seminary, I apprenticed to become a professional tattooer, then founded and co-owned an award-winning tattoo studio in Portland, Maine for over 18 years.
- ❀ I completed an in-depth, 2-year Shamanic Apprenticeship Program.
- ❀ After experiencing amazing results using EFT for myself, I became a Certified Advanced Practitioner and then an Accredited, EFT Master Trainer for EFT International.

Ironically, when I graduated from art school, I felt unprepared to make a living as an artist, so I pursued a career as a Tarot reader. Then when I graduated from seminary, it seemed easier to launch a career as an artist than to promote a healing ministry, so I started using tattooing as my primary vehicle for healing work. Once I'd developed my technical chops, I incorporated intuitive guidance, psychic reading, Reiki, shamanic techniques, EFT, and other forms of spiritual and energetic healing into my tattooing practice. I put all of my heart, mind, body, and soul into perfecting this craft and working to make my business grow and thrive. This was my full-time work from 1999 until I walked away from my brick and mortar studio on Winter Solstice of 2017.

Some people have mused at my progression from art school to psychic healer, to seminarian at the oldest Protestant Seminary in the country, to medicine tattooer, to Modern Medicine Lady. It may seem unusual, but the whole process has always made sense to me.

These experiences not only increased my technical abilities as an artist, but also my sensitivity to people and skill at facilitating the transformational opportunities that often arise during the process of tattooing, teaching, and mentoring. Spending the last 19 years holding the space for each person's process and coaching them through real pain has given me a unique capacity to support my students, clients, and mentees, enabling them to move beyond their fear and discomfort with more grace and relative ease.

As the intensity of our planet seems to increase daily, I've been called to serve beyond the safety and comfort of the walls of a brick-and-mortar studio and a thriving tattooing practice. I know what it took for me to reach this place of ease and calmness. Through this book and my programs and teachings, I share those steps and some hard-won wisdom with you. My goal is that you'll also be able to reach a place of comfort and confidence with your own empathic nature.

Here are a few things to keep in mind as you read:

Take your time. This book was written to be a comprehensive resource to help you manage many different aspects of living as an empath. While you may find yourself wanting to race to the finish, I invite you to pause, breathe, and give yourself the time you need to digest this very dense material.

This is your ride. I write this from my experience, my observations with clients, and many years of my own trial and error. Your mileage may vary. I offer everything for your consideration; only you will know whether or not you agree with it.

Wherever you are is perfect. At its very core, this is a book about love. The most powerful healing and growth only happen with the medicine of kindness. It starts as an inside job. Acceptance is the key at every point along the journey. Whether you're taking your first baby steps into empathic awareness, clawing your way out of a black hole of despair, abuse, and/or addiction, or are a seasoned practitioner on a spiritual path, *you are worthy.* You are okay and you matter.

Identify, don't compare. Measuring ourselves against other people is epidemic in conventional society. Perhaps as you read further, you'll find yourself thinking *"Well, maybe I'm NOT an empath after all. I haven't had some of the experiences that Jen talks about."* Please know that each of us develops and grows in our own way and at our own pace. Regardless of where you are on the empathic spectrum, you are SO welcome here. Each of us deals with both the trials and the gifts of our own unique situation. Empathic abilities often shift and develop over time. It has taken me over 35 years to get to the place I am today. It's through consistent and persistent practice that I can use my abilities with such ease and effectiveness today.

> *"The best time to plant a tree was 20 years ago. The second-best time is now."*
>
> *— Chinese proverb*

Start with an open heart. Even if you don't agree with everything I say, or you think you already know what I'm writing about, I encourage you to approach this material with an open heart and a beginner's mind. The three things that block us from growth faster than anything else are:

1. Thinking we already know something and concluding we have nothing else to learn.
2. Deciding that since we already tried it before, it won't work for us. Or that, if we haven't tried it before, we are different from others, so even if it works for them, we'll be the 1% for whom it doesn't.

3. Giving up before we've given something a chance to work for us and/or taking shortcuts and not following directions.

I encourage you to cultivate curiosity. Instead of reading something and focusing on what you already know, try asking yourself, "What new perspective am I finding? What can I take from this? How can this serve me today?"

Willingness is the key. Resistance is a natural response to growth and change. Some of what I invite you to try may feel awkward and unfamiliar. The single most effective and immediate thing you can do is to pray or simply ask for the "willingness to be willing." As I embarked on my own healing journey, I often noticed that praying for willingness didn't open doors for me because for some reason I still felt resistance to this request. It was only when I sincerely asked for the willingness to be willing that the way would open.

Baby Steps. Significant, lasting change seldom happens overnight. It's rarely bold, sweeping gestures that create profound shifts; it's the daily, incremental actions we take. You didn't get to the state you're in over a few days.

Changing how you live your life and, ultimately, who you are and how you identify yourself in this world is a process. It took me decades to reach the point where I was truly comfortable in my own skin and could live on this planet in love and contentment. Allow yourself the time to do this thoroughly and well. Break things down into actionable steps. You are better served by focusing on a small section of this book and working with it in-depth than by trying to tackle entire chapters in one fell swoop. When I mentor one-on-one clients through this system, we often spend months digging into the five keys of Empathic Mastery, then continue to circle back to the basics again and again.

100% Responsibility. The most effective way to claim your power is by owning your part in every situation. 100% responsibility means being fully present to your thoughts, your feelings, and especially, your choices. This can be challenging for empaths, because when we absorb the energy of the world around us it can seem like we're being *made* to feel a certain way. Taking 100% responsibility means agreeing to accept that, once we recognize what we are experiencing, we get to choose how we proceed. *Own your choices.* If you decide to put this book down and binge-watch all eight seasons of *Charmed*, then do it mindfully. From now on, you are in control of your choices. You decide at every turn what you will do next.

Radical Honesty. There are many questions scattered throughout this book. Each one is an invitation for you to explore the thoughts, feelings, beliefs, and agreements that make you who you are today. You will get the most out of this book and the exercises in it when you are willing to practice radical honesty with yourself. Taking 100% responsibility means that you can speak the truth and still decide to do something different. But to really heal, we need to be willing to own our stuff and admit to what is and isn't working in our life. This honesty is between you and yourself. Whatever answers you discover, consider them valuable information. I invite you to approach yourself with compassion and to release all judgment for whatever truth you discover. Keep your truth safe and sacred to yourself (and to your very trusted guides and loved ones) while you sort out your answers. Even as you choose radical honesty for yourself, you can still decide how much you wish to share with anyone else.

Be coachable. Transformation happens when we're willing to listen, willing to examine, and especially, willing to change our perceptions and try new things. While most of us will give lip service to the idea that we want a better life, being coachable or teachable is often the difference between success and coming to a grinding halt after the first lap of the race. Being coachable depends on three primary things:

1. The ability to listen and accept feedback and suggestions.
2. The willingness and commitment to implement lessons and advice you've been offered.

3. Recognizing when you have hit a wall and you need help, then asking for support that you accept.

As you consider these three qualities, I'll ask you two things:

Are you willing to be curious, compassionate, and accepting towards yourself as you embark on this journey?

AND

Are you coachable? What will it take for you to be able to say "yes?"

A Brief Glossary of Terms

There are certain words and phrases that I use throughout the book which bear explanation. The following are definitions for how I am using them, so you and I can start on the same page.

Awfulizing: A term I use to describe those times when our fear and our mental chatter (see "monkey mind") get together and run worst-case scenarios until we've worked ourselves into a lather.

Bubble Up: This is a term coined by a client of mine. They used it to describe forming a bubble of light around themself, particularly when they needed to protect themself from empathic overwhelm. This is part of how we can form, then fortify, the filters and shields that surround our physical body. I'll describe this process in depth in Chapter 6. I have found it useful as an anchoring phrase to reinforce the exercise where we cast a ball of light around ourselves. I will often say, "Bubble up" when my friends and I are going into any kind of intense environment.

Clients: These are the people (and sometimes animals) I work with as a professional. While my methods and means have evolved since I began as a young psychic, the core of my work has always been to support people in finding their truth, healing their wounds, and growing to achieve their potential. When I mention clients, I'm referring to the people I've served professionally in all of the different modalities I've worked with as my career has shifted and grown over the last 35 years.

Cords: Refers to fibers of energy that connect one human being to another. Some of these cords are natural and healthy, like the ones shared between a mother and her young children. Others are out of balance or even harmful. Cutting cords is a term often used to mean severing the dysfunctional ties that bind us in relationships that do not serve us as they are.

EFT/Tapping: EFT stands for Emotional Freedom Techniques, as originally named by Gary Craig. It is also called tapping, because it is a form of mental/emotional acupressure that uses tapping or light pressure on specific acupuncture points to shift thoughts, feelings, and sensations. While it is remarkably simple, it is also an extremely effective method of identifying and releasing a wide variety of issues. Please refer to Chapter 5 for a chart of all the tapping points. Also visit EmpathicSafety.com to get your Empathic Safety Kit which includes a comprehensive tapping tutorial video.

El Mundo Bueno: In her novel *The Fifth Sacred Thing*, the author Starhawk wrote about two intersecting worlds: El Mundo Bueno, the Good World, and El Mundo Malo, the Bad World. The basic concept is that there's a membrane that separates the two realities (the author describes it as being like the skin that forms on boiled milk). El Mundo Bueno is the world where things go well. Everything is in positivity and life is aligned. When challenges arise, they resolve themselves for the better. El Mundo Malo, on the other hand, is a world where wounds fester, problems amplify, and negativity is contagious. There's a way in which the worlds reflect each other, but the outcomes are very different. We can move away from the membrane and travel further into El Mundo Bueno. Or we can find ourselves moving away from the membrane to descend further into El Mundo Malo. Obviously, whenever we recognize that we're in El Mundo Malo, we want to be working our way back towards the membrane and across that barrier again.

Empath: A person who is highly sensitive (mentally, emotionally, energetically, and even physically) to others and to their environment. Empaths sense thoughts, feelings, and sensations from the world around them and often experience these sensations as their own. By my definition, empathic sensitivity operates on a spectrum, from people who are sensitive to other people's expressions of emotion or pain, to those who are so open that they can't distinguish between themselves and others, not only sensing human emotions around them, but also being aware of paranormal/multidimensional entities and realities.

The Force: Originally from the *Star Wars* film series, the Force refers to the energy that composes and connects all things in the entire Universe. Many traditions allude to this energy field, which can be tapped into and used. The Force is similar to what scientist Wilhelm Reich called Orgone, the source of all life energy; to the Prana and Chi of Eastern traditions; and to the Field of Infinite Potentiality as explained by Pam Grout in her book, *E-Squared*.

Holding Space: This is a term that is used often among healers, coaches, and other transformational business owners. When someone (including ourselves) is going through any kind of intense process or experience we avoid rushing in to fix the problem. We don't try to prevent or stop the mental, emotional, or spiritual pain. Instead of jumping to solutions, advice or trying to put a positive spin on the challenge, we acknowledge the magnitude of the experience and bear witness to its depth. Our job is to create a safe place for both of us to be present to what simply is and to support the one going through it to show up for their thoughts, feelings, and sensations as they are able.

Mala: A Sanskrit word, a mala is a set of 108 beads similar to the Catholic rosary and is used for meditation, prayer, and chanting. Each bead serves as a placeholder for a prayer or mantra. Like a rosary, you hold the mala in your hands and move from one bead to the next.

Monkey Mind: A Buddhist term for the ceaseless, agitated chatter of our minds. Monkey mind is the part of us that starts going through our grocery list or replaying an argument we had earlier in the day while we are at a concert trying to enjoy the music, having an intimate conversation with a loved one, or simply trying to fall asleep. Awfulizing is a variation of monkey mind that I find particularly unhelpful.

Muggle: A term originally coined by J.K. Rowling in the *Harry Potter* series to refer to the ordinary, non-magical people living in the everyday world. Most empaths I know identify as *different* from the people around them, in the same way that Harry knew he was different from the rest of his muggle family. I use the term muggle to refer to people who are not empathic, magical, highly sensitive, or unusual in some other way.

Narcissism and Other Personality Disorders: Personality disorders are types of mental disorders where people display rigid and unhealthy thoughts and behaviors. Someone with a personality disorder has trouble accurately perceiving and effectively relating to situations and people. This causes significant problems in all aspects of their lives. Often people with these issues do not realize they have a problem because their thoughts and actions seem perfectly natural to them. Since they cannot see their own part in the equation, they frequently blame others for their problems and the challenges they face. This can be deceiving for the empath because they pick up on the personality disordered person's cognitive inability to grasp their culpability. Thus the empath will often sympathize with their dilemma and want to help. People with personality disorders are often bright and charismatic and can often woo others into relationships. For empaths, the adoration and initial emotional intensity can be very easy to fall for. These days there's a lot of buzz about the attraction between narcissists and empaths. Simply put, for the narcissist, it's all about them, and for the empath, it's also all about the narcissist. At first the narcissist revels in the attention the empath gives them and the empath feels their pleasure and gets drawn in by their inflated charm, appreciation, and glowing attention. Unfortunately, this honeymoon period rarely lasts and a volatile game begins that is often very hard to escape unscathed.

Past Lives/Reincarnation: Since we can never definitively prove that our soul has lived a previous life, this is an idea that some of us believe while others do not. It has been suggested that perhaps we recall the memories of our ancestors encoded in our DNA. I personally believe we have the capacity to recall both. I speak a fair amount about other lives in this book and about fairly vivid memories I have had. I've always had a sense of the past and of memories that do not stem from this lifetime. As I've grown older these memories have expanded and my recall has become more detailed. There are two things that generally trigger memories for me:

1. Working on an issue that's affecting me deeply. Sometimes it's a chronic pain, sometimes emotional distress no amount of talking or medication seems to resolve. As I dig into the issue and begin to explore its roots, memories bubble up to the surface.
2. When I meet other people who feel distinctly familiar even as I meet them for the first time. When I spend time with certain people, their presence stimulates recall. Images, feelings, thoughts, and sensations come flooding back to me.

Now, it's entirely possible that I simply have a very active imagination and this is my mind's way of processing things. Some of my memories have been quite uneventful and boring; I'd hope that my imagination would come up with more interesting stories than those. That said, while I can never prove the veracity of what I recall, I believe I've been here many times before. The past life experiences I recall are often as concrete and vivid as any memory I have from this life. Regardless, these stories inform my healing process. When I examine them and give them a voice, I experience miraculous healing.

Ping: Originally a term in computer science for sending a query from one network or computer to another to determine if there is a connection. When I refer to "pinging" someone, it alludes to when we energetically or psychically query someone else to try to get a read on what is going on with them, or simply to connect with them.

Pronouns: To someone born in a body that reflects who they perceive themselves to be, using the apparent pronoun of "she" or "he" usually goes without notice, except on the rare occasions they are accidentally misgendered. It can definitely feel jarring to be called "young man" or "young lady" when you are the opposite. However, as more and more people are finding themselves somewhere outside binary gender roles, identity pronouns are becoming more of an issue. As an ally and friend of a number of trans people, I've witnessed how invalidating and dehumanizing it feels to be addressed or referred to by the wrong words. Many people are choosing to adopt the words "them" and "they" as gender-neutral alternatives. Therefore, unless I am specifically referring to a real person, I'll be using this gender-neutral pronoun. It may feel a little awkward at first, but I assure you it's possible to adjust and at a certain point you may even choose to adopt this more inclusive approach yourself.

Psychic Vampire: Unlike the vampires of classic horror movies who literally drink blood, a psychic vampire either consciously or unconsciously feeds on other people's energy, particularly their emotional energy. Psychic vampires can be quite charming at first and, like narcissists, can rope you in before you realize what you've gotten into. One sign that you're dealing with a psychic vampire is that you feel exhausted and depleted after spending any time with them. You may notice that they provoke emotional responses from you, and/or incite you to go to emotional places that you don't want to go.

Spoons: Spoons is a concept coined by blogger Christine Miserandino to explain what it's like to live with a chronic but invisible illness. Long story short, "spoons" has become shorthand for how much energy we have in our reserves at any given moment. When someone says, "I've used up all my spoons," it means they have nothing left to give until they've had a chance to recharge again.

Table of Contents

Part I

Introduction: How I Got Here

Everything changed the day I almost drove off a bridge. One minute I was cruising down the highway and the next I was staring straight into a river gorge. Even though I'd made a vow to myself that no matter how bad it got I was committed to staying alive, I was struck by the revelation that I could end up dying anyway -- by distraction. That was the moment I realized I wasn't in control of whether or not I'd continue to white-knuckle my way through my depression and manage to keep passing the open windows.

Obviously, I didn't careen into the river hundreds of feet below. I corrected my wheel in the nick of time. Fortunately, there were no other cars on the bridge. As I swerved back into my lane, I knew that what I was doing wasn't working. If I wanted to make it to 25, I was going to need more help and guidance than I could muster on my own. At that point I was a hot mess. I was clinically depressed, anxious, and coming off cigarettes, antidepressants, and birth control pills, all of which I'd decided to quit cold turkey without any medical supervision. I'd just graduated from art school with no concrete plan of how to make money as an artist. I'd decided to leave my home state of Massachusetts and everything familiar to start a new life in Ohio. But instead of launching a promising career as a newly graduated artist and videographer, I found myself plummeting into an abyss that I hadn't the first clue how to get out of.

As I reflect back on this crucial time in my life, I understand it more clearly. All I knew then was that I felt this nameless, relentless, nagging distress, and despite all my best efforts and a cocktail of prescribed meds, I was lost and overwhelmed. What I know now is that I was a wide-open empath who was overcome with the pain and negativity of the world around me. I also know that I was making everything worse with a daily candy habit. The sugar would send me into temporary fits of giddiness followed by hours of dark, uneasy moodiness, during which I was convinced the world was going to hell in a handbasket. It was this pain that brought me to my knees and allowed me to surrender and ask for help.

The journey of recovery started for me by admitting I was powerless over a raging sugar addiction and the subsequent eating disorder, body hatred, and distorted thinking that went with it. Though it began with the choice to abstain from sugar and eliminate bingeing from my life, it didn't take long to discover that these issues were not the cause but the symptom of my greater problem. I can tell you that if you want to figure out why you're self-medicating, stopping will bring the answer to the surface faster than anything else. My recovery process peeled away layers of the onion. It began when I quit harming myself with cigarettes, sugar, and alcohol. It continued as I started to explore my triggers for picking up these drugs of choice. Eventually, it led me to examine how I approached all of my relationships. I slowly learned to set healthy boundaries, to stick up for myself, and to ask for what I needed.

As I became healthier, my intuition and ability to support others grew exponentially. Like so many of the empaths I've met along the way, I felt a deep calling to serve this planet, but as an intuitive, empathic woman, I knew I first had to learn to manage my sensitivities so I could navigate the world with more grace and ease. At the core, it was my own need to find calm in the eye of life's storms that led me to my healing path. In time, this inspired me to train and develop skills so I could become a healer and mentor for other sensitive women, who struggle like I did.

I wish I could say I never experience empathic distress anymore, but that's simply not true. There are still times when I realize that I've been sitting with feelings of unidentifiable uneasiness and anxiety. Even with all the tools and techniques I've acquired over the past 30-plus years, there are still periods when I'm consumed with a physical sense of foreboding. But now when I experience what I call "empathic PMS," I can recognize how far I've come. Instead of spending days running around like a chicken with my head cut off, bingeing on chocolate and wondering why I feel so lousy, I've learned to check in with other empaths and confirm my suspicion that this all-too-familiar feeling goes beyond me because they also sense a disturbance in the field. Even when I become gripped with unexplainable sadness or a visceral sense of dread, I'm now able to remain mindful and fairly calm about it. I know from previous experience that the best thing I can do in these circumstances is to sink into my place on this Earth, settle down, anchor, and prepare for whatever storm comes next.

Things have gotten significantly better than they used to be for me. I recently returned from a month of travel. Every week I left home for 4-5 days. Over four weeks I attended a retreat, a conference, a professional training, a concert, and a few business meetings. I'd spent many hours on the road driving in congested traffic, sleeping in hotel rooms, inhaling chemical odors, and eating less than ideal food. There would have been a time when I'd have been totally melting down after a day or two away from the safety of my home and kitchen. I would have been using every single remedy and healing tool I had available. I'd have needed at least a week of down time and extra sleep to recover. More than likely I would have postponed or canceled plans after my first week of travel.

This time was different.

Where there would have been a time when I'd have been taking Rescue Remedy nonstop and each breath would be intentionally deep to manage my anxiousness, it dawned on me I didn't need to use my emergency kit. Not even once. Sure, driving in hectic NYC traffic is still stressful, but once I was out of the car, I felt fine. Best of all was the fact that after a night of sleep to reboot from the road I had bounced back entirely. It was then that I realized how much more resilient I've become.

While for the average person this may seem insignificant, as someone who has struggled mightily whenever I left my safe and familiar home base, the ability to spend a month outside my usual routines is a big deal. Being able to function in this world is the first gift of empathic mastery; using our abilities to make a positive difference on this earth is the second. One baby step at a time leads to resourcefulness and resilience that might seem inconceivable at first. Keep going anyway. As a former hot mess and delicate flower, I'm thrilled to tell you "it gets better."

Just a week and a day after I led my first Empathic Woman Retreat, I learned that a very dear and special client (whom I'll call Susan) had just taken her life, leaving behind her young son, devastated husband, and many confused and heartbroken friends. Susan had struggled for years with an untreatable condition that left her in constant, agonizing pain. On one hand, I totally got why she chose to step off this mortal coil. In the time I'd spent with Susan, I'd heard enough of her story to know the physical and emotional pain she endured daily. On the other hand, I felt deep regret that, as a highly sensitive person, Susan couldn't find answers to turn enough of her pain around to help her stay alive.

As days flowed into months, I thought of her often. Then, during a conversation about this book, it dawned on me that she'd been an empath who lacked the tools to cope with all the stress, pain, and suffering she was absorbing. It made me wonder: if Susan had had more resources, could she have made a different choice?

Fast forward to a few months after Susan's death, when another empathic friend (I'll call her Debra) decided to go on a spiritual pilgrimage, hiking sacred sites in Asia. She chose to share her entire journey publicly to raise money and understanding for suicide awareness. Debra's story is similar to Susan's, in that both of them were highly sensitive, intuitive, empathic women who struggled with absorbing all the pain and suffering of the world around them.

Both of them dealt with depression and both of them seriously considered suicide. The difference is, on the day Debra decided would be her last, she made a phone call to say goodbye to a dear relative and received the support that allowed her to choose life.

As I considered these two empathic women, I knew I wanted to dedicate this book to Susan and Debra and all the other empaths like them. I write with the hope that if more Susans can find support, they might not need to conclude that suicide is the best solution. I have concluded that, while I'm dedicating this book to Susan and Debra, I *also* write this book for me.

I write it for my younger self, who spent her days overcome with fear, ravenous hunger, and visions of an apocalyptic future. I also write it for whomever I might become in a future incarnation, so my next self may be spared years of struggling to make sense of the world as a highly sensitive old soul.

It's my sincerest prayer that, somehow, this book ends up in the hands (or on the tablet) of future versions of my soul. I write this book to be the guide I desperately needed as a teenage girl who was awakening to her abilities. And yes, I write this book for all the other empaths who might be able to avoid at least a few of those hurdles if they are given tools and information that can make a difference.

As I have traveled this healing path with myself and others, I have come to believe that:

- ❀ Every choice we make is an attempt to reach for something better.

- ❀ Real healing happens when we embrace our true selves, warts and all.

- ❀ We are innately resilient and capable of healing.

- ❀ Most pain is temporary; the keys to moving through it are acceptance and love.

I've also found that as long as we keep basing our current decisions on conclusions we formed as five-year-olds, we simply won't get the relief we seek. While understanding the reasons we keep doing counter-productive things is certainly helpful, when we carry an emotional charge around an experience or perception, no amount of strategic action or personal insight will create sustainable shifts. In addition to teaching you the system I have developed to gain empathic mastery, this book was also written to offer tools and techniques to address underlying root causes.

By no means do I suggest that I have all the answers. I'm most definitely human and have my blind spots and growing edges, but I've also learned a great deal since I swerved away from the guard-rail of the bridge thirty-three years ago. I've discovered a number of things that have created a lasting difference for me. To retro-actively heal the younger me and to save myself time in my next life (plus, hopefully, to save you time in this one), I've created this guide for the care and feeding of sensitive souls living in this muggle world.

Perhaps this book will speak to you; perhaps it won't. I invite you to consider what I share and try it on, see how it fits, and use what works for you. I'm genuinely delighted that you are reading this book. We may never meet in person, but I hope that you will consider me an ally and a sister empath who cares about you and the path you choose. I hope you find answers to the questions you have, as well as to ones you didn't even realize you had. I write this with love, and with my best wishes for your highest and greatest good. May you and yours be blessed in all your endeavors.

Empathic Emergency Kit

aka But I Need Relief NOW!

Over the decades as I've worked with empathic women, I'm repeatedly struck by the sense of urgency and distress so many of them express. When you've been emotionally hemorrhaging for what seems like an eternity, holding a book of this size may feel like just one more thing to add to your already overflowing plate. That's the catch-22 of being so sensitive.

In order to shift you must learn to do things in a new way, but this effort takes a level of energy and commitment that empathic overwhelm has drained from you. I'm going to share a few things right now that will give you the most bang for your buck. This can get you started so that you can begin experiencing the calm and focus you'll need to pursue more lasting changes.

1. Learn and practice the Earth-Sky Meditation. You can find it in Chapter 6, *Protect*. This meditation is at the very core of all of this work, and even before you have started to do specific work to release the stuff you've been carrying around, this will help you to feel calmer, more grounded, and more insulated from the energy of the world around you. The more you practice this, the stronger your results will be. You can download an audio version of this meditation along

with the rest of the Empathic Safety Kit at EmpathicSafety. com

2. BREATHE! Consciously inhale light, loving kindness, and peace. Deliberately exhale negativity, overwhelm, and distress.

3. Eliminate sugar from your diet. Of all the things I've done, abstaining from sugar has had the most dramatic and life-changing impact. I started by quitting all processed sugar and corn syrup. After a period of withdrawal and cravings that lasted a few weeks, I felt better than ever before in my entire life. I won't lie, there have been times when I've fallen off the wagon, and after periods of ever-increasing anxiety, moodiness, empathic overwhelm, brain fog, inflammation, weight gain, and exhaustion, I've had to admit more times than I'd like to count that sugar is poison on all levels for me. I go into greater detail about why this is the case in the food and detoxing section of Chapter 5. Now, if sugar really isn't your thing, I invite you to take an honest inventory of your relationship with food, alcohol, drugs, tobacco, sex, shopping, social media, television, and/or any other addictive/self-soothing behaviors that are impacting the quality of your life. What are you doing that is altering your perception of the world? What are you doing that may be compromising your ability to stick up for yourself? What are you doing that stops you from moving forward and drains you of energy and enthusiasm?

4. Refer regularly to my Empathic Safety Kit. Visit EmpathicSafety.com to access the kit, which includes additional bonus content, extensive resources, video tutorials, and an audio of the Earth-Sky Meditation for you to follow whenever you need it.

5. Find me on social media by doing a quick search for @ EmpathicWoman and @ModernMedicineLady on FB. As

of publication, I am regularly posting content on Instagram, Facebook, and YouTube. I often jump on to do live videos that focus on support and solutions for empaths. And I post lots of resources that are good for the care and feeding of sensitive souls.

6. Keep coming back, one breath at a time, one word at a time, one page at a time and...

"Don't give up before the miracle happens."

—*Anon*

Chapter 1

Are You an Empath?

Why Me?

Being an empath can really suck. Many people who struggle with sensitivity and empathic abilities wonder why this is happening to them. Why *is* it happening? You were born this way. Why are you female? Why do you have curly hair? Why were you born in America instead of Japan? Just as you were born left-handed, right-handed, or ambidextrous, you were born sensitive. Why is it happening? It just is.

In my humble opinion, the more important question is, what are you going to do about it? That's what really matters. That's what we will be discussing in this book, so you can not only come to terms with being this way but also claim your gifts and own the power of being this way.

Being Willing To Change

In the coming chapters I'm going to invite you to join me in making some agreements so you can live a life in which: (a) you are not driving yourself crazy, (b) you are not being driven crazy by everybody else, and (c) you are not driving other people crazy. This might sound like a tall order, especially if you've been struggling for a long time.

Ironically, when we feel like we've "already tried everything," there's often a part of us that remains invested in holding on to the challenge. When something has been really difficult and a solution is offered, it can feel oddly embarrassing when it actually works. Why didn't we do it years ago and avoid decades (or even lifetimes) of suffering?

Changing means letting go of what we thought was true, and perhaps even our established identity. Changing means being open to the possibility that you can learn something new, even in material you've learned before. This can feel threatening but, if you're reading this, I imagine you've reached the point where you are sick and tired of being sick and tired. I suspect that the temporary discomfort of embracing these principles will beat the ever-lovin' pants off the alternative.

I'm not going to lie to you and say this will be effortless. If the size of this book alone indicates what's in store, you probably already suspect you'll want to buckle your seat belt before we take off. What I will say is this: if you are willing to commit to doing this work and are open to changing what you believe about yourself, it is possible to go from being a hot mess who is actually adding to the chaos (I was one of those), to being a calm, grounded anchor of light in the eye of the current planetary storm.

What Is An Empath?

You've heard the word "empathy," and you've probably heard the words "empathetic" and "empathic." The term "empath" was originally coined in the science fiction world of the 1960's.

Back in 1968, *Star Trek* aired an episode called "The Empath." A few years later (sometime in the mid-70's, when I was 11 or 12 years old), I saw this program and discovered empaths. More importantly, I recognized aspects of myself in this character. The empath was an alien woman. Some other, mean aliens were experimenting with her. They wanted to understand how her people dealt with sympathy and compassion. Kirk, Spock, and McCoy had beamed down to this foreign planet and, as often happened on *Star Trek*, they got the crap kicked out of them and were captured. After the fights, the mean aliens would send the empath into the prison cell. She was mute, so she'd just look at the prisoners and cry, the tortured expression on her face conveying, "Oh, I feel your pain!" The anguished empath would then go to the prisoners and touch them.

As she placed her hands on their wounds, the cuts and bruises would slowly vanish. As she relieved them of their pain, the wounds would show up on her own body. At this point, the men would be fine, but the empath would be weakened. She'd be lying in a puddle on the floor, totally exhausted. Then, slowly, she'd rally and perk back up again.

When they used the word "empath" in this episode, I thought, "That's what I am." I also formed the belief, "That's what empaths do." I learned a couple of things from that episode. I learned that, as an empath, you take on other people's pain. And I learned that the way to heal other people is by completely absorbing their pain and transmuting it.

As empaths, most of us are naturally skilled at sensing other people's wounds and challenges. We can often absorb them and feel the sensations in our own body. But the truth is, *this isn't such a hot idea*. It's not the only way to operate as an empath, but many of us either learned, or naturally do, exactly this. Let's just say that taking on other people's pain and suffering to heal it is not a great approach. While it can be done (and can actually work), it's simply not sustainable. Right now our planet needs all hands on deck to support the profound changes that are occurring. Right now we cannot afford to be exhausted and out of commission as we recuperate each time we try to help.

My next exposure to the term "empath" was when I was 17 and in my first semester at college. There was this guy who was an empath. He recognized me as an empath, too. We started talking about what it meant to be an empath. We were especially fascinated by what it felt like to be two empaths in the same space. We noted that it was like being in a hall of mirrors; repeatedly reflecting off each other and amplifying the thoughts and feelings between us. In some circumstances this can be really powerful and fulfilling, but in others it can be more like audio feedback -- louder and more distorted the longer it goes on. This is particularly true before we learn how to manage our abilities.

Gee, Toto, This Isn't Star Trek Anymore

My basic definition of "empathy" involves the ability to sense other people's feelings and to understand and imagine what they are experiencing. It is more than sympathy, more than simply thinking, "Oh, isn't that sad?" Deep empathy is more than intellectual. It's an emotional awareness through which the body, mind, and heart perceive another person's experience. What others are expressing, thinking, and feeling, empaths tend to experience viscerally -- physically, mentally, emotionally, and spiritually. In other words, an *empath is someone who can feel someone else's feelings.* This can include other people, animals, plants, and even the greater collective consciousness of this planet.

Empaths can generally distinguish between their own experience and that of others, but for the extreme empath, there may be very little distinction between self and other. They not only sense other people's feelings, but are basically open vessels that take in everything in their environment.

Are My Abilities Demonic?

One of the most controversial issues around this whole subject is the question about whether gifts of intuition, empathy, and psychic awareness are spiritually dangerous and should be avoided. The truth is, some conservative faith traditions label all forms of divination, sensitivity, and mediumship as evil. Sadly, there are still people on this planet who believe that people like you and me are misguided, manipulated by false gods, and therefore a bad influence. They believe that these natural gifts and abilities are inherently harmful, or at the very least to be avoided.

A while ago, I received a message from a woman whose empathic sensitivities had started to awaken. She shared her family's fears about her abilities being demonic. She felt overwhelmed by her new experiences, which is common for many empaths who are newly awakening.

If this is happening to you, I want to reassure you that this is completely normal. Of course it's overwhelming at times; you are like an exposed nerve. You're feeling everything. If you're one of the unfortunate people who woke up all at once, you find that you're suddenly flooded with information.

Here in the U.S. where I live, some traditions are extremely xenophobic. They basically believe that if you are not just like them, then there is something wrong with you. This is particularly true in some conservative religions, where anything outside of the ordinary is considered sinful, wrong, and "the Devil's work." There are people who believe that being gay or transgender is demonic, too. I will say this once again: in the same way that being queer is just the way you're born, being blue-eyed is just the way you're born, being left-handed is just the way you're born, for some of us, being empathic is just the way we're born. It's what we are, and it's who we are. I sincerely believe, with every fiber of my being, that it has nothing to do with the Devil or demons.

Yes, as empaths we are vulnerable to picking up on evil. We are sensitive to it, since we are sensitive to picking up negativity in the world. Just as empathy and psychic ability can be used for good, they can also be used for harm. I suspect that those who are concerned about the Devil associate these natural abilities with the way some people choose to misuse their gifts.

Empathy is a trait. Like many other traits, it can be used for both good and ill. It is simply an innate characteristic. Unfortunately, there are still some people who have a worldview that says something different. God bless them and their perceptions of us, and their perceptions of all the queers, no matter what form of queer they are. They don't get us. But this is our world, and you're welcome to be part of it. I invite you to come to my worldview. I invite you to come to a place where you are welcome, where God is love, and where, by God's will, we were born this way.

The Science of Empathy: Mirror Neurons

A few months ago, I was watching an emergency room drama on TV while working on a project. I wasn't really paying attention until I noticed that the plot centered around a teenage girl who kept experiencing every physical symptom exhibited by the people around her. They dragged in the Amiable Psychiatrist (played by Oliver Platt) because her family thought she was acting out to get attention. Long story short, the doctor noticed how she was responding to other people's pain and concluded that this girl had especially active "mirror neurons." This was the first time I'd heard of mirror neurons, and I was thrilled that prime-time television was doing an episode about a character that I would consider an empath. It's so exciting to me that science is now acknowledging phenomena that many of us have experienced all along. Some of us have the capacity to pick up the thoughts, feelings, and even physical sensations around us, and now neuroscience has identified mirror neurons.

I am neither a doctor nor a scientist, so I will explain this only briefly (if you're interested in learning more, there's a lot of great information available; see the Resources section at the back of this book). Simply put, mirror neurons are a special kind of brain cell that responds both when we take action and when we see another person taking action. It "mirrors" the other person's action as though we were doing it ourselves.

Mirror neurons were first discovered in the 1990's by a team of Italian neuroscientists. One of these scientists, Giacomo Rizzolatti, MD, believes that these neurons might actually explain how we can feel empathy and "read" other people's minds. The implications are significant for those of us who identify as empaths. The origins of our sensitivity may literally be "all in our head" (although I believe this is but one part of a significantly more complex energy body system), but this science validates that our experiences are not merely the product of overactive imaginations. Mirror neuron research is still in an early stage but, in my opinion, simply knowing that there is a physiological explanation for why some of us are more sensitive than others is priceless.

The Spectrum of Empathy

Empathic abilities exist on a spectrum. On one end are people who are so insulated and self-contained that they are oblivious to energy, thoughts, feelings, and sensations being experienced outside of their own body. On the other end are people who receive input through all of their senses and often are so sensitive that they pick up "extra-sensory" information that transcends the limits of time and space. Empathic abilities range from simply sensing other human beings' emotions and experiences all the way to picking up absolutely everything going on in the world around us.

This can include awareness of electromagnetic fields (EMFs), radiation, and Wi-Fi, along with the ability to perceive the vibration or history of inanimate objects around us. There can be perception of things that have happened in the past, or things that will happen in the future. Some empaths may feel as though they have no filter around time. Some are aware of ghosts, spirits, and other paranormal activity. Some are even conscious of (and, at times, in communion with) extraterrestrial beings. The more empathic someone is, the more they tend to perceive things outside of conventional "reality." Life can be really hard for empaths who live where no one else senses anything out of the ordinary.

The Empathic Spectrum

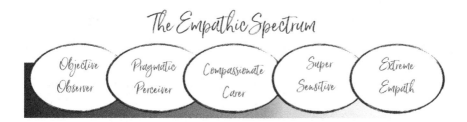

Objective Observer — Pragmatic Perceiver — Compassionate Carer — Super Sensitive — Extreme Empath

On one end of the spectrum are the people who are extremely obtuse. They have little to no empathic ability at all. You could hit them over the head with an emotional sledgehammer and they still wouldn't feel much of anything. I call this type of person "the Objective Observer." They are like the political comedian and talk show host, Bill Maher. They generally have no sense of anything spiritual, anything outside of the ordinary, and their attitude is, "If you can't prove it, it isn't real." They're all about reason and rationality, and most of the time they have extra dense and impenetrable emotional and psychic filters.

Next is "the Pragmatic Perceiver." This is a person who has some capacity for empathy, but they do not absorb or embody anything outside of themselves. They're usually able to function effectively in the world because they're not constantly flooded with mental and emotional stimuli.

Then there is what I call "the Compassionate Carer." These people are really good at observing and understanding what's going on with other people. They are mindful of what's happening, but their energetic filters are still solid enough that they're not being bombarded by the external information that surrounds them.

Next are those I call "the Super Sensitives." They are the people who are pretty sensitive all the time. Super Sensitives pick up what's going on in the world around them and often sense other people's feelings. They have a need to caretake and be of service to other people. This behavior can be interpreted as "co-dependent," but I have a different take: I believe the reason these people have such a strong need to serve is that they themselves are relieved when others are no longer in distress. They feel compelled to help people in order to stop feeling their pain. Unfortunately, constantly trying to fix everyone else's problems makes it pretty difficult to function in the world.

The final group is made up of people like me, who are at the far end of the spectrum. These are what I call "Extreme Empaths."

When they are around other people, unless they've done work to protect themselves, they automatically pick up on everything. They sense what other people are feeling. They have a hard time being in places where there is a lot of activity. Extreme Empaths are not only sensitive to what's going on with the people and the world around them, but also to non-physical energies. They will walk into a haunted house and know immediately that it's haunted. Some of them even have experiences with extraterrestrials or other paranormal phenomena that ordinary people have no capacity to perceive or comprehend.

I created a quiz on my website called, "What's Your Empathic Type?" Go to EmpathicWoman.com to see where you score on the empathic spectrum.

The Impact of Being So Sensitive

There are many consequences to being so sensitive. Not only does it affect your ability to navigate daily life, but it also tends to make for environmental sensitivities, sensitivities to food, medication, airborne pollutants, electromagnetic frequencies, etc. This can include reactivity to pretty much anything.

For those who identify as empaths, the spectrum can range from those who sense other people's moods to people described as schizophrenic because they are having non-physical experiences. It is not uncommon for highly sensitive, empathic people to worry that they're crazy, especially if they live in a culture where these kinds of abilities are not recognized and most of the community is at the other end of the spectrum. Think about how many times you have heard, "You're overreacting. You're too sensitive. Just suck it up and chill out. Stop worrying about it. You're always blowing things out of proportion. You're such a drama queen." This may be useful advice for some, but it can be extremely difficult for sensitives to just suck it up and stop reacting.

Stress and tension tend to affect how susceptible you are. If you're calm, relaxed, and grounded, it's much easier to manage your sensitivity. As the world heats up with ever-increasing planetary crises and people become more and more anxious in response, it's much harder to filter information. For many of the people I work with, it's common to become overwhelmed with information and unable to process or push it away.

Why Are Empaths So Sensitive?

After many years of working with sensitive people as a healer and an intuitive, I have formed a theory. I have come to understand that many empathic people are missing vital pieces of their protective filtering and shielding systems. I believe there are several reasons for this.

One is that you were just born this way. You come from a long line of extremely intuitive, sensitive, empathic people whose filtering systems are simply more fragile than most. It's just the nature of who and what you are, part of your ancestral legacy. Periods of extreme challenge or trauma can also wreak havoc on filters and shields. After an intense ordeal, the energy body may be damaged and depleted. It then becomes more vulnerable, more susceptible to leaks in the protective bubble. Living through a very challenging childhood is another way these filters can be worn down. And, of course, glorious misspent youths (like mine) are another way to compromise those filters.

Many with these sensitivities are prone to feeling anxious for no apparent reason. We have a tendency to be more emotional, even more volatile than ordinary people. As a result, it's not uncommon that we start smoking cigarettes, smoking pot, and/or drinking alcohol. We may turn to food or other substances to try to self-soothe. This is a double-edged sword. In the short term, these substances bring relief. But in the long term, they actually cause damage to our energy systems rather than sustaining the relief they originally seemed to provide.

Damage to your filters doesn't necessarily come from multiple traumatic events. A single intense experience can cause shifts. I was talking with someone whose ability to filter information totally shifted after she suffered a brain injury. It varies with each individual.

The bottom line: as empaths, we do not have the density of energetic protection that regular folk have. It is much harder to control our exposure to both sensory and extrasensory input. One of the reasons I feel this book is so crucial is that there are probably millions of empathic women and men on the planet right now. Many are absolutely maxing out on the sheer volume of data they're being bombarded with. They don't know what they are, or why they're feeling the way they do. They have no tools. They're living with muggles who tell them they're too sensitive, they're overreacting, or, even worse, they're actually crazy.

I've gotten lots of feedback from people taking the quiz on my website telling me that it was really validating. They've said things like "Holy shit, I cried when I took the quiz, because I thought I was the only one," "I can't believe there's an answer for this," and "Oh my God, that's what I am? That's why I feel this way? That's what's been going on for me?"

We live in a dominant culture that does not acknowledge that empaths exist. I think being an empath in this society is similar to being queer, in that a significant portion of our mainstream culture does not generally recognize or accept it. We receive very little support, validation, or acknowledgment. This is terribly isolating and lonely for so many of us. Sometimes people find their way to places where they begin to hear about others like them. They come in thinking they're broken. They've been told that it's their fault. They think that if they could just figure out how to control it or shut it down, they'd be okay. But that's not how this works.

The Empath's Energy System

One of the things I've noticed, for both myself and many of the people that I've worked with, is that highly sensitive, empathic people tend to have different energetic and emotional filters than most people. Most of the information available right now is about how to become more psychic and intuitive. If you look into spiritual trainings, most tend to offer programs like, "So You Want to Learn How to Channel" or "Learn How to Read XYZ." I believe that most empaths don't need to learn how to be more psychic. We need to learn how to ground and protect ourselves. We need to learn how to manage what we already know and how to process the information that's coming to us.

Most of us were born psychic. We were born intuitive. We were born open and receiving. We need to learn how to protect ourselves, not how to be more open or get even more information. Most of us are suffering from "TMI" already. What we need to learn is how to harness our abilities.

Let's begin with the energy body. Different systems have different ways of looking at the energy body, but most assert that, in addition to the physical body, we have a personal space that extends out beyond our form. Some call it an aura. Others describe it as a ball of energy that extends beyond us. What I am talking about is an outer energetic layer that serves to define and protect our personal boundaries like a bubble. You've probably noticed that when a close talker comes into your personal space, you can feel them encroaching on your boundaries. That energetic barrier between you and the other person is what I'm referring to. That personal space, that boundary, is essentially an electrical or energetic field that extends beyond your physical body.

For the average muggle, that electrical field is like an insulated glass window. Most of what hits that window bounces right off. Unfortunately, instead of insulated glass, most sensitives have a set of rickety old screens. In extreme cases, there's just a cracked set of shutters flapping around an empty frame. If there's a windstorm, the ordinary person can look out his window and watch the trees whipping around, but remain unaffected. It's a different story for the empath. As soon as the first little breeze comes by, we feel it. It affects us immediately because it's blowing right into our house. Now, imagine that that windstorm is the emotional climate of the world around us. Ordinary people are able to sit back and watch it on TV. We, on the other hand, experience it directly. It enters us in a way that it doesn't enter regular people. We end up being flooded with all the emotions, thoughts, feelings, ideas, concerns, and pain from everything that's going on around us. Often these emotional storms leave damage in their wake.

There are layers to the energy system. The outer layer, shell, or sheath, keeps most extraneous material from getting in. Next, there's a thicker layer, rather like fiberglass insulation, that some extraneous material may penetrate, but will still be filtered by. Finally, there is a primary barrier right before our actual skin that protects our core. Most people have a fairly thick ball of energy around them. In contrast, many empaths' filters are either profoundly thin or never developed at all. Sometimes, even if the outer sheath is not missing entirely, it lacks strength and resiliency. It's often porous; for various reasons, holes have been torn through it. Thus, all kinds of information can enter rapidly, even when we don't want it to. This is one of the reasons many empaths tend to have issues around weight. It's not always excess weight -- we may be either thinner or heavier than average. But because we have self-protection issues, the body may compensate for an inadequate energetic sheath by adding a layer of insulation. We add extra padding to the physical body in order to protect the energetic body.

Energy Body

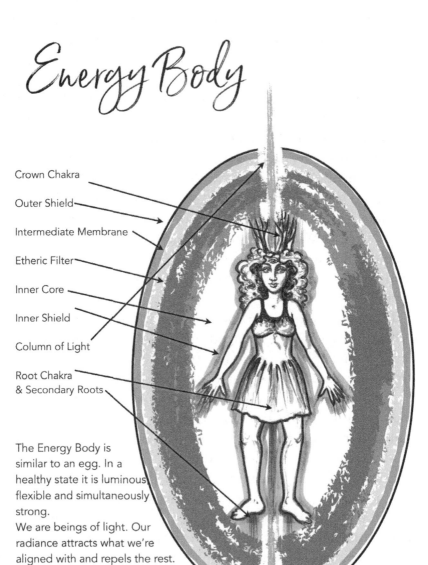

Crown Chakra

Outer Shield

Intermediate Membrane

Etheric Filter

Inner Core

Inner Shield

Column of Light

Root Chakra
& Secondary Roots

The Energy Body is similar to an egg. In a healthy state it is luminous flexible and simultaneously strong.

We are beings of light. Our radiance attracts what we're aligned with and repels the rest. When our system is depleted or compromised we become vulnerable to absorbing & carrying negativity.

Impact On Our Energy System

Traumatic experiences, emotional or physical intensity, too much stimulation, too much data coming in non-stop; all of these wear down our protective barriers. You may have started out with reasonable filters, but if you experienced repeated difficulties -- especially if you were a child with challenging, erratic, unpredictable parents or caretakers -- you were often placed in situations requiring constant vigilance in order to anticipate incoming chaos. This meant you had to decrease your filtering system in order to more rapidly sense and protect yourself from danger. This is another way that people become empaths.

Some of us come from long lines of empaths. Perhaps you've heard stories of grandmothers and great-grandmothers having "the sight" or prophetic dreams. Some of the things to look for in your family history are tendencies towards nervous conditions, depression, or mental health issues. If there is a lot of this in your family, chances are there's empathy in the ancestral line.

It doesn't ultimately matter whether you were born an empath or you became one because you got dipped into emotional paint thinner. Regardless of how you got here, you must learn to rebuild your sheath in order to operate effectively in the world. It's debilitating to be constantly bombarded with other people's thoughts, emotions, concerns, and pain. A robust sheath keeps us from absorbing information, energy, and sensations not just from the present moment, but also from the past, or even rippling backward from a potentially dominant future. When we are deluged with TMI from another time, it can prevent us from experiencing full awareness of the here and now.

As you learn to fortify your outer sheath, you will become better equipped not only to survive, but to thrive in daily life. You won't cease to be an empath because you've developed your sheath; the better protected you are, the more effectively you will be able to use your empathic gifts. With your sheath intact, you can actually use your empathy to be of service, rather than being a perpetual hostage to the wild ruckus of your sensitivities.

So many things can challenge an empath. It's one thing to run into a friend and immediately sense their feelings, allowing you to be a compassionate support to them. It's another thing entirely to be on a three-day bender of emotions, hardly knowing what you're feeling or why you're feeling it. Perhaps you've been having regular panic attacks, or experiencing a deep sense of uneasiness without being able to put your finger on any particular source. Perhaps you've been thinking, "I don't understand this. Where is it coming from? I'm uncomfortable but I have no idea what it's about." Often it's because you've absorbed other people's turmoil.

In some cases you may be experiencing emotional prophecy. This is when you sense things that haven't yet happened in this time stream. Where psychics have the ability to view coming disasters with some detachment, we empaths usually feel them in our bodies. We're like animals sensing an earthquake before the actual tremors begin. We'll often feel these tremors far in advance.

For example, I started to experience inexplicable panic, unease, and disorientation about two weeks before 9/11, as well as a few days before the mass shooting at Pulse nightclub in Orlando in the summer of 2016. This has been happening since I was a preteen: I experience a period of acute distress, pressure builds up, and then when the actual event occurs, I feel the pressure release like a rapidly deflating balloon.

Catastrophic events are like big stones dropped in the river of time. They send out ripples to the past, present, and future, simultaneously. The more beings impacted by an event, the more significant the ripples. As empaths, we feel these ripples -- they hit us repeatedly before the event even occurs. We don't have the ability to perceive it the way a classic psychic does. We just feel it. We feel the panic. We feel the stress. We know instinctively that something is coming.

Psychic or Empath?

What is the difference between an empath and a psychic? The simplest explanation is that empaths experience, while psychics perceive. Most empaths receive information as though they are living through it. This ranges from thinking others' thoughts to feeling others' emotions or physical sensations. One of the empath's biggest challenges is the inability to distinguish their own sensations from those of others. Conversely, most psychics can easily differentiate their own thoughts, feelings, and flashes of intuition from those of another source. Psychic information tends to come in through a much more intellectual channel. Psychics normally get information through one or two dominant sensory processing modes. Even if they are telepaths (having the ability to read other people's thoughts or to nonverbally communicate with other telepathic people), there is still a boundary between self and other. Telepathy is like picking up the psychic phone and having a conversation -- you know who's on which end of the line.

Along with telepathic abilities, psychics may have what are called "clairs." A "clair" gives the ability to perceive things beyond normal sensory contact. It literally translates as "clear." Essentially, any way we engage with the real world and process information can be experienced as a "clair." Clairvoyance is the ability to see things. Clairaudience is the ability to hear things. Clairsentience is the ability to sense things (it's actually another term for extreme empathy), and claircognizance is the ability to know things. Clairtangency, also known as psychometry, is the ability to receive information through touch. In addition, there are the less common clairalience and clairgustance. Clairalience occurs when someone smells odors that are not currently present, like a deceased loved one's perfume or cigarette smoke. Clairgustance is the ability to taste things that are not present, or to look at something and taste it without putting it in the mouth. I have a hunch that many gifted chefs and cooks have this ability. Some mystics have expanded on the "clairs" to include qualities like eloquence, embodiment, and empathy. For the purposes of this conversation, I am speaking only of the "clairs" which correlate with sensory awareness.

Psychics tend to specialize in one of these "clairs," usually the one that corresponds with their dominant mode for processing "real world" input. This can be true for empaths, too. You have probably noticed that many people use sensory language to describe their experiences. For example, when somebody uses language like, "I see that," "Look at it this way," or other phrases describing a visual experience, then chances are they are a visual processor. A person who says things like, "I hear what you're saying" or "That's music to my ears," is more of an auditory processor. Someone who is more in the feeling department is likely to use phrases like, "I know how you feel," or even "I get it." Next time you have a conversation, notice the other person's language. Do they tend to use words that are visual and colorful? Do they describe things in photographic detail? Do they use language that's emotional? Are their descriptive words dramatic or physical? "I was devastated!" "That was heartbreaking." "That makes me sick!" Or do they use language that's drier and more intellectual? These are all clues to their primary modes for processing input.

The Temptation to Shut It Down

After struggling with being an empath, some people wonder whether they can just turn it off to block all the feelings that flood them. Unfortunately, trying to shut down this sensitivity is like filling a pressure cooker with gasoline: it's only a matter of time before it explodes. Those suppressed feelings become combustible. The more exertion and restraint you put into avoiding them, the more volatile they become and the more powerful the inevitable explosion. Shutting down your feelings as an empath is worse than futile, it's harmful. It's about as useful as going out into a hurricane with an umbrella.

It's much more effective to cultivate mindful awareness of what's ours and what isn't, and to recognize how the present experience is triggering reactions from the past. Instead of denying or attempting to shut down empathic intensity, we are far better served by strengthening our personal filters and shields. Perhaps the most difficult thing to master is the acceptance of discomfort. Even though it can feel really unfamiliar (and even scary) at first, it's better to be present with uncomfortable emotions than to try to shut them down.

Remember, we live in a culture that does not embrace pain. We are trained from infancy to avoid it. As a result, when we feel sadness, anger, or anything unpleasant, there is an urgency to fix it or shut it down. Because of this habit of denial and suppression, when "negative feelings" finally do rise to the surface, they can be expressed in extreme ways.

Dramatic tantrums and hysterical sobbing are familiar caricatures of anger and sadness. However, it is possible to experience emotions without having them hijack your life. There is a very big difference between feeling a feeling and acting it out. You can be angry. You can be sad. You can be scared. You can have any number of feelings and be mindful of them, acknowledge them, and accept them, without turning the volume up to eleven and creating a telenovela. You can create space for feelings without letting them consume all the oxygen in the room.

When I was younger, emotions ruled me. If I felt sad, anxious, or angry, the feeling became my reality. My perception of everything was filtered through my emotional gaze. If I was having a particularly fearful day, it meant the world was a dangerous place and it was only a matter of time before something terrible would happen. If I was feeling blue, it meant that I was doomed to struggle with depression for the rest of my life and nothing would ever go right.

Instead of understanding that emotions are only part of who I am, I gave them total authority in my life. I often made myself miserable because my dire conclusions only amplified my distress. Learning to question the veracity of my emotional instincts has been incredibly freeing. It has allowed me to become comfortable with the fact that feelings are just feelings, and often they don't go away immediately. Emotions are like the ocean. They ebb and flow. They come and they go. The more we resist them, the more we dam them up, the more powerful they become. But if we just allow them to be, they pass. Resistance to emotions is one of the best ways to exacerbate them.

It's often easier to see how emotions amplify distress and distort perception by watching someone else. A number of years ago, my friend Tina's teenager missed their curfew. Tina considers herself an intuitive, and all night long she kept seeing horrible images of her child drowning in a river after falling off a bridge. She was convinced she was having premonitions and that her child was dead. The next morning the kid came home. In reality, Tina's fear was so extreme it distorted everything. What she imagined was a premonition was actually just a tortured fantasy from her distressed, overwhelmed imagination. The moral of this story is: "Just because you're psychic doesn't mean it's true."

Part of the work we'll be doing in this book will be learning to accept both your feelings and the feelings that come to you from others. In chapter four, you'll learn the fundamentals of *Recognition*. You'll learn to recognize where feelings are coming from and you'll receive tools to help you work with them. You'll learn how to acknowledge the feelings and then, in the following chapter, how to work with them until you're able to calm your mind, body, and emotions. One of the best places to start is with conscious breathing.

Acceptance and the Willingness to Surrender

Empaths feel the pain and suffering in the world and they want to alleviate it. I often read comments such as:

"Oh my God, I'm having *all the feels*. The world is in *so much* pain. What can I do?"

"I sense all of the suffering that's happening around me. How can I help?"

"My coworker is having a really shitty day and I'm absorbing all of it. How do I support them *and* protect myself?"

"This is so hard for me to handle. How do I deal with this?"

"I wish I could help them. I wish I could fix this, but I don't know where to begin or what to do without getting even more overwhelmed!"

The most gracious response I can muster is that everyone is entitled to their own feelings. Everyone is entitled to their own journey. It is not my job -- or yours -- to fix anyone else. It is not my job to make somebody figure out the shit I think they need to know. It is not my job to be the savior who knows the right answer for somebody else. I can offer suggestions. I can offer information. I can offer my own experience, strength, and hope. If it resonates for somebody else, that's great. But if it doesn't, it is not my responsibility to take away their pain, to deny them their experience, or to protect them from their own process or their own journey.

Fundamentally, I must surrender the outcome. The key to all of this lies in profound acceptance of what *is*. Only by every single one of us being 100% present with our own journey will we, as a planet, start taking responsibility for the choices that we make.

One of my spiritual teachers is a woman named Florence Scovel Shinn, who was a writer and new thought leader back in the 1920's.

At the very core of her teachings is the radical idea that everything real comes from Divine Source and all else is an illusion, Shinn wrote: "Jesus Christ said: 'Resist not evil,' for He knew in reality, there is no evil, therefore nothing to resist." When we surrender and trust that all is unfolding in Divine Order, all will be well.

Now, I'll admit that I come from some pretty high-strung people who are gifted at awfulizing nearly anything. Not only that, but both of my parents worked in human service fields, so I was raised to worry over people's problems and to let my sense of injustice mature to a rich, full-bodied *whine*.

Part of me still contends with the message that *Life Is Not Fair*, and that all this "Pollyanna" thinking just denies the inequality, unfairness, and corruption that is destroying our planet. While I can't confirm or deny whether these Debbie Downer and Richard Revolutionary statements are ultimately true, I can say that whenever I surrender and focus on the perfect unfoldment of the Universe's Divine Plan, things go with much greater grace and ease (even when I hit detours) than when I fret with indignation and concern.

As long as we keep siphoning off other people's pain and trying to help them circumvent their process, people will continue to participate in behaviors that do not serve them as individuals or all of us collectively. When we continually try to engage with other people's challenges and lessons, we prevent their true growth.

The path of willingness is the key to any shift or change. But before we can reach willingness, we must be *willing* to be willing. Prayer is a wonderful tool for this – prayer to whomever or whatever you believe in. Whether you believe in a life force or intelligence that is greater than yourself, or in divine energy in any form, when you can acknowledge that there's something beyond yourself that may be able to support and help you, help will come. You can even appeal to your ancestors for that help. One of the most powerful prayers that exists for me is simply: "Grant me the willingness to be willing." The willingness to be willing to surrender to whatever comes next is the key to functioning effectively and lovingly, and being able to continue down the path.

This ties into the classic Serenity Prayer (written by Reinhold Niebuhr), which is one of the most powerful prayers in the world:

Divine Source, Grant me the Serenity

To accept the things I cannot change,

The courage to change the things I can,

And the wisdom to know the difference.

It really is true. There are things I *cannot* change. There are things that I'm incapable of affecting. For example, I sincerely doubt I'll ever influence Donald Trump to become a different person. There is nothing I can do to change him. But I can adjust my own attitude and the energy I project towards him. I can cultivate compassion and love despite our differences. I can also choose to hold the perspective that there is a greater reason -- even though I do not understand it -- for why we're going through this time of global upheaval and conflict.

But there are also things I *can* affect. I can increase the information that you, reader, have about what it means to be an empath. I can be present with you. I can offer support and share my own experience about this healing journey. As empaths, we can find the willingness to be willing to surrender the things we cannot control, and the willingness to be willing to surrender the outcome of that which is beyond our capacity, and to truly let go of the outcome.

How do surrender and acceptance differ from one another? Surrender is being willing to let go entirely. It's the trust fall:

giving in to gravity with faith that you will be caught. It's not just surrendering the outcome, but truly handing it over to the Universe. With surrender, if I have a problem, I open my hands and allow it to be taken from me. I cease to grasp at it, clutch it, or attempt to control it anymore. My heartfelt prayer is, "Here. Here. I'm opening up my hands. Please God, take this from me."

With acceptance, I acknowledge and choose to accept something as it is. I find acceptance an easier quality to cultivate, because I can accept something without having to surrender it. From my perspective, acceptance is step one. Surrender is step two. You work with both of them. You start by accepting something and then, from that place of acceptance, you surrender it

The Characteristics of Empaths

After reading the previous sections, you may already be convinced that you're pretty far along on the empathic spectrum, but you might not be sure exactly where you land. Here are some characteristics that will help you determine where you fit on the empathic continuum. This list of characteristics isn't arbitrary or absolute. These are the general behaviors and traits we are inclined to have. None of these are exclusive to being empathic, but the more of them you identify with, the more empathic you are likely to be.

Empaths are creative.

Empaths have a tendency to be creative, whether in the classic visual arts, music, dancing, or some other form of expression. It could be through food. It could be through writing. It could simply be through the way that you love to experience the world.

Empaths are drawn to beauty and nature.

Empaths are drawn to beauty. We're attracted to color. We find solace and comfort in nature. We're drawn to things that are lovely and harmonious. We experience art, writing, movies, music, food, stories, nearly everything, deeply. We take things in on a deep emotional and visceral level. Empaths can often experience full immersion, so we are also prone to bingeing (including binge-watching).

Empaths absorb other people's feelings.

I've already said a good deal about this, but it bears repeating: in an increasingly loud and confrontational culture, we get blasted by people who have no emotional containment, as well as those who are deliberately projecting their shit all over the place. We feel and absorb that all too easily.

Empaths absorb the energy from our environment.

We also pick up what's going on in the world around us – the messages, the media, the things that are happening everywhere all the time. There are several levels to this:

1. Our close relationships with people and other living beings like our pets and the wildlife living in our direct vicinity.
2. Those who are just living and breathing every day in our town, state or even country.
3. Global awareness of all the animals, plants, insects, even the air, and everything else that surrounds us.

Instead of recognizing that we all function as cells in the body of one great, living planetary entity, it's unfortunate that we live in a time where we've been taught to perceive ourselves as isolated individuals. In reality, this planet is a colony, like a hive of bees. We are all interdependent members of this colony. We are interconnected like a vast neural network. It's natural for everyone to be firing off and receiving energetic, emotional, and mental signals, to and from all the other cells in this global body. That's the way nervous systems work. There's non-stop intercommunication between everything.

Empaths are baffled by small talk.

Need I say more? Truthful expression is especially important to empaths. You know when people are speaking the truth. Empathic people have a tendency to be naturally truthful, as well as extremely literal. You want to be sure you're communicating clearly so people grasp what you are saying. You want to be understood. You want to be impeccable in how you speak the truth.

Unfortunately, when it comes to muggles, more than half the time they simply do not have the capacity to fully comprehend what you are trying to express. Empaths choose their words carefully. It is not uncommon to lie in bed at night and replay the day, combing through what you could have said or done differently: "I can't believe I said this instead of that." Because it feels so essential to get the message right, you may worry: "I hope I didn't hurt them by saying 'like' instead of 'love,' or by mentioning that so-and-so was my best friend instead of talking about them first."

Empaths are good judges of character (usually).

Because you can sense the unspoken thoughts and feelings of the people around you and pick up on their energy or vibe, it is generally easy to determine who is a good, kind, reliable person.

However, there are two common exceptions: (1) when your need to rescue someone in pain hijacks your common sense, and (2) when you meet a narcissist, whose very nature can override your alarm system. (More on that in the next section!)

Empaths are capable of deeply intimate connections.

Even though you may tend to be shy or introverted, you can form tight bonds with kindred souls. Unless an empath has been hurt to a point of irrevocable mistrust and wariness, they are naturally loving and inclined towards unconditional love for most beings they meet. Empaths can love instantly, especially with other empaths. When an empath meets another one there is often a flash of recognition: "You are my tribe. You are my person. I love you dearly."

Empaths frequently come from a legacy of anxiety, addiction, and abuse.

Many empaths tend to be anxiety prone. Other family members are often like this too. To put it bluntly, many of us empaths come from a long line of hot messes. We've inherited a legacy from generations of people who were inclined to imagine how awful things were going to be, who always envisioned the worst-case scenario, and who issued warnings about why we might not even want to try something new. In many cases this inclination to perseverate on a future of darkness and disaster is a learned habit which can feel hard to break. Visualizing the worst possible scenario or outcomes driven by evil is kind of like eating sugar, taking drugs and scratching poison ivy all rolled into one. We know it is not good for our health on any level but in the moment that rumination can feel deviously delicious.

In addition, it is not uncommon for empaths to have grown up in households (or school systems) where they needed to be hypervigilant to avoid harm. As with the proverbial chicken or egg, one could ask, "Does hypervigilance provoke empathic abilities, or does empathy run in families who abuse substances (and subsequently act out) to cope with being so sensitive?" While I certainly have met empathic people who had pleasant, loving childhoods, I know many more who grew up enduring alcoholism, abusive treatment, or even sexual abuse.

Enduring a childhood of relentless danger and harm wears down the filters and shields of our energy body. On one hand, we become more sensitive because our protective shields are depleted; on the other, we amplify our sensitivity to anticipate anger and volatile behavior, and to learn to protect ourselves. In some cases we are the children of children of alcoholics. Perhaps the cycle of abuse appears to have stopped on the surface. There may be no actual substance abuse or physical harm, but the impact of these 'isms' does not go away simply because our parents broke the cycle of violence. In some ways this can be even more baffling because -- from outer appearances -- life seems fine. Yet parents who grew up under siege do not put away all of their coping skills and dysfunctional behaviors simply because they are now out of harm's way. They are still prone to the same fear, hypervigilance, worry, and concern that they grew up with. There is often an unspoken uneasiness, a moodiness and even depression that haunts the families of adult children of addicts. Highly sensitive children will pick this up and, since there is no glaringly obvious "bad" behavior going on, there is often even more of a need to probe the subtle and persistent distress going on under the surface. Obviously, dealing with most of these characteristics can be a huge challenge. I'll talk at greater length, as the book progresses, about how we can deal with them.

Empaths and Narcissists

The need to rescue or people-please clouds our better judgement. When we are particularly depleted or open, the discomfort we feel from other people's pain provokes a desire to help them even if this is not in our own best interest. We may be able to see clearly that someone is wounded and will not be a trustworthy or reliable person to engage with, but our sense of urgency gets triggered by the intensity of their pain. This causes us to second-guess our better judgment and help them anyway. This dynamic is perhaps one of our most challenging and harmful behaviors, and many of us will engage in it at some point in our empathic lives. Helping others comes naturally for us; if anything, it is almost an imperative. Empaths actually have to learn how *not* to help others. Before we learn how to protect ourselves by establishing solid psychic, emotional, and practical boundaries, we can end up giving much more of our time, energy, and resources than we can afford to share.

The dangerous, sometimes even lethal, combination of empath and narcissist is a fatal attraction; the empath is a moth to the narcissist's flame. Narcissists *love* being loved. They *love* being reflected positively by the empathic beloved. The first blush of romance between empath and narcissist is intoxicating. The narcissist is on their best behavior. They are charming, they are considerate, and they bend over backwards to woo the empath. While this is happening they are getting all kinds of positive strokes and validation from the empath, so the empath only senses the best, brightest side of the narcissist. They are both fed by this engagement, and both may believe they've finally found "the one." This honeymoon period can last for weeks, months, or sometimes even years. However, once the bond has been established and the narcissist no longer needs to attract the empath, their behavior begins to shift and become more selfish.

At this point the empath is all in; they have pledged their loyalty and care deeply for the needs of the narcissist. As the narcissist starts making outrageous requests while simultaneously giving less and less emotional support to the empath, the empath starts scrambling to meet their increasing demands. When the narcissist tells the empath things like "You are overreacting. You are being too sensitive. What I am asking is totally normal, you're being unrealistic," the empath may feel baffled and confused, but their desire to fill the ever-increasing emotional void of the narcissist keeps them in this painful dance. Narcissists are deceptive by nature.

In the same way that most empaths are hyper-aware of their part in the picture and deeply committed to speaking the truth (at least most of the time), narcissists are constitutionally incapable of perceiving their role in any problem or challenge. They will take all the credit for anything good, but place all the blame for a problem on anything but themselves. After enough disregard and mistreatment, many empaths will decide to leave. However, while a narcissist may not even love or care about the empath anymore, it is a great injury and insult to their fragile ego that someone would ever have the audacity to leave them. Ironically, even when they are the ones leaving, they will still be angry at the empath for abandoning them. This is a point in the relationship that can become very tricky, especially when children are involved.

Sadly, I know far too many empaths who married classic narcissists when they were young and innocent. It is often the birth of children that causes the whole house of cards to collapse; the empath's attention is suddenly on the children instead of doting, 24/7, on the narcissist. While the narcissist may even have been the one who insisted on having children, whom they see as reflections of themselves, they resent that the empath is not there for them the way they used to be. Conversely, the empath's priorities shift to raising their children with the best life possible. The empath sees the narcissist's volatile, irrational behavior through the lens of what their kids are witnessing. The scales fall from the empath's eyes. This is often when they realize what a disaster the whole relationship has become.

This is the point where things can get really messy. Behaviors like gaslighting, stalking, badgering, and involving the kids in the narcissist's twisted game are all too common. I've frequently witnessed what one of the empathic women I know refers to as "Domestic Violence by Proxy," where the custody of children, child support payments, and alimony are all used as ways to punish the empathic spouse. I wish I could tell you that there is a simple solution to this, but in cases where the relationship has developed roots, it usually takes vigilance, self-awareness, clear and steadfast boundaries, the courage to stand your ground, and good legal support. Perhaps the biggest mistake empaths make when ending relationships with narcissists is persisting in the hopeful belief that the narcissist has the capacity to care about anyone other than themself. This simply isn't the case.

Narcissists first charm empaths, then they destabilize them and cause them to doubt themselves. Next, they become baffling and frustrating because they do not and cannot behave in ways that empaths can predict or understand.

However, narcissists are sensitive to losing the critical supply of attention and concern from their empath. They may do a sudden 180 and become kind and considerate just as the empath is about to throw in the emotional towel and simply stop giving any F's about them. If this doesn't work, they will frequently revert to manipulative or even vicious behavior, because human beings are wired to choose negative attention over indifference. If there is one thing I can tell you from my travels around the sun, both with my own encounters with narcissists and from witnessing some of my most beloved friends endure their abuse, it is the following:

1. Narcissists will *never, ever* admit to being wrong, to causing you pain, to manipulating the situation, or to bringing you harm.

2. Narcissists will often perceive themselves to be the injured party and sincerely believe they are the victim and you are the perpetrator.

3. Narcissists are remarkably skilled at turning the tables and putting other people on the defensive. When someone calls them out on their behavior and accuses them of being abusive, they will put it right back on the victim and accuse them of everything they are doing.

4. Narcissists have ninja powers when it comes to manipulating others to meet their needs. Their emotional survival depends on other people's attention, so they have masterful coping skills. They know how to lie undetectably. They know how to anticipate how far they can push someone before they go too far. They may be the most charming person you've ever

met, they may make you feel better than you have ever felt before, but they can (and will) make you feel lower than a worm. At their core, they are suffering greatly. Theirs is a mental illness that often decimates their lives and the lives of their loved ones. There is no winning with a narcissist. They are cognitively incapable of perceiving their own part in any of this and, unless they are very rare, they will never change.

5. Stop putting your bucket down a dry well. This engagement is futile and you will *never* get your needs met here. This can be especially hard to accept when the romantic phase was so glorious in the beginning.

6. Accept that you fell for a narcissist. Forgive yourself and move on. Find support from people who truly love and care for you. Honor your needs with self-love and self-care. Ask for help from people who can actually give it to you.

7. Get the support you need to heal from this. Take some time to really probe what drew you in, what signs you may have missed, and what to look for now that you are older and wiser.

8. Finally, if you have found yourself in a series of relationships with narcissists and/or abusive people: *please*, I urge you with every fiber of my being, hit the pause button! Take some time -- not just a few weeks or even a few months, but upwards of a year or more -- and find a good healer/counselor/practitioner/mentor who can help you release this fatal attraction. Learn to become comfortable in your own skin and sitting with your own solitude. Get to a point where you love yourself so much that you'd rather be alone than ever love another mismatched, misaligned asshole again in your life. As George Washington once said,

"It is better to be alone than in bad company."

Empaths Out and About

It takes a lot of effort to be wide open while wandering around in the world, so it's common for empaths to feel exhausted after being out and about. This is because you exert so much mental, emotional, and psychic energy trying to process what you are sensing, while also trying to shield yourself from all the intensity. It is very common to feel emotionally drained after you've spent time with other people. It's particularly tiring with people who are not deliberate or conscious about their actions or feelings. Feeling their feelings, trying to process and heal things for them is exhausting. Perhaps you find yourself feeling aggravated, irritated, or angry for no evident reason. Actually, there are two reasons for this. One, because you feel other people's feelings, you're actually experiencing their anger, irritation, and aggravation. The other is that you've reached your saturation point. You're overstimulated from sensing other people's stuff so you become irritable yourself.

As mentioned earlier, not only can we sense things happening in the present moment, we are often capable of sensing emotions, energy, and information coming from a different time. It may be an event from the past, or it may be something yet to occur in the dominant stream of the future. You're perceiving the ripples. Sometimes this comes from sensing the emotional echoes left in a space. You walk into an old house and feel the sadness of people who lived there before.

A number of years ago, as newlyweds, my husband and I went house hunting. A bunch of those houses felt really funky, but there was one that still sticks with me. It was a quaint little white Cape with all the original late-50's kitchen appliances. Everything was tidy and just so. The downstairs felt neutral, but then we walked upstairs. There were two small bedrooms on either side of this little house. First we looked at what appeared to be the master bedroom. This made little impression on me. Then I stepped across the threshold into the other room, which contained a narrow bed with a pair of men's slippers beside it. This cot had been slept in so long it had a deep groove in the center from the weight of the sleeper. As I looked at this bed and those slippers, I was suddenly overwhelmed with profound grief and sadness. I instinctively "knew" that the slippers belonged to a widower who had moved out of his marital bed when his wife died. He was able to keep it together during the day and throughout the rest of the house. But at night, all of his grief would come pouring out in that little chamber, where he'd cry himself to sleep. Just writing about this brings back that sorrow and my empathy for his suffering. I will never be able to confirm that the download of information was accurate. We were not interested in the house and our realtor had no idea about its history. The truth is, even if I did ask, I sincerely doubt the elderly homeowner would admit to a total stranger that he cried himself to sleep every night.

The thing is, whether the exact details of what I felt and saw in my mind's eye were spot on or not doesn't really matter. The energy in that room was distinct and palpable. I went from feeling totally fine to completely verklempt in mere seconds, as soon as I stepped into that room. Because I've had enough other experiences where I was able to confirm what I sensed, I feel confident that this was more than my imagination.

It is also possible to feel the emotions of a physical place. There's a spot on the highway near me where the energy is strange. When they built the road, they blasted the face off a huge, rocky cliff instead of excavating around it. It never made any sense to me because it was only a matter of moving about 50 yards sideways. I imagine what that did to all those rocks. They'd been there for millions of years and suddenly some humans came along and blew them apart. "Why did you do that to us? That didn't make any sense. For your convenience, because you wanted this road to go straight instead of curving around us?" Not only will you sense or feel what's going on with humans and animals, you may also pick up the sadness, fear, anxiety, and disruption of geopathic stress to the Earth itself. This is particularly noticeable when you're in a place where people have no regard for other living things. They just cut down trees, blast rock, and simply don't care about the impact of their choices on other beings who can't express their distress to ordinary humans. These are areas where you feel off-base when you enter them. When land expresses geopathic stress, humans pick up on it even when they're not conscious of it. Therefore, interestingly, when it comes to roads, these are often spots where there are more car accidents than usual.

If I haven't stressed this enough already, being "a sensitive" means that you're sensitive. It means that you can pick up on everything. You don't get to choose. You don't get to decide that you're going to be sensitive with intuition and emotions, but you don't have to deal with a reactive physical body. As mentioned earlier, sensitives are susceptible to an entire range of things; EMFs, Wi-Fi, radio signals, allergens, food, alcohol, drugs, etc.

Television is another challenge. This is particularly true for live news events. I really want to stress that right now it's extremely important for empaths to avoid watching live disasters on television. I mean it. If you take away only one thing from this book, I hope it is this: unless you are well grounded and shielded and have done the necessary spiritual work to anchor light and transmute stress, stay away from TV news. Television amplifies every experience. It brings the event right to you. You're already getting the download from the world around you and it's being magnified by the broadcast. You're not only experiencing the event itself, you're experiencing amplification by every single person watching the event and having their emotional reaction to it. On 9/11, the 24-hour news cycle played the Twin Towers crash over and over again. This exacerbated, recapitulated, and re-stimulated our nation's terror and grief. As an empath, it is very important to start recognizing that there are things we must be careful about. We need to be especially mindful of not exposing ourselves to harmful media.

Long-distance travel is another source of distress for empaths. It's not unusual to have a meltdown after you've been away from home for a few days. It takes a great deal of bandwidth to adapt to a new environment. It's disorienting to be in a place where every single bit of stimulation is new. Your sensitive system is shrieking, "Oh my God, I am in a new place and there's all this new information, and I have to process every single bit of it *right now!*" Empaths tend to be hypervigilant in new environments. We need to make sense of all the fresh data, to understand what's happening and calibrate our systems. To add to this challenge, in order to "know" an unfamiliar location, empaths tend to become more open than usual. This can be depleting and wearing to our already delicate systems.

It used to take three days for me to have a total meltdown. It didn't matter where the unfamiliar place was, I hit my wall. I was okay traveling as a kid and even a teenager, but by my early twenties it got much harder for me as my abilities increased. I would become so agitated it often felt as if I was losing my mind.

While any new place can trigger a meltdown for the unguarded empath, once we are familiar with an area, specific location can make a big difference. It is important to factor in the volume of the population, the culture and personality, the level of noise and crowding, and the overall intensity. For example, Portland, Maine (the closest city to where I live) is like a pee-wee softball team compared to, say, New York City, which is like the top of the Major Leagues. Judging the magnitude of what you're up against can make a huge difference.

Many empaths find it easier to be in less-populated areas and prefer to limit their time spent in congested urban areas. This can be true for schools, too. For empathic children, being in large school systems can be profoundly overwhelming. As an empath, Maine is a good place for me. It's one of the least populated states in the country, so I'm not bombarded with as much information as I would be in a more populous place with less space per capita.

Have you ever noticed that you initially feel energized, perhaps even elated, in crowds or urban areas? After a little more time, however, this excitement turns into overwhelm and anxiety. For me, the first two or three days in Manhattan or Vegas are full of, "Bring it!" Then, all of a sudden, it's, "Oh, fuck, too much!"

There's a part of us that is fed by these energies, especially at the outset. It's almost like emotional eating. When you take that first bite, it tastes yummy and it feels really good. But soon you start getting full and feeling crappy. That's what happens with hectic energy. Those first couple of bites can be pretty delicious, but after you've received a bit more than you can handle, and then a lot more than you can handle, it becomes a problem.

After experiencing the downside of being in hectic settings, empaths will often start to avoid busy areas and crowds. It's common to dislike being in public places with more than a few people around. We tend to avoid concerts, parties, and other events where we'll be packed in tightly with lots of other people. Empaths are usually great at connecting very deeply one-on-one. However, social situations can be overwhelming and difficult to navigate. In part, this is because we're picking up on too many people's information all at once. We don't always know how to process who's feeling what, what's going on, or how to navigate multiple conversations when there's information coming from several different sources at the same time.

Imagine being in a room with multiple radios or televisions playing on different stations. Each is playing at a similar volume, so as the noise mingles it becomes extremely hard to distinguish what's what. Muggles do not have this challenge to the same degree. They rely on the conventional five senses to process the obvious information in the space, therefore they can be more selective about what they perceive and can focus on one conversation or experience at a time.

I've noticed that a lot of empaths identify as introverts. Being "*on*" all the time like an extravert gets very exhausting, and downtime, solitude, and calm environments are what many of us need to restore and protect ourselves. However, not all empathic people are considered introverts. Personally, I fall right down the middle, on the Myers-Briggs scale. I'm what's called an ambivert: depending on circumstances, I can go either way. I'll often say, "I'm an introvert that plays an extravert on TV." I get nourishment by being with one or two friends, in small groups of people where the space is safely contained, or if I am leading or participating in a very focused and positively oriented larger group.

However, large crowds and chaotic groups are almost always overwhelming, especially the chaotic, jacked-up herd energy of certain kinds of sporting, political, or entertainment events. When a stadium full of people is excited, emotionally invested, and lathered up with a singular goal, it can be very overwhelming to be around. I find it challenging just hearing the roaring crowds of football games on television.

There's a rain barrel effect: the more stimulated your system becomes, the more overloaded with information the whole heart, mind, body, and soul get, the more allergies you become susceptible to developing. When a system has been abraded and irritated repeatedly, all it takes is a drop for that barrel to overflow. We become more allergic as we age because we've absorbed so much over time. We'll start having problems with food, chemicals, mold, dust, yeast, dander, and more. Ironically for many of us, the more foods and other elements we eliminate from our life, the more things we recognize are a problem. Sound familiar? Fortunately, as I have committed to working the principles in this book, all of the above has gotten much easier for me. I now have significantly better filters and shields. I have also released a great deal, so my "rain barrel" now has room to accommodate new experiences before it overflows.

Premonitions, Global and Personal

Empaths are often affected by disasters, even when they have no personal connection to them. We frequently feel anxious or fearful days before tragic world events occur. This distress precedes consciously knowing anything is happening well before any breaking news. A few days before Hurricane Katrina occurred, before I even knew anything about weather forecasts or evacuation plans, I walked around feeling as though I had a dull aching wound in my gut. I felt the waves of sorrow and grief rippling out from New Orleans for weeks afterward. As mentioned earlier, I experienced moments of extreme distress before 9/11. Before catastrophic events happen, I'll feel inexplicable waves of panic and anxiety. I'll feel horrible in a way that no self-soothing can fix. This distress tells me that something bad is coming.

One of my most intense experiences happened the day my husband and I attended a Paul McCartney concert. I felt anxious even before we headed south to Boston, but I wasn't sure whether anticipation of the crowd and the excessively loud noise was provoking my panic, or if it was something bigger. Nothing I tried made me feel better. I was a train wreck. Sadly, later that evening I learned that a dear friend had been hospitalized at the same time I had been experiencing those feelings. Although none of us knew it at the time, my friend was only one month away from his death by a rare and very swift degenerative disease. I had been trying so hard to manage my feelings that I tried to convince myself that I was upset by the prospect of a noisy concert, but the truth was that I had been feeling a tragic event coming down the pike.

How many times have you imagined events in your mind, only to discover that they've actually happened, days, weeks, or months later? I don't think this one needs a lot of explanation. You see things ahead of time and get hunches, premonitions, and feelings about them. You may dream about friends or family members and later discover that they dreamed about you at the same time (this used to happen to me a lot when I was younger and hadn't established the kind of sleep filters that I have now). Dreams are one of the more effective ways that we all connect with each other. We can reach out across time and space to one another, even beyond death.

Another manifestation of empathic awareness is when you sense the phone is going to ring, or you think of someone at the same moment you receive a text message from them. Perhaps you call a person and they tell you that they were just about to call you. Empaths often know what other people will say before they say it. All of these experiences are common for the highly sensitive empathic person. It is not unusual for this to be happening on a daily basis.

Sometimes we'll get an urgent feeling to contact a dear one, only to learn that they're having a particularly difficult time when we reach out. Perhaps you discover a loved one is sick or is going to be dying soon. As you look back at it, you realize that there was a very clear reason you felt the urge to make that call. Again, this has to do with being sensitive, to picking up what's going on. And that's not something everybody has.

When I was younger and less aware, my premonitions were especially intense. Over time I have learned to identify their characteristics. Consequently, I'm more able to recognize premonitions for what they are. This gives me an ability to contain my distress in a way that I couldn't before I learned to distinguish what's mine and what is coming from outside myself.

Connections Beyond This Time and Space

Animals, especially pets, are often drawn to empaths. Animals notice you and come to you. They love you. Babies and children love you. Little kids in stores will just light up and say, "Hi!" Cats are especially sensitive to empathic people. They enjoy it when they're not up against a rigid shield. Most cats love climbing right into your energy body.

Perhaps you had imaginary friends when you were a kid. I want to clarify that "imaginary friends" is the term grownup people often use when they see a child connecting with unseen beings. "Imaginary friends" may be people on the other side, deities, nature spirits, devas, beings from parallel realities, and more. It's not that you had "imaginary" friends. It's that you were often connecting with other beings, with spirits, angels, or ghosts in the house. Your parents said, "Oh, isn't that cute? Isabelle is talking to her imaginary friend again."

It is very likely that you preferred being in nature as a child. You probably prefer it still. Part of this has to do with the fact that nature is quieter. Nature is a calmer place to be. It's easier to keep your energy body and emotions in a state of comfort there. You are replenished by the natural world. You are nourished and fed by being connected to the Earth. It is easier to be more grounded, to feel less off-center or out-of-balance in nature. That's why we tend to be drawn to it.

Perhaps you're attracted to stories about magic, spirituality, and characters with special or supernatural gifts. I believe that's because we are so hungry for information or reflections of ourselves that we crave stories in which we can recognize ourselves.

Perhaps you feel like an old soul. You feel that you've been here before. You may even remember being here before. You may have vivid past-life recall. You may even have come into this life remembering specific things. Sometimes you may awaken to those memories later in life. I have met a number of very sensitive people who did not "wake up" until they were in their thirties, forties, or even fifties. Some of us are born wide awake, some of us awaken later. Being an old soul or recalling multiple lives doesn't necessarily mean you're an empath. But I have found empaths are often old souls who've lived multiple lives.

Perhaps you've experienced a weird familiarity with a place you've never been. You've never been there, yet you know exactly where everything is. You know the lay of the land. You know the roads. You know the territory. It's completely familiar. There are a couple of different causes for this. You may actually have been there in another life, so you are recalling something from another time and place.

However, it's also possible that you've tuned into the place and tapped into the local people. It's as if you've plugged into a Universal Data Bank and GPS. You're synced up and able to follow the energetic currents of the land. Every location has its own rhythm and a flow. There's a unique pattern of movement that all places have. Well-traveled paths, trails and roads have more obvious energetic signatures than the more secluded or out-of-the-way areas, but even these spaces carry the signatures of all the beings that inhabit them. Empaths can pick up on these signatures and follow streams of familiarity which have been reinforced by all the energy that's already traveled there. It's like taking a carabiner and hooking onto a zip line. You can link onto this energetic zip line and let it guide you to where you need to go.

Empaths who are tuned in and managing their abilities will tend to have a good sense of direction. Conversely, empaths who are not controlling their sensitivity can feel really chaotic, get lost, and end up in some rather strange places. It's because all the emotional and psychic static makes it hard to stay on track and follow the best path. This applies both literally, to actual travel, and symbolically, to life in general.

Perhaps as a child you were especially fascinated (or even obsessed) by a particular historical period. Ancient Egypt and the American Civil War are periods many are drawn to. The Civil War is a fairly recent time when many souls experienced profound trauma. This is amplified by the collective experience and consciousness because much of this national ordeal has remained unreconciled. People still come back with raw, unreconciled memories of the Civil War.

One of my nephews used to dress up as a Union officer every Halloween when he was little. One day when he was five, he and my mom were playing together in the backyard, pretending he'd just come home from the Civil War. They wandered into the (imaginary) family cemetery and my nephew said to my mom, "And Meema, you were buried right there." My mom just thought, "Okay..." and shared the "cute" story with me later. I believe this was an example of past life bleed-through: the vivid remembering of an event that happened in another time, but feels as if it is happening now. This is much more common in young children because their connection to other incarnations is still fresh. The mental and emotional data of their current life has not yet begun to accumulate and crowd out past-life memories. These days, my teenage nephew has little recall of or interest in the Civil War.

The spiritual essence of a soul can coalesce around events. The awareness, consciousness, and even details of the experiences are retained. This happens through traumatic events, intense emotion, or deliberate and persistent spiritual practice. Past-life memories are stored in a similar way. Memories lock in during acute trauma. Memories will solidify due to intense emotion. Deep, passionate love will anchor memories, as will other intense feelings. Memory retention also anchors through spiritual devotion. It is not uncommon for dedicated Buddhists to recall their Buddhist (and other) lives. There are many instances of people who've been identified as the *tulku*, or reincarnation, of a rinpoche, a monk or saint from a previous century.

You can find a sweet representation of this in the 1993 Bernardo Bertolucci film, *Little Buddha*, wherein a group of monks go on a worldwide search for the reincarnation of a former Lama, who happens to be living as a little white boy in Seattle (watching Keanu Reeves as Siddhartha is almost comical, but there are many jewels in this film that make it worth watching). When non-spiritual seekers experience past-life recall, it's usually because of a traumatic event or an intense love. As it is written in the Song of Solomon 8:6, "Love is strong as death."

You may experience what feel like memories, but they're coming from a completely different time and place. You might be remembering something from your soul's past, future, or even from an alternate stream of reality where another aspect of yourself resides. Or, as an empath, you may even recall events and thoughts that aren't yours and never were.

One of the ways I know that I'm receiving a telepathic download of someone else's experience is that, even though I perceive it as if I'm recalling a memory of my own, it relates directly to the person I'm with. It rises up out of the blue as it's triggered by a conversation or an interaction with that person. It feels similar to having my own memory, but I instinctively know it's not mine. I will see, sense, and/ or hear things as if I was there and recall the event as they would.

Impact of Past Lives

For many empaths the veil between this current incarnation and previous ones is more transparent than it is for muggles. We often come into this life recalling prior lives and recognize others we've known before. Perhaps you've found yourself visiting a place you've never been before but knowing exactly where everything is. Indications of a past-life connect are familiarity, affinity, and unexplained memory.

When I meet someone I knew in a past life, I will recall both of us there. I have my own sensory recall, which often includes our engagements with each other. In the same way you can "know" the distinct essence of a person now, you can also recognize their essence in other times and places. There is an almost immediate sense of familiarity and connection with these people. It feels like a reunion with an old friend or family member, often upon first encounter. Memories often continue to unfold as your current connection deepens, parting the veils that conceal other times together. While I have had numerous experiences like this over the years, there are two that have been especially notable.

This past-life connection is with one of my oldest and dearest friends, whom I'll call Christine. I met Christine in high school and we've been thick as thieves since our early twenties. Early on in our friendship, as we were hanging out in the front seat of her car, I had a glimpse of us together as teenage girls in the French court of Louis XVI. Interestingly, Christine is actually a distant descendant of Marie Antoinette and she also recalled this life. I've been fascinated by Marie Antoinette from a very early age. As a girl, I sought out books about her, was totally obsessed with the fashions of the period, and had a morbid curiosity about guillotines. French came easily to me when I started studying language in seventh grade. Even now, after more years than I care to mention, I still have some (rusty) basic language skills. A side note: I have minimal French ancestry and my family never made the remotest reference to French culture, whereas my identity as a Celt was reinforced from the time I was barely walking (everyone on my mother's side regularly commented on "what a pretty little Irish colleen" I was).

Years later, during a therapeutic breathwork session, I had a more vivid recall of that time. I remembered we had been cousins, and a specific event came back to me, which occurred shortly after the storming of the Bastille. I won't go into the gory details. Prior to the revolution, we had been devoted to one another like two plump kittens raised together since birth. We lived totally pampered, entitled lives until the whole financial and political system blew up. Like so many other aristocrats at the time, we met our demise because of our perceived excess. In truth, we were naive, sheltered girls who were younger than our years, we had wanted for nothing, and our lives were rather vapid and pointless. We existed merely as decorations of the court. Our parents' capacity to spoil us rotten was regarded as a sign of the health and wealth of Louis' reign. We had no power. We had no influence. We were utterly subject to the whims of adults, who wielded all the authority. But to the revolutionaries, we represented everything that was wrong with the current system and we were made to pay the price for our riches.

Let me assure you that I have done a lot of work to clear the distress from this life. In addition to releasing the trauma around our untimely ends, I have also spent quite a bit of time working on the effect this had on my beliefs and feelings around wealth, worthiness, entitlement, safety, visibility, and the right to shine. I will go into greater depth about how to heal this kind of karmic wound in later chapters.

My second example involves an entire family. Years ago, a beautiful woman I'll call Joy walked into my studio to inquire about my services. There was a deep sense of acknowledgment between us from the get-go. I did some work for her, then she left and went on about her life. A little over a year later, I ran into her again. This time our bond was even more apparent. We recognized each other and both suspected we had at least one previous life together. We sensed that we went back to the convents, where many spiritual seekers and old souls had sought refuge during the second millennium. Years continued to pass and, as I met more of her family, I experienced a similar sense of familiarity with several of them. Then I had a session with one of the EFT practitioners who works with me.

I was addressing my sensitivity to sound, trying to get some relief from how overstimulated and distressed I felt anytime I heard loud, abrupt, or jarring noises. Though I started simply by acknowledging my current reactivity, I was soon unwinding back in time. The next thing I knew, I was standing in a room with clay walls in front of a large water cistern. I could hear a roaring rumble off in the distance and the sounds of terrified people and horses. The air felt increasingly hot and hard to breathe. I was a teenage boy. I was home alone because I had returned from work early. My whole family was still outside. I was scared and confused and trying to deal with the rising heat. As I tapped on all the feelings and images that came up for me, the Jen of today knew that the Joy of today had been my mother. Her current sister (also my friend) had been my older, married sister. Her current toddler, my baby brother. And her very spiritual Uncle Ernesto, my grandfather.

As these memories started to pour in, I knew I was on the outskirts of Pompeii. I was right on the verge of my death. All of my family members had perished already. As I struggled between surrender and survival, they appeared before me and invited me to let go and join them in crossing over. I transitioned from that life and body. I released all the panic and the pain as I went with this "soul pod" to what I can only describe as an angelic realm. For a few moments, I gained the special perspective you get when seeing the whole picture. I grasped that this was an immortal contract, which is stronger than time and space because it is formed in the heavenly dimensions. These special people are all part of my soul family and we have shown up together many times.

We are here to do the Great Work together, to support each other and to amplify our mutual light as we do it. I have no doubt that as time goes on we will learn more than we know now. Indeed, when I shared this section with Joy, it triggered her own memory of being in the court of Louis XVI. Some family groups incarnate together as biological families (as Joy's family does), while in other cases (like mine) there is no close genetic tie, but the soul remains part of the same family.

Chapter 2

The Impact of Living in the Muggle World

Dealing With Pain: Not-So-Healthy Coping Mechanisms

I believe that living beings always seek ways to feel better. When we do not have good, effective, healthy options, we will go with the next best available thing. There is always a reason we engage in a behavior; often as an attempt to soothe, support, or heal ourselves in some way. Because there's so little support in this world for highly sensitive souls, it's fairly common for empaths to turn to drugs, alcohol, food, sex, television, or other addictive habits to deal with the intensity around them. Unfortunately, this is a real catch-22. We rarely process or assimilate any of these things well. Empaths simply don't have the same capacity to get away with self-medicating recreational substance use that normal people do, and normal people are not immune to the worldwide epidemic of addiction. We are more susceptible to intoxication, more vulnerable to developing dependencies, and we have a harder time letting go of things that regular folk easily let roll off their backs. In the same way that empaths take in far more information than ordinary humans and subsequently cannot process it effectively, our capacity to metabolize drugs and alcohol is compromised as well.

Back in the days of my glorious, misspent youth I heard a phrase which has stuck with me: "Reality is for people who can't handle drugs." It was a tongue-in-cheek twist on the clichéd saying, "Drugs are for people who can't handle reality." But even then I knew there was some truth to it. In the same way that some folks can't hold their liquor, I noticed that while everyone around me was obliviously stoned and blissed out, my own awareness was heightened and whatever thoughts and feelings I may have been processing were not soothed. Instead, they were amplified. Let's just say that this is one of the biggest reasons that my career as a hippie stoner was extremely short-lived.

Excessive smoking of either tobacco or marijuana will create holes in your aura over time. Ironically, many people smoke cigarettes to establish boundaries. They use the excuse of smoking to take a break from stress and hectic activity. In the short term it helps, and even feels like you're creating a smokescreen between yourself and people you want to avoid. The paradox is, you may be smoking to reinforce your personal space, but you're depleting and ultimately destroying your energetic filters and shields. Smoking provides a temporary, false sense of safety. It does create a smokescreen for you, but at the same time it weakens your real systems of protection.

Marijuana is different from tobacco, in that many people are aware of using it to open their minds and expand their consciousness. Used appropriately, either plant can be a powerful teacher and ally. But used to excess and/or to cope with difficult thoughts and feelings, things can quickly go sideways. While marijuana can serve as a psychic enhancer and spiritual teacher, it can also cloud our capacity to discern things accurately. Too much and too frequent use can even put us at risk of picking up energy that may seem pleasant, but which actually disguises something much more malevolent.

Alcohol is even more effective at making us feel numb and disconnected. Like smoke, it can poke holes in your aura. It renders us unable to distinguish or discern what we're feeling, what's happening, or whether we're picking up on something real or imaginary. Alcohol impairs our mind so we can't tell whether we're experiencing old triggers, current internal conflicts, or something that's external to us. The less sober we are, the more difficult it is to be mindful, precise, and present. Alcohol makes us more vulnerable to psychic vampires, narcissists, and even negative spiritual entities. They don't call it "spirits" for nothing, just sayin'.

Intoxication is never an acceptable justification for bad behavior, and it makes us significantly more vulnerable to predators. Drugs and alcohol can put us in situations where we can be badly harmed, both emotionally and physically.

It's understandable that we sometimes want to numb out because there are times when it's extremely uncomfortable being an empath. Plus, we live in a culture that has industries dedicated to avoiding pain. We are conditioned from the time we're born to *not* feel our feelings, that there is something wrong when we feel pain. A baby cries, and one of the first things people do is stick something in its mouth. Sometimes babies are hungry and they need to be fed. But sometimes they're in a state of distress and the answer isn't just to stick something in their mouths.

Unfortunately, this culture always looks at pain as a sign that something is wrong, and we are taught that it should be fixed. We do not live in a society that is equipped to deal with discomfort. There are few models for sitting with pain or holding space for grief and suffering. It is extremely rare that we are taught any means for self-soothing other than putting something into our mouths or grabbing the nearest pleasurable distraction. Few of us were ever taught that it's normal to feel uncomfortable or distressed, that these feelings are going to be with us, and they're going to move and flow. We are conditioned to resist intense sensations or negative feelings. Why wouldn't we turn to something that makes us feel better and brings us temporary relief, rather than surrendering to the discomfort of pain? Nobody ever taught us that the latter was an option.

This avoidance of pain and discomfort is by no means specific to empaths. Susceptibility to drugs and alcohol is a human condition at this point in time. As the intensity of world affairs continues to heat up, the human population borders on 7.6 billion (at the time of this writing) and we witness one man-made or natural crisis after another. Pretty much anybody on the planet is going to try to find ways to manage the discomfort, but I believe that those of us on the highly sensitive end of the continuum are more vulnerable, largely because we are more susceptible to absorbing and reacting to practically everything. For so many empathic people, the first time we feel true relief is when we get stoned, drunk, or have our first orgasm. Most empathic children are in a perpetual struggle to manage everything swirling around them. Even if we experienced the idyllic childhood of a '70s sitcom, this initial, intoxicating experience may be our first opportunity to relax, let go, and not feel like we're in a state of hypervigilant distress.

While avoidance of emotional pain has been going on for God knows how long, we now live in an era in which physical pain is no longer accepted as an inevitable part of the human condition. Human beings used to fight, farm, hunt, practice swordplay -- activities where they'd fall down, get scraped, cut, hurt, injured -- because they were living life. We now live in a time where people go nuts when their kid scrapes their knee. I've known people who rush their children to the doctor the first moment they show signs of the slightest sniffle. Many people spend their lives going from bed to toilet to couch to car to office, then back, and are rarely exposed to any significant physical risk. (Except, perhaps, type two diabetes and heart disease from their crappy diets).

There's no sense of proportion. We live in a society where people are insulted by pain. They're insulted by disease. There's an idea that, "This should not be happening to me! I shouldn't be uncomfortable." There's so much resistance to the idea that pain is something natural. Sometimes we feel intense sensations but it doesn't mean anything is wrong. Yet most of us are looking for immediate relief. Commercials on TV blare, "Have a headache? Take an aspirin." "Feeling anxious? Take some Ativan." "Can't sleep? Try Ambien." All of which is ironically followed by a list of side effects narrated by a suave announcer who croons, "May cause death," as if you are being invited to lunch at Grandma's.

I recently read a statistic that the fourth leading cause of death in the U.S. is from pharmaceutical complications. When combined with healthcare malpractice, it's the number one cause of death in this country. If we were not so desperate to avoid feeling pain, to avoid feeling emotions, to avoid just being witness to where we are at any given moment, would these numbers be nearly so astronomical?

As a society, we resist and avoid, instead of just surrendering. "Okay, somebody died, I'm going to be grieving." "I hurt myself, I'm going to feel some physical pain. I need to ride it out." We are living in a dominant paradigm that does not know how to manage this. If you are an empath who chooses to imbibe, I invite you to pay close attention to how the medicine you choose is actually affecting you. As you read the following questions, please be as honest with yourself as possible. This is really just between you and you:

- ❁ What are the reasons you want to continue to partake?

- ❁ If you consider cutting down or taking a break from it, what kind of resistance comes up for you?

- ❁ How is this affecting your clarity?

- ❁ How is this affecting your memory?

- ❁ How is this affecting your ability to make swift decisions with good outcomes?

- ❁ How is this influencing the company you keep?

- ❁ How often do you experience flashes of brilliant inspiration while under the influence, but later find yourself unable to implement the ideas?

- ❁ How does this impact your energy and vitality?

- ❁ How does this impact your motivation and follow through?

- ❁ Can you set a goal and keep moving toward it, or do you find yourself back on the couch getting buzzed and watching Netflix more often than working on your idea?

- ❁ Are you frequently moody, blue, anxious, foggy, and feeling groggy?

If you noticed red flags as you considered these questions, I encourage you to consider trying abstinence for a while, particularly after you have gotten further into this book and have started to implement the tools and techniques I share with you. While your "drug of choice" may have served you well initially, it is possible that it is now exacerbating your already sensitive, over-stimulated system. The only way to really know if this is the case is to experiment with putting it down (at least for a few months) and see if things improve for you.

I will say, though, please don't jump the gun and go cold turkey right now unless you know this is making your life completely unmanageable. Instead, take a little time to develop some new and more effective tools for self-soothing, so that when the inevitable emotional shit starts hitting the fan (as invariably happens when we give up a substance or habit), you will have something in place to bring you relief.

Empaths and Weight

This topic is worthy of a book of its own, as weight is often one of the glaring effects of being highly sensitive. Some empaths inflate their bodies with extra weight, while others get really thin. An overwrought energy system can get so worn down and depleted that it cannot absorb nourishment. Paradoxically for some, this makes their body hold onto every calorie, while others simply can't retain weight. In Western society, being thin is regarded as desirable, but in some ways this is the more difficult side of the coin. A skinny empath can't eat enough to put any weight on their body, and they haven't got the protective insulation of their larger counterpart. Ultimately, the solution is the same for both large and small empaths: they must learn to release the stuff they are carrying around and to fortify effective shields for their energy body, so their physical body is no longer trying to compensate.

For empaths, what you eat does not necessarily correlate with what you weigh. Yes, emotional eating is one reason for extra weight -- it's a time-honored way to cope with psychic overwhelm. Another, more subtle, reason is that the body can compensate for deficient energetic shielding by holding onto extra padding in order to protect itself. It's our body's natural defense system kicking in to prevent us from taking in more than we can handle. An empath who eats a clean diet, exercises regularly, gets enough sleep, etc., and is still carrying extra weight is probably trying to manage more energy than a smaller version of their body can handle.

I have found that weight can manifest either to serve as a protective shield or, in cases like those of very evolved yogis with big bellies, weight serves as insulation for a conduit that is running a spiritually high voltage. If you're at a point in your journey where you've got your filters and shields well-fortified, you're managing your empathic awareness, remaining calm and grounded, and eating an optimal diet for your body, but you are still heavier than modern standards encourage, perhaps the amount of energy you're channeling is causing your body to require more density and insulation.

Don't Judge Your Rainbow by Colorblind Standards

Perhaps you've have had paranormal experiences. Not all empaths do; it depends where you fall on the spectrum. If you're an Extreme Empath, you may very well have had paranormal experiences, because your filters are so open that you can sense beyond conventional boundaries. Those who fall in the middle, the Compassionate Carers, can be very sensitive to other people's feelings and what's going on in the world around them, but they're probably not having conversations with ghosts and dead people. They're not the ones experiencing the really weird and wacky encounters -- the extraterrestrials, entities, and other extraordinary beings. The Super Sensitives and the Extreme Empaths, with their wispy-thin filters, are the ones likely to be aware of everyone and everything.

A crucial survival skill for any empath is the ability to distinguish between conventional consensus reality and paranormal reality. This is the essential line between applying empathic abilities and being considered mentally ill. We must comprehend that most people do not have relationships with dead people. Most people do not have relationships with ghosts. Most people do not engage with extraterrestrials. As a matter of fact, most people do not believe that any of the above actually exist, and consider those who claim to perceive such things as either crazy or possessed of a highly overactive imagination. Since they have no capacity to perceive any of this, why would they believe in it?

Having worked with many empathic people, I've learned that empathic sensitivity is like having the ability to perceive colors that ordinary people can't see. It's as if we live in a world of color-blind people. In the same way that a color-blind person cannot see the entire rainbow, muggles cannot perceive the paranormal. It's difficult to function in a society where you're the only one who can see the rainbow. Unfortunately, the color-blind version of the rainbow is the dominant rainbow model in our world today. This doesn't mean we aren't seeing things they can't see. We are. But while we may perceive things beyond the ordinary, we need to recognize that there are places where it is safe to share this, and there are places where it is *not*. It's important to remember at all times that "normal people" are not having the same kind of experiences we are.

Compromised filters can become so damaged that there's no longer any ability to distinguish between current reality and, say, Nazi tanks rolling down the aisles of your local supermarket. That's when words like "psychosis," "schizophrenia," and "dementia" start being bandied about. I have come to believe that a number of mental health diagnoses are the direct result of decimated shields. In extreme cases, people's connection to the time-space continuum is shattered. Their capacity to distinguish between spiritual dimensions is broken, as undifferentiated information pours in relentlessly. It's entirely likely that they do have extrasensory perception, but they have lost the ability to recognize that other people are experiencing life in a different way. To me, the difference between being an empath and slipping into mental illness lies in losing the capacity to discern what is consensual reality and what is not, and losing the capacity to function in the world as a result.

Perhaps you've felt like you could sense ghosts and spirits around you. Perhaps you've dreamed about deceased friends and family members and it felt like more than a dream. This is something that non-empaths may also experience. But as an empath, you're more receptive to those connections. It's more likely that you'll have connections with the people on the other side.

Perhaps you've had a bad feeling about something. Maybe you chose to avoid it, then were relieved to discover that something unhappy occurred right when you might have been there. Or, conversely, you ignored your feelings and ended up experiencing some kind of an accident, disaster, or problem. The last time this happened to me I totaled a car! There's that sense of something coming, of disturbances in the field, of tremors in time like earthquakes rumbling deep below the surface before the actual event occurs. We feel those waves and tremors.

We're living in a time when so much information about being this way has been lost. If we had people with intuitive abilities in our family, we may not even know about them. I was really fortunate. I got to hear stories about my great-grandmother Elizabeth, for whom I was named. One story concerned her son, a young fisherman who died at sea. He was knocked overboard in a freak accident and drowned. That night she awakened to find him standing at the foot of her bed, saying, "I love you. I'm okay. Goodbye."

Vivid Dreaming

Another characteristic of empaths is vivid dreaming. The dreamtime is a place where empaths tend to work a lot out. We often receive a lot of information in the dreaming. You've probably noticed that dreams have different flavors. Some are lovely and restful, some are prophetic and powerful, some are weird and stressful. We use dreams to process physical, mental, emotional and even spiritual issues that we haven't been able to fully integrate while we're awake. I've witnessed many empathic women who are plagued by insomnia, nightmares, or sleep terrors/paralysis. The challenge is that when we are not able to wring out the psychic sponge before drifting off to sleep, we'll take all that energy and distress into our dreams to try to resolve it.

Because we are overloaded with worldly energy, we often end up in a place known in shamanic traditions as the Middle World. This is the place where the weirdest dreams occur. The Middle World can also be regarded as an astral plane. It exists parallel to this world and often reflects the mental, emotional, and psychic energy being felt and processed within and around us. It is the realm of the emotional body, the egoic world. When someone experiences a traumatic event and a piece of their soul fractures off, this is the place where it often goes.

While some folks get to experience lovely flying dreams and journeys to spiritual realms on the regular, it's not uncommon for empaths to spend a lot of their dream time in the Middle World. We go there to try to find things, to reconcile things, to deal with unresolved issues. Dreams in the Middle World are more like nightmares than pleasant rides on rainbow unicorns. They tend to be more challenging. These dreams are rarely restful. When you go to the Middle World every night, it can be exhausting. The Middle World is not an easy place to navigate. It can be rather like a Hieronymus Bosch painting. When you land there in your dreams, you frequently pick up on the collective anxiety and collective fears around you. In order to shift the tendency to go there, some adjustments are necessary.

First off, wind-down time is necessary. Instead of going right from screens and activity to trying to sleep, it helps to create a transition period between activity and rest. Drinking a cup of soothing herbal tea, taking a warm bath, reading a gentle book, massaging your hands, feet, temples, neck and shoulders with a comforting blend of essential oils in a carrier oil are all ways to start easing into a night of sleep. Second, releasing the concerns and energy of the day is the key to not carrying all kinds of empathic debris into your dreams. (EFT/tapping, which I explain at great length throughout this book, is one of the most effective techniques you can use to let go and settle down before sleep.) Third, inviting Divine Source to protect and guide your sleep helps you to avoid the swamps of despair and discomfort that we can wander into when left to our own devices. I like to say a prayer before I drift off, asking that my dreams may be sweet, gentle, and helpful. I'll admit I don't always remember to follow all of these suggestions before I go to bed myself, but when I do, sleep is much sweeter and easier than when I forget.

Inherited Fears and The Repercussions of a Challenging Childhood

Have you ever experienced chronic, inexplicable fears or phobias that seem to have no origin in your current life experience? There are so many reasons you may be receiving this information. Sometimes you're around a strong broadcaster and you're picking up their phobia. Other times you may be experiencing reactions or triggers from a previous life, or even a future one. It may also originate from messages encoded into your DNA. Intense reactions, traumas, and difficult times have the ability to mutate genetic code, which you then inherit from your ancestors. You may have been born with a legacy of anxiety, phobias, and fears which started far back in your familial line. A few years ago a study conducted with mice revealed that fear could be passed down genetically. This study involved mice who were exposed to the scent of cherries at the same time they were subjected to distressing pain. When exposed to the same scent, the offspring of these mice reacted with the same fear, even though they'd neither experienced the pain themselves, nor encountered the mice who did.

Around the same time, a study involving the children of holocaust survivors drew a similar conclusion: that trauma is passed down to offspring through their genes. The ramifications of this are monumental. First, it means that not only are we impacted by our own experiences, we are born carrying legacies of suffering that can go back for generations. Second, it means that if we do not address our own reactions, fear, and distress, it is likely that we will pass them down to our children, and potentially their children and beyond. Third, if trauma has the capacity to alter our genetic code, then healing our response to it should be able to alter that code too.

In many ways this is a cloud with a silver lining. We are not individually responsible for all of our suffering. By changing our relationship to trauma, we can heal more than just ourselves. I personally believe that when we heal our inherited wounds in the present, this healing ripples back through time and can heal our ancestral line. I hold a vision that, as enough of us do this powerful ancestral healing work, we will actually start changing the fabric of time and space. We will transform reality not just for ourselves, but for the generations who came before us. In the same way that science fiction time-travelers alter the future by going back in time and changing the course of events, we can heal the past by altering the present moment, which subsequently ripples forward and transforms the way we perceive our life to this point.

Now, perhaps what I'm talking about sounds a little far-fetched to you. Perhaps you can agree that healing ourselves will positively impact future generations, but the idea that it can heal the past is less believable. I can't prove this to be true at this point in time. However, in much of the healing work I have done, both for myself and as a facilitator for others, I have seen ways that healing ourselves can affect our extended families -- even when they are not directly engaged with our process at all. Even if this seems too woo-woo for you, I invite you to remain open to the possibility that what we do today can heal both the past and the future.

Maybe you had a difficult childhood. This might have been due to faulty parenting or other harmful care, or it could have been challenging simply because you were an empathic kid. In many cases it's both. You were different from nearly everyone else around you. People recognized you were different, and it was hard. They'd identify you as Other and declare, "You are not one of us." If you're like most of the empathic people I know, chances are you didn't really get where other kids were coming from. They probably baffled you. You'd be thinking, "Why are you like that? You don't make any sense to me. Why are you interested in those boring things? You want to do what? Okay... I guess."

Most muggle children do not have the emotional intelligence that empathic children have. Most children are not self-aware enough to recognize what's going on or what makes them tick. Heck, for that matter, many muggle adults don't know what's driving their bus. Ordinary children have limited impulse control. They're often rambunctious, motivated by reward and pleasure, and not considering the consequences of their actions.

Empathic children are often old souls who come into this life sentient and conscious. They recognize, "I'm in a kid's body, but I know who I am. I know there is more to this world than cartoons, ball games, and cereal. I feel like I've done this before." Being around non-conscious, non-empathic children can be incredibly uncomfortable. It can even feel dangerous. Ordinary kids can cause empathic kids a great deal of mental and emotional distress. At times they can be cruel, even abusive, ostracizing and/or bullying their bright, quirky, creative and highly sensitive, empathic peers.

You've probably been navigating these empathic abilities since you were a child. Give yourself credit for making it this far! Show some love to your "inner child" and when you come across a kiddo who is empathic, help to be the beacon that shows them, "It gets better."

Common Mistakes Empaths Make

As we come to the end of this chapter, I want to talk about one of the biggest mistakes I think many of us make when it comes to trying to control our abilities. I know what it feels like to be so overwhelmed by all the thoughts, feelings, visions, energy, and intensity that I just want to go back to bed, pull the covers over my head, put my fingers in my ears, and sleep for a year so I don't have to deal with all of it. I also know what it's like not to want to feel these things, and yet not to be able to stop them.

For me, it was as though there was a radio playing in the room all the time. I wanted to get away from it but I couldn't turn it off, so I walked out of the room. But even after I left the room, I could still hear it blasting away. I struggled with this psychic noise for a long time. I struggled with it as a child, as a teenager, and as a young adult. I tried a number of ways to find relief. I tried self-soothing with high carbohydrate comfort foods and sugar. I tried smoking marijuana but unfortunately this had the opposite effect. I tried drinking alcohol to excess. I tried distracting myself with romantic relationships and lots of sex. I tried the psychopharmacology route because I thought that perhaps my constant mood swings and melancholy were due to a chemical depression. I tried the hormonal route, thinking that maybe if I got on birth control pills (and then off of them) or some kind of herbal tonic for women, it would make a difference for me. I tried the dietary approach. Sugar makes us more sensitive to outside stimulus and at the time I was bingeing M&M's like there was no tomorrow. Going sugar-free definitely helped me, but it did not change things enough. Eventually I started looking for spiritual solutions.

I started checking into psychic self-defense, as well as working with New Age healing modalities. I trained as a practitioner in techniques like breathwork and Reiki. I began using affirmations all the time. I even recorded audio cassette tapes with long lists of personally crafted affirmations that I could play on auto-repeat all night as I slept. I had affirmations written on my dashboard, in countless journals, and I would recite things to myself over and over while I drove from one place to the next.

Much to my chagrin, most of these actions brought me only 20 to 40 minutes of relief. They did help me to feel better in the short term, and they also gave me the energy to go forward with my life. But they didn't solve the underlying problem, which was that I was being constantly flooded with the energy and psychic static around me. Within a very short period of time I would slip back into that same aching sensitivity. I was having the visions, I was feeling the feelings, I was thinking the thoughts, and I was going down the rabbit hole and landing in places that just felt too uncomfortable to bear. I desperately wanted it to stop but it wasn't stopping. Some of my new grounding techniques were helpful, but none were providing a real defense from the endless onslaught of external noise.

One of the most frustrating challenges was trying to discuss feeling so overwhelmed with my various spiritual communities and groups. I'd try to describe my sense of foreboding and the moods I was constantly flooded with, and somebody (almost invariably a guy) would say, "Well, just let it go." I would think, "What the ever-loving *fuck* do you mean by 'just let it go'?" It baffled me. It still baffles me. At that point I started wondering if there was something wrong with me. Why couldn't I let it go? Why was this so hard? Was I doing something wrong? Was I just fundamentally broken? Was there something so different about me that these solutions just couldn't work? Was I doomed to feel this way for the rest of my life?

In time, and out of desperation, I sought further help. Eventually I found a counselor who, by the grace of God, was also an empath. She was older and wiser, and had learned a lot about how to manage her abilities. She was the person who started me on the path of sorting this out, of learning to understand what it meant to be who and what I am. It's been a number of years since I started down that path. I've done a lot of work since those early days. What

I have realized is that the biggest mistake I made was to underestimate what it means to be an empath. I underestimated myself. I underestimated my needs. I underestimated my sensitivity. I was trying to act like a normal person, as though if I acted like a normal person *hard enough*, somehow things would be different.

The second part of the mistake was that, because I thought I could just will myself to function like a normal person, I was seeking solutions that worked for ordinary people. I assumed that those ordinary solutions were going to work for somebody like me. The truth is, while those solutions can be fantastic for people who are not empathic, for people like you and me, they just don't cut it.

Why Ordinary Solutions Don't Cut It

Why don't these solutions cut it? Why can't empaths "just let it go?" As stated above, the biggest mistake we tend to make when it comes to trying to control our abilities is that we underestimate ourselves and we overestimate ordinary solutions. We do not give ourselves enough credit for how different we are. We imagine that solutions that work for ordinary people will work for us as well. But for many empaths, the bottom line is that these solutions are simply not thorough enough.

I believe this to be true because I've worked with hundreds of highly sensitive, empathic women over the years. At a certain point, I began to recognize that these amazing women and I shared some very particular traits. I began to see that they were different in the same way I am. We are more sensitive. We have the ability to receive information in ways that ordinary people don't. This affects how we experience the entire world.

As I stressed earlier, empaths are like finely tuned instruments. We can pick up more, and subtler, information than ordinary people can. In addition, we often have receivers that enable us to take up information at a much faster rate than average people. We get overloaded because everything comes in so fast and strong. Our drives max out because data is constantly being downloaded faster than it can be processed. As a result, empaths tend to carry a greater load inside than most people. Because we tend to be so porous and absorbent, whenever we are around a lot of other people's thoughts and feelings, we're unable to stay separate or detached. Instead we feel it deeply, we absorb it, and then we embody it. Imagine the way water turns black when India ink is poured in. The water can't just "let go" of the ink and revert to clear. The ink and the water have become intermingled and cannot be easily separated. This is also true for exposure to dramatic tantrums and hysterical outbursts -- we can't simply separate these things out. This is why the whole "just let it go" approach does not cut it for empaths.

An ordinary person might worry about someone, but they feel separate from them and are able to "let it go." Empaths, on the other hand, have a tendency to feel things as if we are the ones experiencing them. Our challenge is to manage this merging of energy within ourselves, rather than just trying to let it all go. We need to address things in a much more focused and thorough way than the average person does. We also need to take a few more steps than most people in order to start gaining control over our sensitivity. Simply putting a bubble of light around us is ineffective. As long as we continue to hold a load of external chaos within us, putting a bubble around it won't make it go away. Until we address everything we've already absorbed, we will continue to feel all that negativity and we will continue to be triggered by the world around us. It's so much more complex for empaths to control their sensitivities.

Congratulations, you've just completed the first leg of this book -- now the fun begins! We've explored what it means to be an empath, the challenges we face, and reasons it can be so hard to address them. Next I am going to share the solutions I have discovered and developed. As we go forward into the following chapters I invite you to do four things:

1. Even if you believe you have heard something similar before, please keep an open mind and ask yourself, "What can I learn from this now? What new things can I discover that I may not have noticed before?"

2. If you feel like you've tried everything and nothing has worked for you, please give yourself permission to experiment, and also to fail. Most of us do not master things with one, or two, or even ten tries. Most of these exercises and techniques took me years to fully master. I am still learning how to work with them at a deeper level, even after 37 years since I embarked on this path. I invite you to let go of expectations about what your success is going to look like, and instead pay close attention to the small, incremental shifts as they occur. Celebrate your little victories. Be really kind to yourself along the way. One thing that is especially crucial: leave your agendas at the door. Nothing prevents transformation, healing, or growth more effectively than thinking you know what you are looking for and how it is going to play out. In the many years I have been doing this work, the one thing that remains constant is that when I show up for whatever is ready to reveal itself, *amazing* things happen. When I decide in advance what I am going to find, I am almost always discouraged.

3. Choose connection over isolation. Find support. Allow yourself to be vulnerable, ask for help from people who can give it to you, and remember to avoid the narcissists. Sometimes we need our soul siblings to hold the vision for us before we can claim it for ourselves. When our own perspective is distorted or we are depleted, it's the ones who love us for who we really are, warts and all, who can hold up a true

mirror for us and celebrate our power -- even when we can't find it ourselves. There is a saying I especially love: "You can't read the label from the inside of the jar." I believe this sincerely. While every technique and tool I share with you is something you can do for yourself, there are times when it really helps to get some outside help. We didn't get this way entirely on our own, and some healing happens best when we can relax entirely and let ourselves receive support. There is a delicate balance between doing our work and overdoing it. It is a constant dance between compassion and due diligence when it comes to our recovery and growth. Being part of a healthy community of empaths, who are deeply committed to taking personal responsibility for their own recovery, can make all the difference in the world. Finding a counselor, mentor, healer and/or teacher who you really click with is an investment that will be rewarded a thousand-fold.

4. Embrace your shadow and surrender to your discomfort. The greatest jewels are in the deepest, darkest earth. Only when we are willing to explore our wounds, our beliefs, our judgments, our limitations, our triggers, our memories, and the secret vulnerabilities we barely want to admit to ourselves do we really transform our lives and shine. As I said at the beginning of this book, this is not necessarily an easy path. There will be times when it may feel really uncomfortable. There may be times when you doubt whether you are making any progress at all, or if your dreams and wishes will ever come to fruition. There may be times when you just want to sit down with a pint of ice cream, or make an entire loaf of grilled cheese sandwiches, or head out to the clubs and find relief in the arms of some attractive stranger. No matter how hard it may feel at times, I encourage you to love yourself through it. I encourage you to hit the pause

button, call a friend, grab your journal, go for a walk, pet your cat or dog, take a nap, take a bath, go smell the flowers. What I can tell you is that it is all temporary. Even when something feels intense, urgent, and as if it will never change, if you accept it and surrender to it, it will shift. The greatest paradox of the Universe is that whatever we resist persists, while whatever we accept transforms.

Chapter 3

Big Why and Potential Solutions

It's fairly common for empaths to feel a lot of fear. We get caught up in the feedback loop of global anxiety and panic. When we get caught up in the worry and stress, it reinforces the emotional bottleneck our planet is moving through at this point in history. We're on the verge of significant changes and it seems that Mother Earth is starting her birth contractions. As a species, we're being forced to grow. "Change or be changed" is the message at this time. But instead of being able to surrender, accept, and just allow life to be what it is, our collective resistance to this transformation, the terror so many of us feel regarding what may come next, exacerbates our distress.

Back when I was first training to facilitate breathwork, I had a vision of being at the crucifixion, standing at the feet of Jesus. I was one of the women among his tribe of followers. I wasn't a special one, just one of many. But I recall going up to him, crying. I stood at his feet, weeping and imploring, "How could you let this happen? You have the power to stop this."

He just looked at me and said, "They know not what they do. They're frightened of me. They can't handle what I have to say. You know, we just have to accept that this is where they're at." Then he looked at me with dismay and said, "Sorry, kid, they're just not ready yet." I vividly remember repeating in my head, "Oh, yeah... They're just not ready yet."

That was more than two thousand years ago. Today more and more of us are awakening to the truth of who we really are. More and more of us are being born awake, aware, and already knowing. We are nearing the tipping point, but we haven't quite reached critical mass. We are not quite there yet. We're pushing the snowball up the hill. Every one of us is needed to reach the summit. The magnitude and significance of what we can offer *matters*. At the rate things are going, I suspect many of us will be alive to see it happen. We will not necessarily be the ones spearheading the change -- that will be our children, grandchildren, and great-grandchildren. We, however, are the ones who are pushing and giving it the energy and intention to happen.

The two most powerful things we can do to support the heralding of the New Age are:

> ONE: Do our own work, heal our wounds, and release the legacies of limitation and pain that go back to our forebears, and

> TWO: Hold the faith that we will reach critical mass.

When we finally hit critical mass there will be a significant shift. It will be like collectively changing from chrysalis to butterfly. I suspect this metamorphosis has the potential to be far gentler and subtler than we may currently imagine. Often, the struggle that leads up to change is harder than the transformation itself. This has been my experience with the vibrational medicine techniques and tools I use. Change can happen almost imperceptibly, because the shift occurs at the energetic level first. When new frequencies are initiated with enough power, the same vibrations will resonate everywhere. This is the way in which the world will cease to be what it is and will become the New Earth.

Until the quantum shift occurs, we will struggle to navigate the early stages of this evolutionary transition. Some of us are ahead of the curve. We're the mutants who are heralding what humanity can become. I believe that empaths are the next link in the evolutionary chain.

The empaths alive now are the ones who have shown up on this planet before the rest of our kind are all here. We are here to seed this new consciousness. We are like the 82nd monkeys. We're the ones who are building up to critical mass, so that we eventually reach the point where the Hundredth Monkey happens.

The Hundredth Monkey effect was the brainchild of the author Lyall Watson, who first presented the idea in his 1979 book, *Lifetide: a Biology of the Unconscious*. According to Watson, a group of scientists researching Macaque monkeys on multiple Japanese islands put out food for the monkeys every day, then observed them. They discovered that one group of monkeys developed an unusual behavior. The monkeys would get their food, then go to a beach or stream and rinse off the sand before they'd eat. The scientists observed that one monkey would teach another how to wash their food. Eventually, all the monkeys on the island began to wash their food. Then a miraculous thing happened: the researchers started witnessing this behavior on the other islands, in unrelated and geographically separated groups of monkeys. Spontaneously, simultaneously, the information was transmitted and the behavior was adopted.

While the conclusions of the published scientific study were, in fact, much more modest than Watson indicated in his book, he nonetheless believed the phenomenon to be real. Indeed, this metaphor for attaining critical mass to affect evolutionary change is so resonant and compelling that it continues to be explored in books, articles, and films. I suspect this is because it strikes a deep, intuitive chord.

In her book *Big Magic*, author Elizabeth Gilbert talks about the magic and consciousness of ideas. She suggests that ideas exist as entities outside of ourselves that want to be realized. The idea of the Hundredth Monkey effect is that if enough of us start adopting certain behaviors, eventually everyone will adopt them. Just as a guitar string vibrating at a certain frequency will cause the other strings to resonate to the same tone, when enough of us are vibrating at a higher consciousness -- one tuned to willingness, love, and acceptance -- the entire tide of humanity will come to reverberate with a new awareness.

Forcing this change to happen, trying to control it, wrestle with it, or clutch at it will not work. Dwelling in willfulness and fear is counterproductive. We welcome the change. We surrender to letting it happen. Acceptance is the key.

As I mentioned in the first part of this book, I believe that souls reincarnate. I also believe a soul can come through in a number of different ways. Energy cannot be destroyed, it can only be transformed. Some of us reincarnate by jumping from one body and life to the next. Some of us opt to dissolve back into the Universal Consciousness.

Not only do we bring the karma from previous lives, we are also the product of our ancestry. Our DNA carries the stories of everyone who came before us. We are, in a sense, cells in a body that is much vaster than ourselves. We are part of an immortal body. We are part of a body that exists long after our ego and our individual consciousness have come and gone.

The more aware we are of being a part of an organism -- one cell in a greater body -- the easier it is to accept that when we die, we do not simply cease to be. When we are disconnected from the awareness that we are part of something greater, we imagine that our physical death means oblivion instead of recognizing that it's part of a greater cycle of life, death, and rebirth. We fear that our death means complete annihilation instead of renewed life in another form. I believe this fear of annihilation comes largely from modern society's insistence that we are separate. Empaths understand viscerally that we are not separate. We sense that we are part of a greater neural net and that we are all interconnected. We are the nerve cells of this planet. At the same time, we function as individuals. We are unique nerve cells.

Sadly, I hear from many sensitive people who feel disconnected. They feel they are the only one of their kind. They don't know anybody like themselves. Often they are misunderstood. Worse, they're told they're crazy. Isolated empaths who live among muggles are frequently told they are making things up, that they're too sensitive, that they're broken. This is painful, it is lonely, and it makes it much harder to lean into our abilities and use our gifts for good.

As you cultivate your awareness as an empath, you begin to understand that many people on the planet are still asleep. They are not fully conscious. They do not recognize what is making them tick emotionally or driving their choices. Part of our job as empaths is to serve as awakeners. We are the ones who come up next to people and whisper in their ears, "You're dreaming right now. You're sleeping. You may not be ready to awaken just yet, but I want to let you know that at some point, it's going to be time to wake up." That's a piece of what we're here to do.

As I said, I don't believe that we are the Hundredth Monkeys. Perhaps we are the 82nd, perhaps we're the 89th, but we are essential, we are vital, we are crucial. We must exist in order for the Hundredth Monkey to happen. We're not there yet. We still have a ways to go. Collectively, our planet is going through a really intense time because we haven't hit critical mass. We are vacillating between higher and lower levels of consciousness. We are here to support the awakening that's happening. We must continue to show up and serve.

When we get caught up in our own stuff, we're of no help. When we are in the muck, we contribute to the challenge instead. Many of the sleeping people are empaths themselves. They're waking up, but they're in the weeds. They don't know how to manage. Unmanaged empathic sensitivity can manifest as physical, mental, and emotional health problems, as well as addictions, financial instability, challenging relationships, and unrealized potential. It's our job to start being the ones who recognize our kind. We're the ones who can say: "You know, there's a name for what you are. There are ways to work with this. You don't have to spend the rest of your life suffering."

For some of you the internet may be the only place where you've found other empaths so far. Sadly, not all regions appear to welcome diversity the same way many of us do here in the liberal Northeast. If you are an empath living in an area where you suspect most folks would think you have 3 heads if you told them what you are, I offer you so much love. Yet often it's the stories we tell ourselves that keep us from revealing our true nature and connecting with others. Not all empaths dress in flowing purple gowns and crystals crowns 24/7. You'd be surprised how many empaths are in your midst who fly under the radar. Even here in progressive New England, I've met plenty of people who have NO IDEA how many other magical, sensitive people surround them.

In the same way that once you discover a particular make and model of a car, you start seeing it everywhere, often it is our own limited awareness that keeps us believing we're the only one. The truth is, we are everywhere. When we share our truth with welcoming kindness and start revealing more of who we really are, other sensitives have a way of appearing. A friend of mine runs a New Age center in the deep south. Despite her region's more conservative political and religious nature, she lit a beacon for the empaths, intuitives and lightworkers in her area. Because of her willingness to share her truth and shine her light, many others have found their way to the community she founded. New people keep showing up, grateful to have found a place where they feel safe and welcome exactly as they are.

Welcome to Oz

At this time of great awakening, some people are coming into their awareness very suddenly. People reach the age of 35, 40, even 60 and beyond, and something triggers their activation. Suddenly -- bam! -- they're wide awake. All at once, they have extraterrestrials communing with them, angels appearing, dead people talking to them. There are people awakening right now who are suddenly channeling; entities are speaking through them. In an instant they're cognizant of all the life forms around them.

As I shared in the introduction, I was born this way, with my eyes open. I started to understand my psychic and empathic abilities when I was nine. Fortunately, my capacity to control my sensitivities deepened as I got older, but I'm not Dorothy -- I was born in Oz. I've been dealing with having one foot in Oz and the other in Kansas my entire life. I grew into this. I gradually learned to find my way around this sensitivity. Though it was sometimes painful, I had time to discover who I was and how to deal with all the muggles telling me, "Jenny, you've just got a wild imagination." So while it may have been hard for me as a little kid, I didn't experience an abrupt change well after I'd become accustomed to a muggle life! There are so many newly awakened empaths being plucked out of Kansas and dropped into Oz. It can be really scary for them. They need our help and support.

We can help them to understand that, as empaths, we have permission to tell entities, spirits, extraterrestrials, and anyone else we don't want to deal with to leave us alone. We have a right to say, "No, I am too tired. I don't have the bandwidth. I am not willing to channel for you right now." A friend of mine was at Disney World when, all of a sudden, the angelic forces started insisting: "You need to do a love and light meditation in the middle of Disney World *right now!*" She responded, "No, I'm with my husband and my child. I just want to enjoy Disney World. I want to ride the roller coaster. Thank you very much." She negotiated doing some lightwork later and enjoyed the rest of the day playing with her family.

We are allowed to say, "I'm having a normal moment here. I'm busy. I'll get back to you. I acknowledge your request, I hear your ping, but I'm doing something. Thank you, but I need space right now." Or even, "I'm not ready for this yet. I'm not equipped to handle the information you're giving me. I'm not the one you're looking for. Please find someone else who is more adept and skilled than I am." It helps to work with your spirit guides to get support negotiating with other entities and spiritual forces. You can explain, "This is challenging for me. The way we've been doing things is not working for me. If you want me to do this, I need you to help me to understand it. I need you to help me to establish my baselines. I need this to be easier, to feel more comfortable for me.

Please respect that I'm in a human body and this body has limitations. I need a translator who can work as an intermediary, so this transmission can happen in the safest and gentlest way."

Supporting the Possibility for a Positive Future

As empaths, we often have the capacity to tune into the past, present, and future. I don't believe the future is predestined. However, I've discovered what I call "dominant streams of possibility." While specific details may vary, the energy, lessons, and qualities of a time period can be anticipated. I believe that there are likely outcomes. Choice defines and determines where things are going, and one's will affects this greatly. There are primary paths events are likely to take, and our choices will generally direct us towards them.

As empaths, sensitives, and intuitives, we can usually ascertain the path. We can feel the stream the future is headed for. This is particularly true when it's a strong dominant stream. While there are many possible ways for the future to go, there's generally more weight toward one possibility than another. Thus, we can feel into the direction something is headed.

Empaths must avoid projecting into a negative future at all costs. We must carefully steer clear of the vortex of worry that can arise when we're feeling other people's pain and fear. When we fall into that vortex, we strengthen its potential future. If we feel fear, it's absolutely essential that we bring ourselves back to the moment, and back to our calm center. When we don't know what's going to happen next, it's best to just admit it. Sometimes the most useful answer is to simply surrender and hope for the best. We can purposefully envision a positive outcome, rather than fearing a negative one.

An Empath's Rights & Responsibilities

There are agreements we can make in order to live in the world as healthy empaths rather than emotionally distressed hot messes.

When we fail to take care of ourselves, we become part of the problem instead of the solution.

Whether we want to admit it or not, out-of-control empaths can make other people's lives a living hell. When we're not living in a healthy way, not only do we drag ourselves down, we drag a lot of other people down, too. It may not be our fault initially, but once we understand what we are, it becomes our responsibility to recognize our impact and do something about it.

In the next chapters I'll share a system for living in the world as a healthy empath. Once you've learned these methods and put them into practice, you'll be able to cultivate your energy in a different way. You'll create a resonant field to project and anchor light, rather than taking in negative energy and sustaining distress that also affects others. I believe the ultimate work for empaths is learning to anchor light and hold the vibrations of love, ease, wellness, and grace. Instead of floundering in the midst of crisis, we can learn how to beam a positive vibration.

I want to distinguish between simply holding neutral space and being a beacon of calmness. When you become a beacon, you broadcast energy. This is needs to be an invitation, not a non-consensual invasion of other people's minds and energy fields. Unfortunately, I have noticed that there are people with empathic abilities who actually think it's fun to use their powers to mess with other people. When encountering somebody who's fearful, upset, or distressed, instead of simply acknowledging their fear, these people will take the amplified emotions and actively push them back, thus magnifying the negativity the other person is already struggling with. There are those who say, "I think it's kind of fun to be able to fuck with people." I want to say right now for the record: this is not acceptable. Every single engagement we have with other people must be consensual. It is a violation of the Universal Laws of Love and Wisdom to deliberately ignore another person's free will and choice.

Obviously, when we first discover that we're empathic and recognize that we're picking up everybody else's feelings, there can be an inadvertent lack of consent. We don't yet have the ability to protect ourselves or to control what we're picking up. We can't choose whether to be open to receiving a mental/emotional download. At this stage, it can be like walking in on somebody in the bathroom -- "Oops, sorry, didn't mean to do that!" Once we learn to distinguish other people's feelings from our own, we have a choice about whether to continue or not. At that point we can choose to take it to the next level, which is acquiring consent in order to scan someone (other than our own underaged children and pets).

Just Because You Can, Doesn't Mean You Should

One of the fundamental rules I live by -- both as a healer and as an empath -- is that I will not go anywhere near anybody else's energy body without their permission. I need explicit agreement and consent to work with somebody's energy field, to read their mind, to feel their feelings, or to engage with them on any level. If I notice that I'm getting more information than I can process and I'm starting to absorb it, my primary responsibility becomes to detach and protect myself.

If I notice somebody is feeling a lot of feelings, I can check in with them and say, "I'm getting the sense that there's a lot going for you. Are you okay? Would you like to talk about this?" If they consent, then I can offer my intuitive perspective: "I'm getting the sense that XYZ is happening. Is it okay if I give you some feedback?" Again, I wait for a yes or no. If I get a *no*, then it's time to back down and mind my own business. If I get a *yes*, then I will share my perception: "I'm picking up such-and-such," or "I had a flash about XYZ." Again, if they engage and agree, if I feel called to offer support I ask, "Would you like some help with this? Would it be okay if I offered some prayers/energy/Reiki to you/your situation?"

Unless you have been given permission, you do not have an established contract. Whether it's physical or spiritual, intervention without consent is not okay. The best approach is to assume that everything is an invitation which may be accepted or refused. As empaths, our job is to offer what we are called to share, but we must allow people their freedom to choose at every step.

In addition, receiving consent once does not mean you have received it in perpetuity. This is a constant dance. We must repeatedly check back in, confirming and calibrating. We must continue to ask, "Is it okay if I talk to you about this? May I have your permission to support you right now? Is what I am saying/offering making sense to you? Is this working for you?" People's energy, thoughts, ideas, and needs can change in a split second, so it is essential that we keep clarifying every step of the way. We must continue to ask, "Is it still okay that we're doing this? Are you still up for this? Does this still feel right to you? Have you realized anything? Is there any additional kind of support I can give you?"

Consent means that just because you can, doesn't mean you should. The older I get, the longer I have these abilities, the more inclined I am to mind my own fucking business. If you have ever identified as a psychic, this approach can seem odd or even counter-productive. One of the assumptions this culture makes about being psychic is that we should be able to provide information without a lot of input from others. Asking questions continuously can be regarded as a sign of lesser abilities. Many healers and mentors (myself included) can get caught in the trap of wanting to prove the legitimacy of their gifts by avoiding dialogue and not asking clarifying questions. I have concluded that being as effective as I can possibly be and taking time to make sure I'm staying on the right track is far more important than bolstering my ego or proving what a talented psychic I am.

Even though there are people who will turn down help that we believe they need, there are more than enough people on the planet who want our support. There are plenty who are ready, willing and even excited to say, "Yes, please! Give me a hand!" However, it is not our job to be awake, aware, available, and attentive

24/7. As a matter of fact, it's disrespectful. It's a violation of other people's privacy, not to mention exhausting for us. Before I learned how to turn it off, I was innocent, therefore I was forgiven. But as soon as I started to master these techniques, I became responsible for the part of me that was not minding my own business. Once you learn how to turn it off, it becomes your sacred obligation to mind your own business.

Over time, you'll fine-tune your ability to wade in gently, and to understand that not everybody wants to go as deep as you might. Just because someone wants help, it doesn't necessarily mean they are ready to leave no stone unturned. Being of true service means being sensitive to the depth at which people are able to swim. Sometimes you pick up information that someone is not ready or able to receive. Just because you know, doesn't mean you should say it. There are ways to be in a place of compassion for someone without having to use all of your gifts. This comes back to that sticky issue of ego, when showing off our dazzling skills is not only unnecessary, it's actually inappropriate. It may be hard to own, but it is crucial that we check our own agenda when it comes to helping people. Are we offering information because it has been sincerely requested, or because we have a desire to fix something or prove that we are capable of miracles? There are times when the best thing we can do is say to ourselves, "Okay, I'll just be in a place of love, radiate kindness, and keep my mouth shut." What a novel concept!

Once we've gotten initial consent, we can always ask more questions. We can check in and ask, "How was that for you?" Then pay attention. Do they want to talk about it? Or are they consciously or unconsciously communicating, "This is too painful. I don't want to go anywhere near it." If that's the case, you might say, "That's totally understandable. If I was in your shoes, I probably wouldn't want to be going near it right now either. Let's change the subject. What would you like to talk about instead?" Ironically, by giving people permission not to talk about it, they'll often decide to talk about it.

There are ways to give people room to decide if they want to get into something or not. It's just as important for people to own their *no* as it is for them to own their *yes*. We live in a culture where people do not give themselves permission to say "no." People so often say they want things they don't actually want. As healthy empaths, we can empower and support others to claim their "no." We can say, "I want to offer you this information, but it is really up to you to decide whether it rings true for you." Or even, "It sounds to me like there's a part of you that's not really invested in this, even though you're saying that you are."

We can share our solidarity and support without making it all about us, our abilities, what we know, or even how we feel about something. Details vary, but the human experience shares a lot of common misery. When we are supporting others, it's not uncommon for us to relate to some part of their experience. In friendships, this commiseration is totally acceptable, but good friends know how to listen without hijacking every story and making it about themselves. When you choose to serve as a facilitator for someone else's process, it is crucial that you do not let your own story or personal agenda interfere with the work. The most effective way to avoid this pitfall is to *do your own work* regularly. Notice your triggers. Notice when you suddenly feel a strong need to fix something. Notice when someone's story reminds you of your own experience. Notice when someone says something that your mind wants to contradict. Then take all of this information and get the support you need. Effective allies do not turn someone else's process into an opportunity to work out their own issues.

We can recognize that our experience is different and, as a result, we may not understand everything other people are going through. We can grasp this and seek to understand. I work to recognize when it's not about me and when, on occasion, it actually is. I keep my little corner of the world clean, and I do my best. I invite you to do the same.

Finally, believe it or not, we have a choice about whether or not to use our abilities. Once we learn to control our degree of openness by deliberately working with our energetic filters and shields, we get to choose. Not only do others have the freedom to determine whether they want us to engage, to read their minds or to sense their feelings; we also get to choose whether we want to do this with them. We can say, "Not now." Every single time, we are allowed to ask, "Do I want to engage with this person? Does this feel right to me? Does this feel good? Is there a part of me that's getting into people-pleasing? Am I trying to avoid conflict? Am I afraid I'm going to hurt their feelings if I say no?" We can decide for ourselves how and when we want to engage with others.

100% Responsibility

100% responsibility means that each one of us is completely responsible for our own emotions, our own thoughts, and our own feelings. This is true for everyone, empath or not. You are responsible for your own process. It's your job to take care of yourself, and not to expect other people to do it for you. It's fine to ask other people for help. Part of taking 100% responsibility is recognizing when you need support. So is understanding that everyone else is 100% responsible as well, for asking for what they need, recognizing what they're feeling, owning their process, and taking responsibility for it. Sometime this means letting someone fall on their face and learn things the hard way. It's challenging to be 100% responsible, but once you get it and embrace it, the agreement is to do your best. This includes owning when you fall short of the mark.

When you are deciding whether to engage with someone, you can ask yourself, "To what extent do I want to do this? How am I feeling? Where is my energy? What's going on for me around this? What do I really want? How far do I want to take this?" Remember that your job is to be responsible for your own energy and to protect yourself. It is your responsibility and your right to care for yourself. Other people's needs are not more important than your own. That's a big one.

You can choose to have compassion for yourself by going inward and observing how you feel. How do you truly feel about this connection? What is it really doing for you? What might it be triggering inside of you? What kind of stuff is coming up for you around it? Own your part of the process and recognize it. Then you can determine how best to proceed.

Part of taking 100% responsibility is learning how not to feel everybody's feelings all the time. We must learn how to open and close our receivers and to deliberately choose whether to go down that particular rabbit hole. Now, I imagine as you are reading this you may be thinking, "Sure Jen, easy for you to say -- try living in my body for a while!" I will respond by saying that this is a process. It starts with baby steps. We strengthen these muscles by using them. Part of our recovery as empaths is admitting to ourselves that there is usually a discernable "point of no return," where we choose whether or not to cross the line. We may sense someone's distress, particularly if it is intense, but we can choose to avoid diving into that distress in order to understand it. Even with this knowledge, some people's feelings may still breach our filters.

Some people project their emotions really loudly. They may not have much emotional intelligence. They may not have been taught any boundaries. They don't know about 100% responsibility. They're walking around the grocery store in a state of despair and psychically broadcasting at full volume.

In such cases we need to learn how to create stronger filters. It's tricky, because it can be very tempting to get drawn in. Once we've sensed that someone is in need, we may feel the urge to help them. And the thing is, we climb right in. Their energy doesn't just penetrate us. We penetrate them, to get the information. We go inward and we merge. We enmesh with them and feel what they're feeling. This sensation is familiar and intimate. It's so intimate that it can feel like love. I think there's a fine line between what we define as love in this culture, and empathic engulfment.

We must learn how to strengthen our filters to make sure other people's stuff isn't coming into us, but we must also learn to consciously avoid wading into someone else's energy body. Choosing not to probe others is one of the most essential keys to this work. Simultaneously, we must learn how to create a strong container to hold the space for suffering.

Holding the Space

At a certain point in our soul's evolution, we must come to accept that just because someone is suffering, it doesn't mean the suffering is wrong. It doesn't mean that it's our job to fix it. One of the rights and responsibilities we agree to as recovering empaths is to witness deep emotions and to behold profound suffering. We agree to be mindful of intense events, but to allow them to simply be, without attempting to fix them. We avoid trying to reconcile things. We stop trying to change what is not ours to change.

Much of this hinges on our own personal philosophy or world view. I believe that the reality we are experiencing right now is temporary, but we ourselves are eternal. We are more than our thoughts. We are more than our bodies. We are more than just the here and now. As human beings, we are in an evolutionary process. Even through experiences of incredible anguish, oppression, and abuse, our souls are learning and transforming. When we take on other people's emotions and feel them for them, they don't have to deal with the full ramifications of those feelings. If instead, we step back and hold space for people to be present with their feelings, we create room for them to transform and shift their experiences. We can hold space without engaging, without fixing, and without trying to change anything.

Unfortunately, we often try to protect people from their own consequences. With our intuition we can sense consequences in advance, so we attempt to intercede. I believe that a big part of what we are learning as a species right now is how to own our consequences. This starts with recognizing and accepting the consequences of our choices, then supporting people to recognize and own the consequences of theirs.

Reciprocity and Release of Ego

While most empaths hate to see others suffer, many of us have a very high threshold for our own pain. We embrace other people's pain as if siphoning off their suffering is a virtue. There's incredible hubris in believing that we are somehow more qualified to feel someone's pain than they are. This is where ego gets in the way. It's very distorted: "Oh, little old me? I'm just feeling their feelings." But who are we to assume that we are entitled to feel their feelings?

Part of us may be able to step back and say, "I'm sorry, but I am not qualified to feel your feelings for you. It's cocky of me to presume that I could suffer for you better than you can suffer for yourself, or that I could protect you from learning your lessons." The challenge is that other part of us, the one that gets sucked into the romance of being a savior.

Why, if you and I are willing to feel our own pain and distress, would we assume that others are unwilling to feel theirs? I recently worked with someone who had no problem being a devoted caretaker to a friend, but when they needed caretaking themselves, they were totally resistant to the idea of that same friend taking care of them. They were concerned it would be a huge burden of responsibility. I observed, "You had no problem being the caretaker for that person. Why is it inappropriate for the role to be reversed?"

Reciprocity is essential for the planet to function in a healthy way. In order to help this world to heal, we must accept balance and reciprocity as fundamental. We cannot always be the ones who do all the work. When we continually do the heavy lifting for others, it keeps them from stepping into their power and recognizing the consequences of their choices and processes. When we only give, it weakens the people we're trying to support because we're not allowing them to be in a position of power.

In the Wiccan system, initiation to the First Degree involves learning to use the tools, the Second Degree involves sharing those tools with others, and the Third Degree includes stepping back and allowing others to be in their power and to use their gifts. It takes a courageous human being to "surrender pride of place" -- to step back and let somebody else put on the big foo-foo hat and to not be the one receiving all the glory. We live in a culture that is stuck in the Second Degree. Everybody wants to be seen as the authority who knows what they're doing. We constantly take on the role of fixing, caring, and doing for others. This can leave the receiver in a constant state of need, while the giver is trapped as the "expert" who does all the fixing. We need to embrace the idea of empowering people to step into their own authenticity, agency, and power.

It is not our job to tell people what we think they should know. I have discovered that asking questions is a much more effective way to help somebody figure things out. I find it's best to start with curiosity and gauge how on-board they are, rather than telling them things they aren't ready to hear. We may detect an event that created trauma, but the survivor is still protecting themself from consciously addressing it. It is not our job to blow their cover. Revealing information before people are ready to receive it can cause harm. We serve them best when we engage in mindful, active listening. We focus on what they are saying and avoid forming conclusions or rehearsing what we will say in response. We pay close attention to the actual words they are using and the messages beneath the words. Then we reflect back what we hear. It is ideal to mirror their words as closely as possible. It is so powerful to be acknowledged and seen for exactly who you are. When we meet someone right where they are, with an open mind and heart, they can reveal their truth much more easily. Mirroring is the foundation of good communication. It may feel clunky and contrived at first, but as you get used to it, it becomes second nature. Here is an example of mirroring:

Person: "Things at home are so stressful! I feel like I could explode. If one more person asks me to do something I swear to God I am going to lose it!"

You: "I hear that home is really stressful. That sounds really hard. I can only imagine how much you are already dealing with if one more request is enough to make you lose it."

Person: "Yes! It just sucks and my partner is being so demanding. I feel like no matter how hard I try they don't recognize my effort and it's never good enough."

You: "I am so sorry you are having to go through this. It sucks when someone doesn't see or appreciate what you do."

Person: "I wish they could see how much energy I've been putting into our family. I'm bending over backwards to support them. I'd just like some credit for everything I'm doing."

You: "You totally deserve credit for all you are doing. It sounds like you've been working extra hard. I see how much effort you are making."

Person: "I'm glad someone can see it! I just wish that they could. At least having a chance to talk about it helps."

You: "I'm so glad talking about it is helping. Even though they aren't able to acknowledge everything now, how could you give yourself a pat on the back for all you're doing?

The final question is optional. Starting to focus on solutions depends on whether someone simply needs a place to be heard or they are ready to begin shifting.

I believe that the core of the work is about channeling light, channeling love, and bringing healing to this planet. Sometimes we may succumb to the temptation to prove that we're super-psychic, wise, and can fix it all. We can get caught up in the belief that, "If I give you my insight and reframe this situation in a *better* way, then I can prove I know my shit." In my humble opinion, being empathic is not about proving how gifted we are or sharing information for the sake of showing off how much we know. It's about being really present with whomever we are with -- whether it's ourselves or somebody else -- and bearing witness to the truth of the exact moment we're in.

Loneliness and desire for connection are another snare to look out for when deciding to engage with this sort of work. I know when I'm feeling isolated and depleted, I'm much more likely to offer unsolicited support than when I am feeling loved and nurtured. When I began to study healing in earnest back in my late 20s, I committed to the spiritual contract that I do not work without permission. This is absolutely my bottom line, with two notable exceptions:

ONE: If a parent or guardian requests help on behalf of their minor child or other person who is incapable of free will, then I will intercede at their request.

TWO: If I am in a position to be a first responder in an emergency situation and physical intervention is the difference between life and death (or, at the very least, injury), I will act to save someone's life and get them out of harm's way.

If someone is choking or having a heart attack, it's not the time to ask if you can perform the Heimlich maneuver or CPR on them. Just do it. Both of these circumstances are fairly obvious. If you have to ask yourself if unsolicited help is appropriate, chances are it is not. Your shadow pieces are more likely to affect the process when you are not deliberately confirming that you have permission and consent.

Is It Empathy or Codependency?

In America the term "codependency" gets thrown around a lot. Some people will declare that empaths who are trying to help "are being codependent." I don't think this label cuts it. I think it's unfair to dismiss empaths as merely codependent.

Codependency doesn't acknowledge that we actually feel what others are experiencing and want it to stop because it hurts us too. Empaths as a group tend to be caretakers because we feel relief when we help others to find relief. We sense distress and feel drawn to help. When we alleviate discomfort, we feel better too. Of course we want to do this. It makes so much more sense when you recognize that the reason you, as an empath, want to help, fix, and change other people is because you feel their feelings so intensely.

It's like that old joke: Guy (holding a mallet and hitting himself on head with it): "Doctor! Doctor! It hurts when I do this!" Doctor: "Stop doing that!" When there is distress and you are uncomfortable with it, your empathic awareness creates a feedback loop which is amplified by your own resistance. We feel their pain, we react to their pain, and it triggers a sense of urgency within us to do something. As discussed above, this makes it hard for others to experience their pain and explore the lessons and consequences connected to it in their own time. It may seem that bringing someone swift relief is better than letting them linger in their suffering. However, when we rescue them, they often won't make the necessary changes to sustain this relief, so we only end up giving them -- and ourselves -- a temporary fix.

There's a fair amount of cultural shaming around codependency. Understanding that there's a reason we develop these behaviors of caretaking and people-pleasing can help us to break some of these patterns. When we "fix" things, it's not just that our self-esteem and sense of emotional safety improves, it's that we change when they do.

This ability can make us good healers. When we are healthy and approach things from a place of appropriate boundaries and clear consent, we have the ability to recognize when people have made a shift. Have you ever experienced a massage, healing work, or even an intimate encounter, with someone who was not able to pick up your cues? This may have felt flat, or even baffling. They went through all the motions and used the physical techniques, but they made no energetic connection with your body. They couldn't sense how they were affecting you, so there was little flow or adjustment. They didn't resolve the issue, because they only addressed the physical/mechanical part without addressing the energetic part. Conversely, I think the thing that makes responsible empaths remarkable healers is our ability to sense our clients' needs on so many different levels. We can use this ability to feel what's going on and know when we've succeeded in shifting something. For example, when I am doing hands-on work, I can find and hold the spot where the pain is, because I can sense it in my hand. I know when the energy shifts because I can feel that energy shift in my fingertips. This sensitivity is a magnificent gift that can be incredibly effective when used well. But it can be downright lethal when used incorrectly.

I just got off the phone with my dear friend, Deanna. We were discussing a situation with a friend of hers, whose bad behavior had caused them to become estranged. Unfortunately, this friend did something that cannot be taken back: they broke a vow. While they were willing to admit that their action was wrong, they could not say they'd never do it again.

From my perspective, they caused harm to Deanna, who did nothing to warrant it. I have seen her bend over backwards to love and support her friend and I have watched that friend respond with mean, irrational behavior and self-righteous rage. Both of them have had their challenges in life. Both have endured their share of sadness, fear, and emotional distress. Yet where Deanna has been willing to take personal responsibility and diligently works to become a better person, her friend consistently blames others for their problems and simply cannot see their own part in the equation.

Deanna has felt sad over the loss of this friendship, but she knows it is not safe to let this person back into her life. Still, she struggles. She struggles with whether there is anything she can do to support this person. She struggles with whether cutting them out of her life was fair. She struggles with whether she is being a "good girl" when she is not willing to show up for whatever craziness this friend might bring. On one hand, Deanna knows this is a futile situation. On the other, she doubts her choices and considers reversing her decision because she senses the feelings of hurt and abandonment coming from her friend. At the very core of all of this are the questions: "Am I doing enough? Am I abandoning my friend in their time of need? Am I being a good person?" These questions trigger feelings of guilt and people-pleasing. Though Deanna's rational mind knows that her boundaries are not only reasonable but necessary, part of her feels pressure to cave in to this friend's needs and demands.

As we discussed the situation, we likened it to the story of the Scorpion and the Frog. If you've never heard this allegory before, the short version goes like this:

Since it can't swim, Scorpion asks Frog to ferry it across a pond. Frog says, "No way -- you'll sting me!" Scorpion adamantly swears, "I won't sting you! That would be stupid because I'd drown too." Frog reluctantly agrees to carry Scorpion. Midway to shore Frog feels a sharp pain in its side. As they both sink to their deaths, Frog cries, "But why? You swore you wouldn't, now we're both going to drown!" Scorpion replies, "I couldn't help it, it's my nature."

Our challenge is that we want to believe our scorpions when they make that promise. We want to trust that they've changed when they say they did. This kind of willingness to give people the benefit of the doubt and to give them a second, third, or even fourth chance is something empaths naturally do. All too often, we get stung as a result. This is where it becomes imperative to override our natural instinct to care and forgive and to ignore our feelings of obligation and loyalty. There are times when the best thing we can do is to cut our losses and accept a scorpion for what they are. Sometimes the only way a person has a snowball's chance in hell of changing is to live with the full consequences of their behavior. There is a difference between forgiving bad behavior and excusing it. We can accept someone for who they are. We can forgive them for their actions. We can have compassion for everything that made them that way. We can do all of the above without letting them off the hook.

A person can be held accountable for their actions even when they are forgiven. It is actually a disservice to welcome someone back before they've made amends and demonstrated that they really have changed. Simply welcoming them back gives them permission to perpetuate bad habits with no consequence. Instead of worrying that abandoning someone who has repeatedly proven themselves untrustworthy or abusive is unkind, what if we started to see it as the most compassionate choice we could make? We are not the ones abandoning the covenant of friendship. They are, when they choose to disregard mutual agreements and betray us. Truth be told, it is a waste of our precious resources, our limited time and energy, to keep going back to the same poisoned well and hoping that this time it won't cause us harm.

If you are sincerely committed to being part of the solution that will turn the tide on this planet, your boundaries must be strong. Each of us only has so much time and energy to offer. People like this are vampires who only drain us of our valuable essence. There is no time for lost causes right now. There is no time to be wasted on the people who refuse to listen to or accept any of the help they are offered. We simply cannot afford to pour our hearts and souls into bottomless pits, when every second of every day of the rest of our lives can be devoted to serving the ready and willing.

Not Being Overcome by Suffering

All the intensity and downright insanity of today's world can be difficult to process, especially when we are aware of political events and widespread disasters. We can become engulfed with the anguish, overcome with the overwhelm, and not know how to manage it. The first step in dealing with all of this is returning to our own core and restoring the layers of filters and shields that surround and protect us. This is one of the things I'll be teaching you in the following chapters.

We can begin to envision ourselves as smooth rocks in a river of energy. Standing in the stream, instead of absorbing it like a sponge or trying to push it away, we can let the energy flow around us. With practice, you'll become better and better at this. When stuff comes towards you, you'll be able to offer it love and send it along downstream. You can also send anything to the Divine. Whatever you take in, acknowledge it, relax your body, exhale it out and give it to your Higher Power. Give it to God/dess, give it to the Earth, give it away. Just keep letting it go. Love it and let it go. Love it and let it go. Love it and let it go.

Most human energy fields have a certain sponginess or stickiness, because our vessels are not yet completely smooth and filled with light. Therefore, unprocessed energy can become attached, like plaque in a clogged artery. We breathe in the suffering but it doesn't flow, it gets stuck.

Many human beings live in this state of stickiness and congestion because they have not yet focused on their spiritual core. Souls may be in this state due to their degree of emotional maturity, their number of incarnations, the intensity of traumatic events both current and karmic, and more. In the evolved form we ultimately want to reach, we enter a state of pure light which is smooth and radiant. Whatever comes at it slides off it, through it, or is completely transmuted into light itself. Before we begin to clear our karma, our emotional body, ancestral legacies, and energy can be like paste, or like coral, which is spongy but brittle. The energy body is very absorbent in this state. We hold onto all kinds of mental, emotional, and psychic debris. If we attempt advanced transmutation work before we are ready, the world's suffering, pain, and sorrow can become lodged in our energy bodies.

We do nobody any favors (especially ourselves) attempting this kind of compassion work when we haven't developed the ability to release what we've taken in. Without this ability, such work can send us into distress and leave us with even more work to do. We are better off simply focusing on the positive and broadcasting love, while keeping our filters and shields nice and solid. By keeping it simple, if we notice that something needs to be cleared, or we have an energetic disruption, we're able to move things more quickly. If we take on something that's bigger than we expected it to be, we're better equipped to clear away the sticky mess.

In order to do this work on behalf of the planet, we need to honor where we're at. We need to heed our limitations. We must be honest with ourselves about whether we've developed the skill to deliberately draw in global darkness and then transform it, without absorbing and being overcome by it. Once you've done the work, you'll be absolutely golden transmuting things with compassion. You'll be able to draw in suffering, hold it in your heart, transmute it into love and compassion, and send it back out to the world without triggering and activating your trauma body. But until you have achieved such expertise, please do not deliberately breathe in anything that causes you emotional distress. Inhale only thoughts, ideas, and feelings that you can take in calmly and lovingly. If it causes you distress, first learn to relax and release it. Keep it outside of yourself, step back, and send energy to it. Do not step in and try to transmute it by embodying it.

Conscious Breathing Exercise

Conscious breathing is one of the top four tools in my toolbox (the other three are EFT/tapping, mindfulness, and gratitude). Breathing is one of the fastest and most effective ways to get back into your body, tune in, and focus. The way we breathe reflects the way we live. Your inhale directly correlates to your ability to receive. Your exhale directly correlates to your ability to release, as well as your ability to put energy out into the world. There are people who are great at inhaling, but not at exhaling. There are people who are great at exhaling, but not at inhaling. Healthy, flowing energy lies in the reciprocity of both giving and receiving. This starts with your breath. Please join me in exploring your breath with the following exercise.

Find a place where you can be comfortable and settle in. Turn off your phone and put aside any distractions. Take a moment to tune in to your body. Close your eyes. Settle in and get comfortable.

Let yourself feel the surfaces beneath you. Take a moment or two and give in to gravity. Let yourself feel supported and held.

Put your hands over your chest on your heart. Start by taking a normal breath, and notice what this feels like. Just breathing in and letting go.

You may notice that there are places in your body where the breath is stuck, or it's not as deep as you'd like it to be. Perhaps you're already breathing freely and your inhale and exhale are just fine. Take another breath. Breathing in, and breathing out.

Next, we're going to breathe with some intention. We're going to deliberately use the breath to draw in a quality. I think calmness and focus are two really good things to invite.

Take in an extra deep breath, just a bit slower than usual. Let yourself breathe in calmness and focus. Imagine, as you inhale, that you are drawing in a sort of relaxed clarity. Breathe in this calming focus. As you breathe out, release any tension, worry, concern, or distraction that may keep you from being here right now. Again, breathing in calm, breathing out concern. Just letting it all go.

As you continue to breathe, imagine you're creating a bubble or cocoon of light, clarity, and calm all around you. Breathe in that clear, calm focus. Breathe it out all around you, in a circle of safe, sacred space. Breathe in clarity and focus; breathe it out all around you.

As you continue to breathe, notice how you're feeling in your body. Notice what it feels like to be here, right now. And just keep breathing. Take a few more minutes to simply be in your body, breathing in and breathing out.

When you're ready, open your eyes and return to the present moment, here and now.

The Four Steps to Empathic Health

Recognize, Release, Protect, Connect.

Over time, I've come to understand that there are four steps necessary to achieving and sustaining empathic health. By working with these four fundamental steps, you can shift from being distressed to thriving, free to use your divinely given gifts for good in this world. We'll be covering these steps in further detail in the next four chapters.

The first step is to *Recognize*, discern, and understand what is yours and what is somebody else's. This breaks down into two components.

The first is actually knowing who you are and recognizing what your own experience is. For someone who's always felt other people's feelings, it can be quite difficult to distinguish what's yours and what's not. This first phase starts with calibrating your own body, mind, heart, and soul to identify your personal defaults.

The second phase is to backtrack and identify: "When I'm feeling a feeling, does this feeling represent me? Is this how I actually feel, or am I feeling this because I was around someone broadcasting their own issues, I was triggered, and then I started to run their program?" I have found that when we pick up what somebody else is feeling, it's as if a chord has been struck and it starts to resonate within us. Part of the work is learning to distinguish whether the current chord has triggered a deeper octave within us, or whether we've picked up an entirely external process. When something triggers our own stuff, we address it. When we are perceiving energy from outside ourselves, we acknowledge it and let it go.

The next step is *Release*. Once we've recognized that we're carrying around something that is not our own, it is essential that we learn how to release it so our own sense of self can be restored. There are a number of different ways to let things go, but I have a few favorites. Breathing has been my go-to for over three decades because it is so immediately effective, but discovering EFT over a decade ago was a total game changer for me.

EFT, which stands for Emotional Freedom Techniques, is also known as tapping. It is an amazingly effective way to shift and release material we no longer need to carry around. Other useful techniques include forgiveness work, journaling, affirmations, dialogue between the different parts of our self, and conversations with other people's Higher Selves. There's also prayer, chanting, aromatherapy, and working with flower essences. There are so many effective tools to help us *Release*. We'll explore a number of them at greater length in Chapter 5.

Once you've cleared yourself of baggage you no longer want or need, it's time to strengthen your system so you're not simply taking in new negativity. The next step is *Protection*. This starts with restoring weak energetic filters and creating ones that have never existed. You will learn to establish a sturdy, protective shield, one that's appropriately permeable for beneficial energy: an egg of light with a strong shell on the outside to prevent negativity from pouring in.

Once this protective system is installed, instead of constantly feeling bombarded and reactive, you'll start to experience some peace and quiet. There are numerous techniques which contribute to *Protection*, including yoga-style breath and energy awareness, flower essences, stones and crystals, aromatherapy, prayer, and visualization. The establishment of down-to-earth, rock-solid emotional and logistical boundaries is critical.

Once you have established stronger filters and shields, the fourth step to empathic health is to *Connect*. This is about our connection to Divine Source, higher intention, and gratitude. It's about cultivating awareness of a Higher Power, however you perceive that power greater than yourself. This step enables you to charge up your battery. You learn to deliberately fill your tank with positivity instead of absorbing whatever dross happens to be in the vicinity. With this ability, we go from being passive receivers to serving as broadcasters of radiant light. We become anchors for calmness, stability, and love in the world, rather than being dragged down by its pain, suffering, and negativity.

When we become adept at working with these four steps, we cease to be sensitives struggling to manage sensitivity while magnifying distress. We become empaths who generate a calm, healing presence that ripples out into the world. Eventually we can take this up to the next octave, which is to *Act*. We use our abilities to follow the subtle tapestry of information and inspiration, remaining aware of the multiple threads that are simultaneously revealed. We can serve as empathic healers, guides, teachers, leaders, and innovators. We strive to be ever-clearer open channels for the higher and greater good.

But first we must learn and practice the four steps: *Recognize, Release, Protect, Connect.* We cultivate this new way of using our hearts, minds, bodies, and energy systems to deploy our empathic abilities with ease, and to realize our mission for this planet.

Let's begin with *Recognize.*

Part 2

Chapter 4

Recognize

Empaths often experience things without knowing where they're coming from. Recognizing their actual source is instrumental to managing your feelings. When you're functioning "normally," your thoughts and feelings correlate with what's going on in your life and the world around you. There's nothing confusing – you're happy or sad based on your attitude and circumstances. There's no dissonance between what you're feeling and what's occurring within and around you. But sometimes you feel wonky and out of sorts without knowing why.

You may not notice anything unusual at first. Perhaps you're in a mood that will pass. I've often experienced lag time between feeling empathic distress and realizing that I'm feeling it. Fortunately, as I've developed greater agility with the system taught in this book, this realization comes much more quickly. The more familiar you become with your own experience, emotions, body, thoughts, and general mode of operation, the more quickly you'll recognize that you're absorbing external energy.

Identifying an empathic episode begins with noticing, "I don't feel like myself. This doesn't feel normal. Why do I feel so ___?" You fill in the blank: blue, freaked-out, scared, anxious, sad, in physical pain, worried, or any number of other unpleasant feelings, including a deep, underlying sense of dread. The moment you notice that you're feeling off for no obvious reason, you can begin to explore what's actually going on.

RECOGNIZE: Basic Diagnostics: Checking Your Engine

My friend, Britt Bolnick, always says: "Feeling off or out of sorts is your check engine light." Once you get the signal, you'll want to do some diagnostic work to determine what's actually out of balance. Here's an initial set of questions to ask yourself:

- ❀ Is this going on within me alone?
- ❀ Is it about me?
- ❀ Are these my personal feelings?
- ❀ Is this a reaction triggered by my previous experiences?
- ❀ Is this a physical, mental, or emotional response to something I've been exposed to? (Many empathic people are sensitive to food and environmental factors; exposure to chemicals, processed sugar, Wi-Fi, EMFs, and mold can throw off our delicate balance).
- ❀ Is this due to thoughts, feelings, and energy generated by a force outside of myself?

This first step invites you to tune in and discern whether the feelings are yours or coming from outside yourself. You can respond accordingly, depending on your answer. When you take the time to get centered and tune into your truth, you'll usually receive a clear "yes" or "no," or occasionally, "both." The willingness to be unflinchingly (but compassionately) honest with yourself is crucial to this process. Sometimes it's easier to offload negativity as something caused by external factors, when in truth, it's your own doing. Often the answer is actually "both." In these cases, the work is about addressing your personal stuff while letting go of all the rest. When you get a clear "no," you can start backtracking to examine the source of your distress.

When you sense a "yes" or "both," consider it an invitation to look deeper into what's going on for you. Emotional Freedom Techniques (EFT), also known as tapping, is a very effective way to get at what's going on internally. I'll talk about this in greater depth later, but for now let's look at a brief example of this powerful yet gentle tool.

Following the basic recipe, begin by tapping on the side of your hand while saying, "Even though I don't know where this is coming from, I suspect that it's something about me. I'm open to discovering what it's about, and accepting myself as I am." Then, as you move through all the points (see diagram in chapter 5), focus in and speak about the sensations, emotions, and thoughts you're experiencing, and where in your body you're feeling them. Let this continue to unfold as you tap through the points. Not only will you gain insight about where things are coming from, but speaking about it while tapping can help you to move through it. As you gain clarity about what's coming up for you, you can choose to tap on a specific issue.

If you find yourself hitting a particularly tender topic, you can tap to calm and soothe yourself. Instead of adding more details or issues, stick to the thing that's really in your face. Slow down. As you tap or put mild pressure on the points, take a slow, deep breath for each point. Take a sip of water, then come back to the feeling and assess whether it's shifted. If the feeling is still holding intensity, continue tapping or using gentle pressure on the points while keeping the focus very simple until the issue has really settled down. One of the best things about EFT is that you can do it yourself. If an issue feels like too much to address by yourself, a skilled, well-trained practitioner can help you to move through it more quickly and effectively than you may be able to do on your own.

In situations where it isn't suitable to tap and speak aloud, there are some more subtle options. You can focus on the issue and either whisper or speak it in your head. If you are around other people and feel uncomfortable tapping in front of them, you can tap on a photograph of yourself, a selfie on your phone, or you can imagine you are looking at a snapshot and tap silently on what you are visualizing. You can also sneak away to tap for a few minutes in the bathroom or when you take a shower. You can apply gentle pressure or massage your points instead of tapping on them. If you feel a need do some EFT but doing full rounds won't work for you, there are several hand, finger, and wrist points that are more discreet.

RECOGNIZE: It's Not Me. So What Is It?

Perhaps after some consideration or tapping, you realize it's not about you. Maybe you received a clear "no," or just have a suspicion that something is coming from outside yourself. At this point you can ask another set of questions. Start by being present with your hunch and focus on where you feel it in your body. Close your eyes and tune into it. Then open your eyes and while reading through and considering these questions, using a journal, and/or tapping on your collarbone or the side of your hand, ask yourself:

- ❋ Where am I feeling this in my body?

- ❋ What about this feels unusual for me?

- ❋ If it had an emotion, what would it be?

- ❋ What thoughts, beliefs, and/or images am I picking up from this?

- ❋ What else am I noticing?

Make note of this inventory. Then ask yourself:

- ❋ Do I recognize where this is coming from yet?

If the answer is still "no," ask yourself:

- ❋ How long have I been having this feeling? Have I been feeling it for the last couple of hours, or has it been days, weeks, or months?

- ❋ When did I start feeling it? (For example, perhaps you started feeling it at work after a co-worker made a comment).

- ❋ How suddenly did it come on?

- ❋ Is this about the here and now, or is it from another time?

Let this keep unfolding until you have more clarity. Once you've dialed in to when the distress began, you can ask yourself:

- ⊛ What was going on at the moment I started to feel this?
- ⊛ Where was I?
- ⊛ What was happening around me?
- ⊛ Who was I with?
- ⊛ Who or what was in the extended environment?
- ⊛ What did I notice at the time?
- ⊛ Do I know what other people were going through?
- ⊛ Do I have an awareness of what was happening for anyone else?

At this point you might remember, "Oh, that's right -- *Sal* seemed kind of off. They were having a bad day; maybe I picked up on it." This approach is designed to stir your memory. As you tease apart the different elements, you can begin to discern whether you had a direct encounter with somebody and picked up their feelings, they said something that triggered a personal reaction in you, or you experienced a combination of the two. The next set of questions might be:

- ⊛ Did that person's comment trigger a reaction within me that's based on a previous experience I've had?
- ⊛ Did it trigger my inner child? (If you're reacting from the wounds of a much younger part of yourself, this is an opportunity to focus on self-care and doing the inner work to heal those wounds).

If the answer is still not about you, then ask:

- ⊛ Am I absorbing somebody else's stuff?

❀ Is it because they're having a hard time and I just happened to take a hit from that experience, or was I sensing something brewing under the surface?

Usually, by the time you've gotten to this point, you can ascertain what's going on and identify the issue. It can be helpful to use one of the following prompts:

❀ If I knew the answer, it would be…

❀ If I was imagining what the answer would be, it would be…

❀ I have a suspicion that the answer is…

If nothing comes to you, try making up an answer. Our subconscious knows things our conscious minds don't have access to. "Making shit up" is often just as effective as knowing for sure. When you allow your imagination to work this way, you'll often be led to the right answer. It may not be entirely right, because the information is filtered through your own triggers and perceptions. But *that* information is also valuable and useful to work with. Even if you don't have a 100% accurate version of the other person's story, you now have information about your own overlay on the story, and that's your real work. As long as you remember that you're discerning this for yourself (and not insisting you know someone else's truth better than they do) a little bit of grey area won't impact your ability to address the issues affecting you. Whatever information comes to you is the information that *you* need to resolve and work with right now. Unless someone has asked for your help and given you overt permission to intervene on their behalf, it is not your job to fix them in any way, shape, or form. Your job is simply to deal with how their behavior or energy is affecting you, and to heal that.

RECOGNIZE: Your Triggers

As an empath, it's essential to recognize both your natural coping mechanisms and your natural triggers. For example, I'm highly sensitive to noise. It's not usually because I'm picking up on other people's shit, it's just that sound deeply affects me. I don't get concerned when I feel agitated by my husband's drumming, because that's a bug in my operating system. But if I'm feeling something that is not one of my standard responses, I know that something else is going on. I can say, "Oh, wait a second. This isn't my stuff. This is probably coming from someone or something else." Being able to articulate what we're feeling leads us to greater understanding of why we're feeling it, where it's coming from, and sometimes, whose it really is. But it starts with recognizing our own baseline reactions.

You can use journaling and observation to help identify your natural emotional responses. It's very helpful to recognize your personal patterns in response to stress. You may find yourself writing, "When I'm stressed, I crave chocolate, get really cranky, feel exhausted, become totally overwhelmed, start writing snarky comments online, etc." Once you identify your own stress reactions, they can become personal alerts to take care of yourself. These reactions don't necessarily mean you've picked up someone else's shit. It can actually be all about you.

On the other hand, you may note, "If I *suddenly* feel incredibly angry, irritable, or super depressed (or whatever flavor of reaction you experience), it's usually a sign that I've picked up something outside of myself." Deep sadness, depression, and an overwhelming sense of foreboding are generally signs that what I'm feeling isn't mine."

When I notice that I'm feeling those deep feelings, I return to loving kindness. I breathe into the sadness, hold it in my heart, then breathe it back out to the world with compassion and love. Conversely, if I notice I'm feeling irritated by sound, or even if I'm just feeling super bitchy, it's more likely to be my own emotions or depleted state. Nine times out of ten, it's because I'm either overstimulated or overextended. That's when I need to calm myself down, relax, and regroup. At those times, it's best to get away from hectic activity and other people. I've discovered that anger often means I've become overstimulated. I've taken in too much information and I'm saturated, but I'm not actually carrying other people's stuff around. I may be irritated from the outside in, but I haven't necessarily absorbed someone else's anger. I will note that other people's anger can *provoke* mine. In contrast, other people's sadness and despair tend to penetrate me, and I'm prone to hold onto those feelings.

Perhaps the biggest challenge in separating other people's pain from our own is that their pain triggers ours. It's no longer just their pain. It's both their pain and ours. The first solution is to address your personal pain and do what you can to clear it. Tapping on the side of the hand, you can start with whatever it is, wherever it is, and simply acknowledge it. Get as precise and specific as you can:

> *"Even though I'm feeling this sharp prickly sensation in my ankle,"* or *"Even though I'm feeling this dull aching sadness in my solar plexus . . . I choose to relax anyway. I choose to love myself anyway."*

Then move through the points and tap:

> *"This pain, this sensation in my solar plexus, this sadness that's reminding me of ___."*

Continue to tap until you feel an acceptable shift. Work on one little chunk at a time until it feels like it has dissipated. Then, go to the next. Whether you clear this for yourself or are dealing with somebody else's pain, shifting your energy not only benefits you, but the other person as well.

It's like being around a colicky baby; by changing your energy and calming your own body, you can help to soothe and settle the fussy child.

RECOGNIZE: Time, Place, and Experience

Once you've ascertained whether your feelings are internal or external, you can explore them even more deeply. We'll begin with a set of categories: Time, Place, and Experience. These three categories are broken down into different components, or potential ways of addressing them. This approach is at the core of all the work I do, both for myself and as a practitioner for others. In my humble opinion, effective healing always begins with effective sleuthing.

The first category, Time, can break down into Past, Present, or Future. Ask yourself whether your experience is:

- About the past
- Current and present in this moment
- Might be rippling back from the future

Then:

- Where do I fit into all of this?
- Where am I in this timeline?

The second category is Place. It goes from microcosm to macrocosm: Personal, Local, Regional, National, or Global. You will have asked yourself these types of questions during your basic diagnostics, but they're worth revisiting now:

Is this experience:

- ❀ Personal?
- ❀ My own experience?
- ❀ Actually about me?

And:

- ❀ What is happening in my life that could be causing this?

Next, is this something:

- ❀ Local to me, but not about me?
- ❀ Outside of myself, but within my circle of friends and family?
- ❀ Within my community, village, or area?
- ❀ Happening regionally or nationally?
- ❀ Much greater and vaster? Is this global?

This will conclude:

- ❀ This is completely about me.
- ❀ It's about me and my relationships with other people.
- ❀ It's definitely about other people.
- ❀ It's about my city. It's about my state. It's about my country. It's about the planet.

The third component to evaluate is Experience: Physical, Emotional, Mental and/or Spiritual.

Physical:

- ✺ What am I feeling in my body?
- ✺ Is this a physical reaction?
- ✺ Is this being influenced by something physical within me or beyond me?
- ✺ Is my physical environment triggering this reaction?

Emotional:

- ✺ Is this emotional?
- ✺ Is this rooted in my own feelings?
- ✺ Is this something that I'm picking up from other people or circumstances?

Mental:

- ✺ Is this intellectual?
- ✺ Is this about thoughts, beliefs, or ideas?
- ✺ Are these thoughts mine or are they collective or inherited?
- ✺ Is this an attitude?
- ✺ Do these thoughts or ideas feel familiar or foreign to me?
- ✺ Am I picking up information from outside of myself?

Spiritual:

- ✺ Is this of a spiritual or paranormal origin?
- ✺ Could this be about my own karmic expression, or ancestral or collective karma?

- ✳ If this is ancestral does it feel like lingering trauma from specific events, a family agreement/vow that has been passed along for generations and/or inherited wounds/distress that was encoded in my DNA?
- ✳ Am I picking up on spirits or ghosts around me?
- ✳ Am I sensing otherworldly entities?
- ✳ Is this of Divine Source or does this feel like a lower vibration?
- ✳ Does this feel comfortable and safe, or do I need to invite protection?

Past	Present	Future
Personal Physical	Personal Physical	Personal Physical
Personal Emotional	Personal Emotional	Personal Emotional
Personal Mental	Personal Mental	Personal Mental
Local Physical	Local Physical	Local Physical
Local Emotional	Local Emotional	Local Emotional
Local Mental	Local Mental	Local Mental
Global Physical	Global Physical	Global Physical
Global Emotional	Global Emotional	Global Emotional
Global Mental	Global Mental	Global Mental

RECOGNIZE: Pinpointing the Combinations

Each of the components, Time, Place, and Experience, can combine with the others. For example, you may have a feeling about something from your past. Perhaps it was something that happened within your family and you were involved. You then consider it in terms of Place. Perhaps it happened in your family home. So this issue falls into Past, Personal, Relational, and Local (assuming you still live near your family home).

You then look at it in terms of Experience. This Past Experience was with your family. You identify it as a belief your family has carried for generations, which would fall into the Mental category. As you begin breaking these things down, you can get more precise about all of it, pinpointing where it falls in terms of Time, Place, and Experience.

You might ask:

⊛ Where is this occurring on the timeline?

⊛ How large or small, significant or insignificant, is this?

⊛ Is this experience Physical, in the realm of concrete realities? Is it an embodied sensation and experience of the world?

⊛ Is it Emotional, dwelling in the realm of feelings?

⊛ Is it Mental, an expression of thought or intellect? Does it inform beliefs and perceptions of things?

⊛ Is there a contract or agreement which is impacting the situation?

⊛ Is this beyond anything Physical, Emotional, or Mental?

⊛ These questions allow us to break things down so we can explore what's really going on for us.

Let's go deeper and look at some more examples.

Say you have a feeling coming up. You might begin by considering where it falls in the timeframe. Sometimes the experience is something from the Past, so the questions might be:

⊛ Did something that just happened trigger a feeling from the Past?

⊛ Have I recently experienced something that sent me backwards into the Past?

❀ If I'm in the Past, is this *my* memory? Is this my own experience?

❀ Is this bigger than me? Am I feeling something greater than myself?

As of this writing, we in the United States are a nation that is, to put it mildly, *freaking the fuck out*. Part of what's happening is that the impact of previous wars is resurfacing, triggering fear and panic responses in many of us. There are *so* many sensitive people on this planet, most of whom don't recognize themselves as sensitive. Most of us have ancestors who've endured the atrocities of war and oppression. If you go back far enough, every single one of us has ancestors who experienced extreme violence. If you have ancestors from Germany, the trauma of the Nazi regime is carried forward in your genetic code. If you have Jewish ancestry, the legacy of trauma is particularly intense. If you have African or Native American forebears, the legacies of slavery and genocide remain painfully fresh. Recently, countless examples of hate have provoked strong distress and have triggered ancestral wounds we've been carrying for generations.

Every one of us has ancestors with some connection to horrible events. Our cellular memories, our epigenetic experiences, carry forward that history and those wounds. When the political situation starts to resemble other turbulent times, it stimulates those memories and emotions from the past. In terms of Place, this is a Global event that's affecting everybody. People are responding at every level -- Physical, Emotional, Mental, and Spiritual. America's current political situation is hitting all of the experiential components.

In terms of Time, many of us are sensing ripples from the Future while simultaneously being impacted in the Present and triggered by the Past. Memories of the rise of fascism, the Holocaust, and countless other traumatic events throughout the course of time are also pinging our current experience. Anyone who's sensitive is being impacted right now. We are feeling tremors of intensity that transcend time due to the experience of multiple, overlapping events. This is triggering extreme reactivity in many of us.

RECOGNIZE: Danger, Will Robinson!

In Chapter 2, I mentioned a study in which scientists exposed mice to the smell of cherries, then put them in harm's way. The mice then associated the smell of cherries with pain and fear. Going forward, future generations of mice reacted the same way. These mice were not even born when the test mice had the experience, yet they reacted exactly as the original ones did.

What this means for us is that we respond at a *cellular* level to things that resemble challenges of the ancestral past. When this happens, I am a strong believer in using our tools. EFT/tapping, breathwork, flower essences, essential oils, movement, energy work, prayer, ceremony/ritual, visualization, lightwork, meditation, and sending healing to our ancestral line are all extremely useful. When we heal these wounds we can cease being in a place of reactivity and calm our fight-or-flight mechanism. We can then respond appropriately and proportionately to the situation at hand.

From the dawn of humankind, our species has been wired to react swiftly to predators and harm. We are designed to fight for our life, escape as fast as we can, or freeze and shut down. The part of our brain called the amygdala rules our fight, flight, or freeze response. It stimulates the secretion of adrenaline and cortisol in the body. When we sense that we are in imminent danger, this little almond-shaped part of our limbic system overrides calm, rational thought. It obscures our capacity to perceive our options or to consider creative solutions. Once in survival mode, logical thinking short-circuits. We revert to instinctive tunnel vision. Stress and fear cloud our reasoning. We can no longer see alternative options or explore alternative ways to address anything. Our natural reaction is urgency and impulsiveness.

When this cascade of adrenaline and cortisol was released in the bloodstreams of our prehistoric ancestors, they would use these hormones to get out of harm's way and literally run it off. Because they would fight or flee, all of that adrenaline and the extra energy it generated was burned off rapidly. They would utilize all the fuel, so by the time they got out of harm's way, they were fine. The challenge in today's world -- and I think this is part of our problem as empaths -- is that we still get the fight-or-flight trigger but, unlike our ancestors, we pool these hormones instead of burning them off. We still feel the "Danger, Will Robinson! Warning!" alarm, but these days it's more often an intellectual danger than a physical one. We react to a nasty comment directed at us on social media in the same way our ancestors responded to a wild animal chasing them down.

The problem is that our brain and nervous system respond to intangible threats as if they are physical dangers and we're not doing anything to run it off or fight it off. We end up in cascades of reactivity, with our bodies pumping out fear hormones in an effort to cope with existential threats that have no physical form. The stress chemicals continuing to course through our bodies create a feedback loop that keeps our amygdala on red alert. We can't simply think our way out of our dilemma. The fight-or-flight mechanism must be reset. Until we do something to reboot it, this defensive system will keep firing. I strongly suspect that the stress and fear many of us experience contribute to the epidemic of autoimmune diseases we're dealing with today. The impact of living in a state of perpetual stress is probably the single biggest contributor to every other problem on this planet. As empaths, we are particularly vulnerable to this. Not only are we dealing with our own distress, we're absorbing it from the world around us, which further exacerbates the issue. But just as we can act as vortexes of chaos and distress, we can also become anchors for calm and healing as we learn to reboot our alarm systems and find our way to safety and ease.

When we understand that our reaction originates from a cellular, ancestral memory, we can step back and let ourselves know,

"I'm safe. This reaction is about the ancient past. I can bring myself back to the here and now. I can offer healing and light to that ancient wound."

RECOGNIZE: Old Trauma, Old Agreements

In addition to ancestral legacies of trauma, we can also carry karmic past-life experiences.

Unfortunately, because women have endured so much abuse for generation upon generation, most matrilineal lines have places where the wounds dominate and the tether of light that connects us can be incredibly dim. There's familial trauma from the past for nearly all of us, but there's often personal trauma as well, whether from this life or a former one.

Trauma can extend beyond individuals and families. A location or community can carry regional wounds caused by events that happened in a particular place. It could be local, or it could be so significant that it has global impact. For example, in Boston in 1942, shortly after Prohibition ended, there was a catastrophic fire at a restaurant/supper club called the Cocoanut Grove. Between lax fire codes, highly flammable decorations, locked or obscured exits, and the only way out being a revolving door that jammed when too many people stormed it trying to escape, over 400 people died that night. The event was devastating for the region, and the lasting emotional and energetic impact of that disaster affected Boston and the outlying areas for many years. People who were alive then (like my father) still have their stories and feelings. These were passed forward to family members who weren't even born at the time. Like me.

My paternal grandfather was one of the doctors who helped treat many of the victims. I grew up being told stories about this fire, probably in far greater detail than a little girl should have heard. From a very early age I experienced an extreme fear of fire, particularly as I was trying to fall asleep. I suspect this had multiple roots: direct genetic memory of this horrific event; the regional legacy of fear, loss, and grief; past-life recall of other fires; and the dreadful witch hunting period now known as the Burning Times.

The 9/11 attack is an example of an event that impacted our entire nation and significant parts of the rest of this planet. Events such as World War II created such intense global repercussions that virtually no one on the planet has remained unaffected. We can carry the impact from anywhere in time or space. These manifestations of traumatic congestion may have origins that are personal or karmic, familial or ancestral, local or regional, national or global. They can be physical, emotional, or mental. They can arise from the ancient past, be occurring right this moment, or be looming in the future. Sometimes they're so huge that they show up in multiple ways.

Let's imagine a past-life experience manifesting as a physical consequence in this lifetime. In other words, you experienced an injury in a previous life which is still expressing itself in your current body. Here's a personal example. For many years, I had a sharp, persistent pain beneath my right shoulder blade. Even with massage and chiropractic adjustments, it wouldn't go away. During one of the intensive trainings I underwent to become a healer, I decided to work on this shoulder pain. As I tuned in to the sensation in my shoulder, I was suddenly flooded with a vivid image of being stabbed in the back exactly where the pain was. Now I must say, I deserved it. I was not a nice person in that life. I was extremely self-serving, I lacked any moral compass, and I was ready to throw anyone under the bus who couldn't serve me in some way. Before I was able to recognize the source of my current discomfort, I struggled regularly with that stabbing pain. It wasn't until I worked specifically on that memory, owning and repenting for my part in the process, that I was able to entirely release the pain. That pain has been gone for nearly 23 years now. This is an example of a Personal, Physical Experience coming from the Karmic Past.

We can carry physical expressions from our ancestral lines as well. Obviously, many illnesses and physical conditions are passed from one generation to the next. Chronic issues like extremely difficult menstrual periods can be legacies passed from mother to daughter to granddaughter. There is often a correlation between histories of abuse and persistent reproductive problems. People with ancestors who endured famines have been known to struggle with metabolic disorders (like thyroid disease), which cause the body to hold onto weight. During times of starvation, this allowed our ancestors to survive on very little food, but it can manifest as weight which does not correspond to caloric intake or activity in our bodies today. One of the reasons I do so much work on ancestral and karmic healing, both for myself and my clients, is that until we address these roots, we will continue to deal with the ramifications.

Staying in the Past, let's talk about the impact of an emotional experience. An emotional experience may have been the loss of a loved one, an intense betrayal, or any number of other extreme emotional events. It might range from Personal/Karmic to Ancestral/ Local, Regional, National or Global. Tuning in to determine where and when the emotional response came from is tremendously helpful. A client of mine -- let's call her Claire -- struggled with a deep fear of being separated from her daughter. From the time the child was born, Claire had recall of a previous life where her daughter was ripped away from her shortly before she was unfairly imprisoned and executed for political reasons. This fear has affected both of them. Any time they were to be separated for more than a day, they'd both experience extreme duress. The birth of Claire's daughter was quite complicated, and after a long, grueling labor she fell into a deep and much needed sleep, during which her infant was taken to the nursery. When Claire awoke many hours later and the child was nowhere to be found, she panicked. If the previous life hadn't held such an intense charge, it's very likely that she would have checked in with the nurse, asked where her daughter was, and been easily reunited. Instead, because the intense sense of loss and terror from her prior life was still fresh, it informed her entire reaction. Claire and I worked through this issue in a series of sessions. While we were able to reduce its emotional charge by addressing the hospital experience, it wasn't until Claire tapped on the pain from her past life that she found true relief. She released the emotional intensity of the original experience and discovered a new way to interpret the story: the love between Claire and her daughter is so strong that they will *always* find each other, no matter what happens, no matter where they go. Their love is stronger than death.

The Holocaust is a clear example of ancestral impact. As mentioned in Chapter 2, studies have begun to confirm that genetic expressions of trauma and fear have been passed on from concentration camp survivors to their descendants. We can carry both genetic trauma and karmic trauma. Determining whether something originates from our ancestral line or from our soul's experience in another life is not nearly as important as identifying the wound so we can clear and heal it.

Impact on the Mental level can be more subtle. It's not as visceral as physical injury or emotional devastation. As a result, it can also be more insidious. The Mental often has to do with the contracts we've agreed to: the beliefs we have, the ideas we think we are supposed to adhere to, and the rules we follow. Rules like: "No one in this family is allowed to outshine Grampa Henry," "We're just not lucky, nobody in our family ever gets ahead," "Our people had to struggle for everything they have. It dishonors their struggle if things come easily to us," or "In our family, the boys go to college and the girls get married. It's a waste of resources to send girls to school." I could go on and on but I imagine you get the gist. Before you continue with the rest of this chapter, I invite you to grab a sheet of paper and take some time to identify the familial agreements and beliefs impacting your life today.

These mental agreements transcend our families and ripple into cultural and even global concepts. For example, as women we're taught from a very early age to be wary, to be mindful that if we're not careful, we may end up in harm's way. This belief goes back thousands of years and the impact continues to spread across this planet in countless ways. Sadly, we live in a world where this belief is so pervasive that it reinforces an expectation that not only can females be considered prey, but that it's completely normal for males to be predators. It's a belief that we've all bought into: "Well, it's just true. You've gotta carry your keys pointing out in your fist, cross the street if you see men coming toward you, and keep scanning the perimeter for anything suspicious. If you're a woman, you need to pay extra attention. You must always be careful." This is a Globally dominant perception. It's something we've inherited and perpetuate as well. In many ways, all of this stems from a pervasive agreement: we teach girls to be careful of how they present themselves instead of teaching boys that they will be held accountable for their actions and that girls are equals worthy of respect.

All of the above are examples of how Time, Place, and Experience intersect, affecting the Physical, Emotional and Mental aspects of our lives. Except for extreme cases (like 9/11 or school shooting massacres), I've noticed that many people are barely affected by events outside of their personal and familial realms. A lot of "ordinary" people have the capacity to detach from suffering other than their own, which allows their response to be more conceptual than visceral. As empaths, we're vulnerable to picking up pain and suffering whether it's local or global. Our experience can encompass any and all categories and combinations. Take a look at the accompanying flow chart, which lays out all of the possible permutations, illustrating their potential complexity.

Empaths often feel multiple, combined experiences simultaneously. While the average human may sense some of these things (certainly when their own personal triggers, experiences, and ancestral legacies are activated), it will be with less conscious intensity. Those of us who are empathic get all of this stuff on steroids. Becoming clearer about what we're experiencing and identifying the roots -- Personal, Local, or Global; Physical, Emotional, Mental, or Spiritual; Past, Present, or Future -- is invaluable. It enables us to discern, address, and heal our issues.

In the Personal, Present Moment

Sometimes an event occurs -- somebody says something, you see something, you sense something, you feel something -- and you end up being triggered. You're having a Personal response.

It's not because you're feeling someone else's feelings. You are feeling your own, Personal feelings. Something was activated in the Present, in your current space and time as a Personal level of Experience.

It is especially important to ascertain the origin. By now you're probably realizing how many different factors can contribute to why we feel what we feel. It's crucial to start noticing, "Uh oh, I made the mistake of eating junk food, and now I'm paying the price."

For example, I'm really fragrance-sensitive. It used to be that I could not go into a place like Bed, Bath, & Beyond without my lungs tensing up, which would create a deep sense of panic. It was clear that this was a simple case of cause and effect. There was no wondering, "Gee, why am I feeling this way?" It was obvious: I'd smelled something hideous, my lungs reacted, and I became really uneasy. Often, it's more subtle than that.

My friend Irene moved into a new apartment. Within a few weeks she began experiencing physical pain and intense emotional distress. In addition to it being moldy, the building's entire electrical system was wired incorrectly.

Irene's highly sensitive nervous system was constantly irritated by electromagnetic interference. It was only after she relocated and had time to recover that her body and mood bounced back.

RECOGNIZE: Picking Up On Global Events

On the Global Physical level, when natural catastrophes like earthquakes, hurricanes, wildfires, or volcanic eruptions occur, they impact large populations. Empathic people will feel the shock, the aftermath, and the echoing disturbances in the field. For me and a number of my empathic sisters, the Pulse Nightclub shootings in Orlando, Florida started out as Future Emotional and National distress, which then turned into Present Physical, Emotional, and Global distress. If you're picking up something that feels like it's happening here and now, determine where it's falling on the scale of Personal to Global, then assess where it falls in terms of Experience. It might just be physical, or it might encompass the entire physical, emotional, mental, and spiritual range.

More often than not, there will be a dominant signature event in one Time and Place, manifesting as a primary Experience. You may also have issues reflecting multiple time streams. On other occasions, circumstances are compounded: a series of mirroring events happening in the Past, Present, and Future, while impacting physical, emotional, mental and spiritual states of being. The Motherlode is a situation so intense that it affects us at Personal, Familial, Local, Regional, National, and Global levels, in Physical, Emotional, Mental, and Spiritual ways, arising from multiple, mirroring events reverberating from past to present to future and back again. Talk about intense empathic distress!

I can't say why certain events affect us deeply, while other, equally agonizing situations may cause only a slight wobble. When Hurricane Katrina struck in 2005, I felt like a caged animal for days in advance and like I had a spiritual ulcer afterwards. My sense of grief and loss was profound -- I truly felt like I'd been kicked in the gut. Yet other significant global events don't have as powerful an impact. As I was writing this section, a tsunami and an earthquake hit New Zealand, but I wasn't strongly affected. On the other hand, with numerous disasters in Florida and New York, I've been a hot mess. As I started to contemplate this, I realized that many of the events I feel most strongly run fairly close to the ley lines where I live. While this is certainly not an exact science, and looking at map coordinates, there is a fairly wide swath between my little corner of Maine and Miami, Florida, it seems that I am more aware of, and sensitive to, the events that run up the Eastern seaboard. That said, I was also laid low by the tsunami that devastated Thailand in 2004 and the Fukushima disaster of 2011, so I can't say with any certainty why we're more vulnerable to some events than we are to others. It may be our stress levels at the time, or our degree of connection to the place and the people living there. I'm not sure there's any logical rhyme or reason.

RECOGNIZE: Distinguishing Between Fear and Premonition

One of my clients asked about the amazing, holy experiences she'd had while traveling through Southeast Asia. She'd felt not quite in her body, but not quite out of it either; she was disoriented yet filled with energy. It happened most often when she was near a temple or other spiritual landmark. What she described sounded as if she was suspended between the worlds of form and spirit and/or between dimensions. She was starting to experience the intersection between concrete reality and the spiritual realms. If you experience this, you may feel like all the hairs on your body are standing on end. Sometimes you'll get what a friend of mine refers to as "spirit confirmation chills." When I experience those chills, I feel as though I'm being lit up and start to tingle from head to toe. I feel shockwaves of sensation moving through me. It feels like a validation that something is absolutely true. I can also feel unusually large, as if I've expanded and am floating into space. As my client said, "It doesn't feel positive or negative, just overwhelming and very much in both worlds."

In such situations I recommend you put your feet on the ground, breathe in, and get back to being here and now as soon as you're able. A significant aspect of functioning effectively as an empath is the ability to bring yourself back to the present moment quickly. It's so easy for many of us to time hop -- to be in the past or the future instead of the present. Many of us have the ability to ride future streams, traveling down the rivers of possibility. While this may sometimes be useful, more often it doesn't serve us well at all. It doesn't serve any of us to look at the future and project into what may or may not happen. It can be difficult to distinguish whether we're being mindful of legitimate warnings or fear is pulling us into a whirlpool of awfulizing instead. If you notice your brain starting to take you down the rabbit hole of anything *remotely* scary, just back that truck up and get the F out of there. It never serves us to amplify or accelerate fear. The media are selling a lot of beer, pizza, and pharmaceuticals by keeping people scared right now. I invite you to focus on the best possible outcome, visualize solutions, and send light, love, and healing. I think it's very important that we do our best to stay in El Mundo Bueno.

A premonition is a flash of vision, knowing, sounds and/or sensations which have no correlation to the present moment and appear to be about the future. You have no control over the premonition, no ability to stop it. You get a brief download of information, rather like the scroll at the bottom of the news screen. For example, when Donald Trump became host of *The Apprentice* years ago, I had a flash. I thought, "Oh, my God, they're grooming him to be President." It was a 30-second blip. I saw it in my head, and I thought, "There it is." Then I thought, "Okay," and I let it go. I have not spent the last God only knows how many years imagining what a horrible President he would be. But I had that vision, that tiny little snapshot.

Conversely, many years ago I had to get up early to drive a friend to the airport. Let me just say, I am not a morning person, so getting up at 6am to drive her to Boston was pretty unfathomable for me. Nonetheless, she had a morning flight, I had promised to do this, and she was counting on me. There was ice all over the roads. I was experiencing horrible feelings but kept thinking to myself, "Suck it up, buttercup. You just don't want to get up early, leave your comfy bed, and drive a bunch in shitty weather. Sucks to be you. Get up, get out of bed, go drive your friend to the airport." I continued to have this terrible sense of foreboding, but we got to the airport just fine. I was returning just as the sun rose above the tree line. The ice on the roads began to melt, covering everything with a thin slick of water. Just as I approached my town, the car spun out of control. Miraculously, there were no other cars nearby and I managed to regain control. After that near miss, I thought it best to take a different route home. As I came to a stop sign, I hit more ice and the car began to slide. I frantically tried to stop, but the brakes locked up, the wheels froze, I slammed into a telephone pole, and totaled my car.

This is a perfect example of assuming that intuition is just your fear and ego talking. I knew deep down that something untoward was going to happen. I could sense it, but I simply didn't have the experience to distinguish my intuition from my fear.

Unfortunately, most of us have had experiences like this, but this is how we learn to recognize the difference between our intuitive voice saying, "Bad idea, don't go there, li'l bucka-roo!" and our fear and ego creating false resistance. My theory is that fear, specifically projection, results from the indulgence of running a scenario over and over in your head. The difference between prophecy and catastrophizing involves fixating on fear and projecting the vision into darker and darker places, visualiz-ing scenarios we shouldn't be visualizing. We flesh it out and then some. When we begin fantasizing about bad things, we tend to go on and on. Real intuitive information doesn't unfold at a leisurely pace. It tends to come in a flash -- you get the full download in an instant. Fear, on the other hand, has a tendency to escalate and keep on ramping up. It's like a shopping spree where you just keep loading more and more into the shopping cart until you've maxed out all your fear cards and have World War III happening in your head. It's exhausting, but for many of us (particularly if we come from a line of high-strung, anxious people) it can be quite familiar, even habitual.

There is a distinction between fear and concern. It's reasonable to have concern. It's reasonable to look at something and conclude, "This isn't acceptable." There's a big difference between acceptance and complacency, calm and numbness. We can choose to be calm despite the fact that things aren't working. You don't have to throw concern or an appropriate sense of danger out the window -- there's a reason we have those responses. Serious circumstances call for cautious concern. Like a physician preparing for surgery, or a martial artist facing battle, we can choose to remain relaxed yet focused, cool and grounded in the midst of seeming chaos. It's appropriate to acknowledge the gravity of a situation, but we cannot allow fear to dominate our approach to the work.

Many people are awakening to their abilities right now and frequently don't know what to do with the information they're getting. Trust your gut. If something feels icky, it's icky. If it feels disgusting, it's probably disgusting. As the saying goes, if it looks like a duck, swims like a duck, and quacks like a duck, it's probably a duck. If something does not feel okay and your instincts are telling you it doesn't feel like the right place for you right now, don't go there! The more you continue to use your intuition, the more accurate it will become.

As empaths, we need to cultivate our ability to distinguish between fear and fantasy, projection and actual premonition. Going back to the example of the Pulse nightclub shootings, a couple of weeks before it happened, two of my students called, asking, "What the fuck is happening? What is coming? I can feel it." All I could say was, "Me, too!" I will generally start sensing a coming event three to ten days before it happens. Sometimes, if it's really big, I'll sense things months in advance. I've noticed that the greater the magnitude of an event, the greater the disturbance it creates in the space-time continuum, and the more powerfully the shockwaves will roll back and forth across time. Particularly intense events can be so traumatizing, so shocking to the energy of the planet and to our psyches, that their tremors will roll back into the past. Those of us who are sensitive can feel the rumbling.

There are psychics who can pinpoint with great precision where and when an event will hit and what the situation itself will be. As an empath with psychic abilities, these things tend to affect me viscerally, on a physical/emotional level. I feel them like an animal, in my body. I know that a future prophecy is not about me when I experience an unidentifiable combination of grief, sadness, fear, heaviness, dismay, worry, and anxiety, all at once. In short, I feel like crap. I feel "off." I'm unusually tired and out of balance, and nothing about it correlates with my life. I'm not fighting with my partner. I'm not in a weird situation at work. I've done nothing to deplete myself. None of the usual contributing factors are in play. Also, I'm usually on a fairly even keel. My personal emotions are like New England weather -- even when I feel intense emotions, they tend to move across the sky pretty quickly -- so when I have a persistent, low-level sense of foreboding that lasts more than 24 hours, I know something is on its way. I can feel it coming.

I do not believe that because I have the ability to sense it, I have the ability to prevent it. What I do have is the ability to get grounded, to anchor my space, and to hold love and light. When I sense something coming, my job is to acknowledge, honor, and recognize it, then prepare myself for whatever the fallout is going to be. I choose to be a vehicle and an anchor for calm. As empaths, we can amplify both tranquility and suffering. Because we're receivers, we have the capacity to take in positive energy and expand it out to the world, but we also have the ability to absorb negative energy and to broadcast that back out into the world. Learning to calm ourselves down, quiet our energy bodies, and make the deliberate choice to serve as beacons of serenity and hope is a much more effective use of our abilities.

Let's talk some more about the Future. We can learn to sense whether we're perceiving something coming down the pike for us personally, or something more extensive. Personal premonitions can feel really strong. Right before my friend James was diagnosed with a terminal illness, I felt panic. The day he went into the hospital (unbeknownst to me), I was an absolute disaster. In hindsight, I know exactly why: he died just two and a half months afterward. That day was a total shit show. I was beside myself with anxiety and fear. I could not shake it. No amount of flower essences, tapping, or breathwork could calm me down. Because something really intense and personal was coming down the chute, I simply could not manage it effectively. It wasn't until I received news of what had happened that I was able to relax, because I finally understood where the feelings were coming from.

With prophecy and difficult portents of the future, I have found no better way to cope than to surrender, accept what's coming, breathe, ground, relax and batten down the hatches. Having endured that premonition, I was prepared for James' death as it happened. I was better equipped to deal, because I had sensed what was coming and had received a download of the entire situation that day.

RECOGNIZE: If It's Not One Thing, It's Another

As I dug into editing this chapter, I realized yet again how crucial it is for us to learn how to recognize what's actually going on and how to address it effectively. Our ability to recognize helps us to pinpoint where and what we are dealing with. In the same way that a healthcare provider may use X-rays or CT scans to understand exactly what they're contending with, if we take the time to identify what we are sensing, feeling, thinking, and experiencing, we can address things more concisely. The thing is, most of the time there's more than one thing going on. In order to effectively heal, we must often peel away numerous layers. I want to share an example of how complicated this process can be.

A particularly empathic woman I know (let's call her Eloise) had been struggling with insomnia following the birth of her fourth child. We looked at the obvious roots, including a time when everyone in the family except Eloise suddenly fell ill, leaving her to cope with everything on her own. As we peeled away the layers, slowly but surely she began sleeping better, but still not as well as she had prior to her son's birth. Every so often we'd circle back to the sleep issue to see if we could get any more clarity. In a recent session, we began with her concern that she'd never sleep normally again. As we tapped on this, a new piece of the story revealed itself. Eloise recalled that shortly after she'd returned home from the birth, things suddenly became very hectic. All kinds of clueless but well-meaning people started showing up to visit so they could spend time with the baby. Simply standing at the top of the stairs displaying her new son to the sky like the Lion King (while remaining otherwise isolated) wasn't going to cut it for this considerate empath. So instead of continuing to nestle into her "fourth trimester," she suddenly had to hop to it and become the Hostess with the Mostess. A time meant for rest, quiet, and bonding between mother and child was totally hijacked by visitors from out of town. Needless to say, this was extremely exhausting and stressful. Eloise went from a state of calm recovery to being totally *on* and feeling obligated to entertain and accommodate everyone else.

Within weeks of this initial trigger, everyone got sick, including the baby. A series of stressful events began to unfold. We had already identified many of these events and tapped down their intensity, but until this point we hadn't discovered the central issue: being forced to rally, to be awake and energized for everyone else, had put her nervous system on perpetual high alert. At the core of Eloise's current insomnia was the fact that she'd gone from what should have been a slow, gentle grace period to moving at breakneck speed *way* before she or her son had been ready. This had disrupted both their nervous systems and circadian rhythms. Only after we identified the need to reset her nervous system and give her body the message that she could finally stand down and relax were we able to clear this issue.

If you consider all the contributing factors, you can see the intersections. Not only were physical and energetic challenges to this woman's body, nervous system, routine and expectations activated by being forced out of postpartum recovery too early; she was also emotionally drained by having to deal with the energy, thoughts, and feelings of people with no capacity to recognize or respect her boundaries. This was followed by having to grapple with her entire family getting sick and the subsequent cascade of caretaking, stress, and insomnia. And this was just her current experience! In addition, there were similar challenges and unresolved issues mirrored in her familial histories. Each aspect contributed to the problem and every time we peeled away one layer we'd find another. I share this story to illustrate just how convoluted and dense our issues can be. It's rarely just one obvious issue that we can reconcile and be done with. Getting to the roots can sometimes take a good bit of time. We must cultivate patience, because we may be dealing with events impacted by Past, Present, Future, Physical, Mental, Emotional, Spiritual, Personal, Relational, and possibly National and Global issues. It's a lot to unravel!

RECOGNIZE: Creating a Story for Yourself

When you're working to identify empathic feelings -- particularly around future information -- sometimes things can be pretty unclear. I mentioned earlier that you can use your imagination to home in on what's going on. You can play with the idea of, "I imagine this is because..." to create your own story. There's no wrong way to do this. Whatever you imagine will be pertinent to your situation. Now, if you're working directly with someone else and you're in service to them, accuracy will be important. But if you're just doing this work for yourself, then whether or not your story is factually accurate is less important than what it brings up for you, how you feel about it, and what you want to do about it.

To create a story for yourself, you can begin something like this: "Okay, I imagine the reason I'm feeling this way is that I just walked down the street and happened to go into a grocery store where I saw two people arguing. This is what it's about..." There's nothing wrong with creating a story that's based on what you imagine, then working through the stuff you've imagined. After all, it's *your* stuff -- you imagined it. Of course, if you're working with somebody else, it *always* goes back to consent and calibration. You might offer, "I'm getting the sense that this might be about _____. Does that make sense to you? It doesn't? Okay, recalculating. Let's try something different."

As an empath, the willingness to be wrong is vitally important. We need to be willing to understand and admit that we don't have all the answers. There are so many reasons we could be feeling what we're feeling and why this information might be coming to us. Just because something feels 100% true to us does not mean we understand it accurately, truthfully, or effectively for anyone else. Anyone doing healing or psychic work out in the world who has the audacity to claim that they know all and are unfailingly accurate is full of it. When a client or friend says, "That doesn't ring true for me," it's crucial that we immediately recalibrate. We must promptly concede, "Okay, thank you for that information. I'm going to take that into consideration and adjust accordingly." Never, ever tell somebody that they're wrong and you're right. Even if you are right, it may be that you're picking up something they're not ready to acknowledge. To force them to accept something they aren't on board with goes against the fundamental rule of consent.

Staying married to an intuitive hunch or premonition is something I've seen people do many times (hell, I've done a fair share of it myself). There's a kind of hubris that leads us to assume we're picking up everything and interpreting it correctly. There are so many different aspects to how and where information arrives. There are so many different ways we can receive it. Bottom line: we are human vessels and we're fallible. We must always remain humble and be able to admit that we may not be interpreting things accurately. This is relevant wisdom even if confirmation chills are urging us to believe something to be indisputably real and true. If I get that sparkle of certainty crackling through my system and present it to somebody who responds, "That doesn't ring true for me," all I can do is say, "All right," and move on. Perhaps it will make sense to them at some point in the future. Perhaps they will come back to me later and say, "Oh, Jesus Christ, Jennifer, when you said XYZ to me, I thought you were nuts! Then, weeks later, such-and-such happened and I realized that you were telling me exactly what was going on." Just because somebody denies it, doesn't mean it isn't true. Sometimes, it just hasn't happened yet. It doesn't matter -- never, ever force your agenda.

RECOGNIZE: Cultivating Curiosity

Before going any further, I want to put in a plug for curiosity and inquisitiveness. These can be very effective tools when you're feeling unsure and don't yet have a clear way forward. We can approach our experiences by saying, "Even though I have no clue where this is coming from, I'm open to the possibility that I can be curious, that I can simply be inquisitive. I wonder where this is coming from?" Cultivating a sense of curiosity can often open the way to insights and solutions and furnish amazing results.

A while back I was facilitating a session for a client. She'd struggled with a curious physical condition for quite a while. Her conventional doctors were baffled and had told her she was doomed to live with it for the rest of her life. She'd gotten no real answers and no suggestions for coping, other than "Suck it up, buttercup." She was aware of the sensations in her body but couldn't understand why any of it was happening. Because we didn't know the root or origin of her condition, we simply focused on acknowledging her symptoms. When you don't know, curiosity is one of the most effective ways to unpack a situation. My client and I mused together about the things she *did* know.

"I feel this in my *shoulders*. I know it's especially sore when I *first wake up*. When I tune into this I feel *sad and hopeless*. I'm really curious what this condition is trying to tell me. I wonder what it's about."

Fascinatingly, what seemed to be an unrelated memory arose as we worked. As we began to explore, it became apparent that the memory was directly connected to her physical symptoms. There was a strong emotional charge attached to this memory which had eventually manifested in the physical condition. As we tapped on the specific event and released her feelings of hurt, betrayal, and frustration, the symptoms began to subside.

What had started at a distress rating of 9 moved down to a 2, then returned to the way things had felt prior to the onset of symptoms. If we had over-thought things or tried to command a specific answer, who knows whether we'd have made such a clear connection to the root cause.

RECOGNIZE: Truths and Lies

Sometimes a situation feels off, but you're not sure whether it's connected with what's actually happening or whether it's triggering a memory or previous experience. You can ask yourself, "What does this remind me of? Is this situation triggering this memory?"

Here's an example. Many years ago, I was in a relationship with a guy. During an event we attended together, he disappeared for the night. I knew instinctively that he was cheating on me, so when he returned the next day I asked him directly, "Did you sleep with so-and-so?" He looked me straight in the eye and said, point-blank, "No, you're imagining things." I thought, "Okay, I have some history with difficult relationship stuff. Maybe this is just me projecting my fear of abandonment and it has nothing to do with him. Maybe I'm just being anxious because I'm afraid he's going to leave me." But try as I might, the feelings wouldn't go away. Then I started having dreams about him with this other person. My feelings of anxiety and grief persisted, but he kept insisting, "No, no, no, I'm not doing anything." So I told myself, "This must be my own shit."

Two months later he sat me down and admitted, "You know how you dreamed that I had sex with so-and-so, and that you thought that I might be having an affair? Well, you were right." I was simultaneously shocked and relieved. While it stung to learn that he had cheated, the hardest part had been his persistent lying. I'd allowed him to convince me that what I'd intuitively known, dreamt, and envisioned was all my own invention. But I hadn't made it up. It was real. Sometimes, you get information you're pretty sure is accurate. When that information is denied outright, it doesn't necessarily mean it isn't true. It's a very interesting dance between what is real and what is imagined. In this and other cases, I've had people tell me I'm imagining things when, in fact, I wasn't imagining them at all. I'm willing to give the benefit of the doubt, but my experience is that when I sense something, more often than not, it really is happening. At this point, I'm much more likely to trust my intuition. I'm also completely disinclined to get into a relationship with a liar.

I've been talking about how important it is to willingly admit when we, as empaths, are wrong. The other side of that coin is throwing away our truth for the illusion of connection. All too often, we're willing to discount our truth and make ourselves wrong in order to meet our other emotional needs. Distinguishing between your own stuff and other people's when they insist that what you're perceiving isn't real can be a serious mindfuck, especially in intimate relationships. I'm sure that many of you have had this experience. Anytime we choose to stay in a situation where someone makes us doubt ourselves and feel unbalanced, insecure, or anxious, we have to ask ourselves a few questions: "Why am I staying here? How is this serving me? What part of me feels the need to be with someone who's just not that into me?" This is about being brutally honest with ourselves and examining our own agendas. It's about recognizing what we're doing and why we're doing it, not sticking our fingers in our ears and chanting, "La la la, I don't hear you!" The only way out is through. Sometimes, the only way we learn this is through the heartache of doing the unconscious, triggered, dysfunctional shit we do until we get sick and tired of being sick and tired.

Before we develop our filters, we can be so porous and chameleon-like that we may not know who we really are, what we really want, and what truly matters to us. A big piece of *Recognition* is learning how to actually sit with and get to know ourselves. The first step in distinguishing between me and not-me is knowing who "me" is. Before we've had any support around being empathic, it can be terribly easy to discount our truth. When we can't distinguish what we're feeling and whether it's coming from within or without, it can be hard to trust ourselves or to believe our own truth.

I'm now at a point in life where I know myself fairly well. I know my body, my heart, and my mind. I know my energy, so more often than not I can identify when I'm picking something up from somebody else. I can recognize when I'm sensing an impending disaster. I can determine when I'm reacting to something happening in the present and whether it's triggering stories from my past. I can usually discern whether I'm feeling something originating from within myself and which thoughts and emotions are my own. This ability to discern has come from a willingness to sit with my feelings and to be emotionally uncomfortable. It has deepened through a willingness to separate myself from other people and dwell in solitude. Solitude is an essential aspect of surviving as an empath. In order to have any perspective about ourselves, we must be willing to be alone. It takes courage to admit to ourselves who we truly are and who we want to be.

RECOGNIZE: Getting Support with Recognizing

We can't always DIY this stuff. Sometimes we can help ourselves, but other times it takes someone else's objectivity to create the perspective we need to stay the course as we navigate our more challenging issues. We don't always get ourselves into situations on our own, so it follows that we're not always able to get ourselves out of them on our own. At the core of our healing lies the ability to allow ourselves to receive and accept support. It often takes an outsider, someone who's not mentally or emotionally invested in our story, to help us get through the hard stuff. I strongly believe that if I'm going to help others I must be willing to accept help myself. We do better when we don't always try to go it alone. I have a team of people who support and guide me. Contrary to current cultural perceptions, we are not isolated individuals. We are cells creating the body that is this planet. *Asking for and accepting help is our birthright.*

I've had other empaths ask me, "Why is it that I can find solutions to everyone else's problems, but I can't help myself?" As I wrote earlier, my favorite answer is, "you can't read the label from the inside of the jar." When we help someone else, we often have perspective that they don't have. Why should we be able to see our own solutions all the time? Sometimes, seeking good counsel from another source is the wisest move we can make, especially if we're choosing the path of offering counsel and support to others. As the saying goes, "Physician, heal thyself!" Get support. You need to take your own medicine. Sometimes, you can't see because you're looking from the wrong vantage point, so the best thing you can do is to pursue an outside perspective. Get guidance from someone who can ask insightful questions, who can help you to tease out the answers and reveal things you might not otherwise have grasped.

When we first enter this arena, we can be so bogged down with other people's feelings and energy that we cannot distinguish anything. Our perspective is obscured by all the emotional toxins we've already taken in. The key is finding a source of support, then learning to *Recognize* and *Release* energy which no longer serves you. Seek out help and guidance to move those old energies. Once you've had a thorough, professional clearing, it's much easier to do your own routine maintenance. When you're first learning how to navigate your empathic abilities, it really helps to have somebody who can facilitate emotional "surgery" or offer energetic medicine to help you shift things.

Most of us need help -- especially at the beginning of our journey. You can receive support by seeking a practitioner who feels right to you. You might want to work with a massage therapist, a chiropractor or osteopath, an acupuncturist, or a Reiki or polarity practitioner. Most healing modalities can provide help with letting things go, especially with stuff you've been carrying in your body. There are also many great modalities for releasing other people's energy from your body. Some practitioners are not oriented to working with the subtle energy body, but plenty are: EFT practitioners, shamanic healers who do energy work (particularly extraction work), and healers who do chakra work to unblock energy flow in the body, to name but a few. The support of someone who can recognize foreign or misaligned energies within you and then realign them is priceless.

When you're looking for support, you want to find the right person or people for *you*. Even if a practitioner is great for a friend, you still need to be clear that the chemistry is right for you. Unfortunately, not everyone who claims to know what they're doing actually does. Not everybody is as far along on the path as they think they are. I want to offer some important considerations when you're look-ing for the coach, healer, or mentor who is the best fit for you.

Choosing the right mentor (or other practitioner) can be a cru-cial part of the equation if you're serious about investing in yourself and transforming your life. While effective coaching can facilitate swift and immediate shifts, most deep, substantial change involves a commitment of time, effort, and resources to yield the best out-come. This means beginning a relationship with someone who will work with you intimately for a significant period of time, ranging from a few months to many years.

I believe that good coaching, mentoring, and healing happen by empowering you to find your truth, your spark, your energy, and the best path for you. A good coach can hold up a clear mirror, reveal insights which may be hidden, and offer strategy, support and suggestions to help you along the way. Ultimately, though, you are the only person living your life, and you are the one who will be putting one foot in front of the other as you do your work. You are the one investing in you, so you need to be comfortable that you're really making this choice for you.

Bottom Line:

- ❇ When you tune into your inner guidance about a potential practitioner, is it a "Yes," a "Yes, but," or a clear "No"? Does the fit feel right for you?

- ❇ Do you believe that if you show up, really commit to doing the work and persevere when the challenges start surfacing, that this practitioner or community has the tools and insight to guide you to where you want to go?

- ❇ Do you sense that this person has the ability to see and uphold your vision and your potential for greatness, even during times when you hit a wall or feel discouraged?

⊛ If money or fear of failure were not issues, would you jump at the chance to work with this person?

⊛ I've created a resource called the 9 C's of Support that goes into depth about qualities and details to consider when you are seeking support from a community or individual, it's included in the Empathic Safety Kit which you can access at EmpathicSafety.com

Being a Good Client: How To Effectively Use Support

The best relationship with a mentor, healer, coach, or practitioner is based on reciprocity and respect. We are most effective when we acknowledge that this a two-sided partnership. I've heard many stories from friends (particularly massage therapists and people in the allopathic medical fields) whose clients come in expecting them to do all the heavy lifting. Many expect the therapist to fix their problem while they lie passively on the table with no sense of accountability for their own part in how they got there.

In order to get the most benefit from working with a practitioner, it is imperative that we be willing to take complete responsibility for ourselves. This means being willing to invest the time, energy, emotional willingness, and money into really doing the work. It also means being realistic about what you are ready and willing to do. There is a difference between having resistance that you can be coached through and having so much on your plate that adding more will only result in overwhelm and frustration.

Now, if overwhelm, frustration, and overdoing it is your M.O., then the support you need may have to start with eliminating the behaviors that keep you on the hamster wheel. Obviously, as someone who has worked in the field of healing for many years, I believe in the importance of getting support. I know *without a doubt* that I would be nowhere near where I am today were it not for the many healers, teachers, mentors, and advisors I've worked with over the course of my life. As a very young woman I didn't have a clue how to receive support and, to be honest, I was pretty resistant to getting help. But I kept showing up and eventually learned how to benefit from support. Since this is definitely a marathon and not a sprint, you deserve to get as much bang for your mental, emotional, and financial buck as possible. The following is a list of qualities that will help you to reap the rewards of your investment.

- ✸ Find someone who feels right to you. If your gut tells you that it doesn't feel like a good fit, then please walk on by. I can't even count the number of people for whom I've done cover-up tattoos because they didn't listen to their inner guidance when it told them someone was the wrong person for them. Whether it's the fear of hurting someone's feelings by saying "no," the fear of creating conflict by refusing a pushy practitioner, or some other reason all your own, it is essential that you feel truly confident in your choice. Not all practitioners are created equal. Some are too soft and not particularly insightful, and if you are smart (which I strongly suspect you are since you've read this far), you'll probably be able to run circles around them.

  Conversely, there are dominating practitioners with their own agenda. These are often harder to walk away from, because they can be really good at manipulating you into believing that your ambivalence or concern is resistance to your own growth. I have a client who finally left a teacher after more than five years of gaslighting. The teacher used challenging tactics anytime his motives were questioned.

  In this case, the teacher so resembled her father that her 5-year-old self couldn't stand up to him. Fortunately, we worked together and she was able to claim her truth and walk away from this abusive power dynamic. You deserve to work with the people who feel really comfortable and right *to you*. This is obviously more important for an empath than it is for those who don't readily pick up on other people's energy.

❀ Approach the work with the attitude that this person is your ally. Deep work involves revealing your true self, warts and all. Fear of judgment or criticism can bring the healing process to a grinding halt. During your first consultation, pay close attention to how the practitioner listens to you as well as how they respond.

If you notice language that feels triggering or dismissive to you, trust your gut. This work is hard enough without the added burden of worrying about how someone will judge you. If your core issue is expecting judgment and criticism and you are wired to find evidence of this, then perhaps you'll want to keep this in mind as you search for the right support. I also invite you to address this challenge as early as possible in the relationship.

❀ Act *as if* you deserve love, care, kindness, healing, support, and an ever-improving life until you actually believe you do. You've probably heard the saying, "fake it 'til you make it." When it comes to healing our sense of worth and self-esteem, this is often the only way in. Low self-esteem lies like a rug and tells us what lowly worms we are.

The only way beyond this in the beginning is to take action despite the meanies in our head. This is not about ignoring or blasting those voices, but rather acting with the same kind of compassion you'd have for a scared little kid who really needs a good meal and a nap. You hold the space for the fussiness and offer love instead of argument.

❀ Allow yourself to receive support. There is a paradox in healing: no one can fix us or change us without our participation.

We are the ones who must say "yes" to change, yet there are times we simply can't reach the spot that needs help.

A good practitioner works in collaboration with you. They seek to support you and to help activate your innate healing process. This is a fine dance between willingness, surrender, acceptance of support, ownership of everything that brought you to this moment, and the willingness to take the next steps the Universe reveals.

❀ Choose to be transparent. Let the practitioner know what's going on for you. If you are overwhelmed, tell them. If you have a lot of stuff coming up and will not be able to do your homework, let them know in advance.

You hired this person to support and guide you. Give them all the information they need in order to make it easy for them to help you. If they ask you to fill out regular updates or check-ins, please do this as often as you can. Not only will you benefit greatly from taking the time to write down what you're experiencing, it will also help your practitioner to understand what's going on and to be prepared to support you when you do more work together.

❀ If you have any concerns or needs, please bring them up. Even the most psychic practitioner cannot anticipate your wants or needs. Part of your work is learning to advocate for yourself and not expect other people to automatically take care of you. A good client-practitioner relationship is one of calibration and consent. It is an ongoing dialogue that changes as you grow and your needs shift.

❀ Approach this work with the willingness to be willing to regard things in a new way. Allow for the possibility that even the most deeply-entrenched patterns and beliefs can change and that perceptions of even your most sacred cows may be distorted by wounds or patterns of imbalance.

Being "coachable" is one of the most vital qualities any of us can cultivate if we want to truly transform our lives. When a trusted mentor or healer offers you an observation or suggestion, follow it, experiment with it, and implement it when possible. Avoid the "yeah buts" -- putting up roadblocks or creating excuses for why you can't do it. As the saying goes, "Argue for your limitations and they will be yours."

✤ Notice your resistance as you can. Acknowledge defensiveness. Hold it with compassionate detachment. At its root, this is our attempt to protect ourselves from pain and the imagined discomfort of reliving challenging events.

The irony is, the resistance is actually far more painful than addressing and releasing whatever wounds we carry. We've already endured the worst part and we're still here. We are resilient and we are strong. Releasing the pain is far easier than it was to experience it in the first place.

✤ Stay in your heart and out of your stories. Even though sharing the details of what happened can facilitate powerful healing, going on and on about what we are thinking is a great way to stay fixated on the problem.

Being present to our feelings can be surprisingly simple. "I feel disappointed and hurt that my dream isn't working the way I'd hoped" is really different from, "When I was seven my father left my mother, she got really angry and started drinking every day and it got so bad she lost her job and was hospitalized so I had to raise my two-year-old sister and every day we had to go to the park with my mean grandmother who always called me selfish so now it seems like I keep finding people who are mean like my grandmother or let me down like my mother and no matter how hard I try, nothing works and everything always falls apart and it's just not fair -- I don't know what's wrong with me, I want to succeed but no one ever wants what I have to offer, my former business partner walked away with all of our business and now I have to build everything from square one again and if only people could see that I'm better at this work than she is and know the truth about what a backstabbing biotch she really is -- it's just not fair..." Perhaps you've been with someone when they start telling their "story." I find there's a difference in quality between the chattering monkey mind and heartfelt expression; I tend to glaze over after a few minutes of monkey mind rant, whereas I can sit in rapt attention when someone is speaking their authentic truth. Now and then we *all* fall into monkey mind stories. A good practitioner will often notice when this happens and invite you to get back to the essence of what's really going on. Over time, you'll learn to get clearer and to articulate the essence of what you need with greater swiftness and ease.

✷ Keep it simple: instead of trying to tackle everything and the kitchen sink in one session, break it down to the most pressing issue at hand and focus on moving through it until it shifts. As my EFT mentor often says, "this work is about going a mile deep and an inch wide, not a mile wide and an inch deep."

Bottom line: you didn't get to where you are through one singular event, and you won't transform everything with a lone "one minute miracle." My friend Britt says it best: "It's not a pill, it's a process." It takes time to really transform and it is incremental, persistent, regular action that creates significant change.

✷ Accept that you are in this for the long haul and invest in yourself. True change is about sustainable lifestyle shifts and living differently. We live in a culture that seeks the quick fix and advertises the latest business, dietary, or exercise fad with the promise that after only X weeks or months we'll have the life we've always dreamed of. The truth is, as soon as folks stop the program and revert to their old patterns, the old way of being soon follows.

I encourage you to be honest with yourself about whether you are genuinely ready to change and how much you are actually willing to commit. You are the only one who can choose to invest in yourself and you are the only one who can agree to a lifestyle, not a fad.

✺ Create time for yourself to do this work. Grab your calendar and block off time specifically for you, then *show up and do it*. Don't just expect growth and recovery to happen in random moments that you squeeze in here and there. Having skin in the game means making the time to do the work. For example, a friend of mine (also an entrepreneur) enlisted a colleague who was enrolled in the same, long-term program to be an "accountability partner." Although this other person claimed they wanted to grow and change, they consistently missed clearly scheduled, weekly check-in calls because they made other plans to do something "fun." This lack of commitment was reflected in their lack of progress.

In contrast, another person I know decided they were ready to do the deep work to finally release some very old, entrenched wounds. Not only did they show up for every appointment, they also arranged their entire schedule to allow time for decompression and integration for a few days following the work. Needless to say, this person has had far better results than the "fun" seeker.

✺ Accept that this is a journey, not a destination, and that *done* is better than *perfect*. Perfectionism is one of our biggest roadblocks to healing and growth. We so often start new projects with big, lofty plans. Progress, not perfection, is the key here.

It is better to keep trying. As Elizabeth Gilbert suggests in *Big Magic: Creative Living Beyond Fear*, being a persistent half-ass yields better results than being an inconsistent perfectionist ever will. Accept that you are going to stumble. Accept that you will have days when you forget to show up for the work. Accept that you'll have days when you choose to say "fuck it" and go back to old behaviors or patterns. Instead of giving up, instead of claiming failure and using it as an excuse to scrap it all, accept that you'll keep going anyway.

✤ Be kind to yourself when you slip or fall. If you revert to old coping mechanisms and less-than-optimal behaviors, please be good to yourself anyway. I invite you to own your choices. Instead of closing your eyes and pretending you just fell into the pit of old habits, be deliberate

Connecting To Community: Finding Your Tribe

Having a chance to express what you're learning to one or more witnesses can be really helpful. It's valuable to have validation from other sources and to connect with other empaths. While some of us have the good fortune to live in areas rich in spiritual resources and other self-identified empaths, many of us live in the middle of nowhere and don't have in-person resources readily available.

In some cases resources may actually exist, but we don't know how to find them. Fortunately, the internet and the special interest groups that have formed on social media platforms have become great resources for finding kindred souls.

As you begin exploring your options, it's important to take the health and safety habits of any new group into consideration. Before you just jump in with both feet, I encourage you to take some time to observe. Keep an eye out for the levels of awareness, mindfulness, and self-awareness within any group, live or virtual, before you decide to join. Read through the guidelines and terms of membership. Find out what the policies are for sharing and privacy, in addition to offering unsolicited advice and self-promotion. As you explore a community, try to determine the following:

⊛ What are the boundaries of the group?

⊛ What are their terms?

⊛ Who are the leaders and moderators?

⊛ Do the leaders take an active role in the group?

⊛ How large is the group?

⊛ How active is the group? Do posts move so quickly that it's hard to keep track of them?

⊛ Is there noticeable divisiveness? Are "flame wars" occurring?

⊛ Are there any dominant personalities who are behaving badly?

⊛ Is there any kind of snarky or bossy attitude between people?

⊛ Is there a lot of negativity and blame? Are people spending a lot of time complaining about how awful their lives are? Is there a lot of, "poor me" going on?

⊛ Is it a supportive, loving community?

⊛ Is the overall attitude positive and uplifting?

⊛ Are people taking responsibility and owning their stuff?

⊛ Are they doing their work?

⊛ How are newcomers welcomed?

⊛ Does this feel like a place you would like to visit on a regular basis?

⊛ An important factor to take into consideration: because you have no cues other than the posts in a forum, working in a strictly virtual community can intensify your empathic nature. You must therefore remain mindful of how you're extending your energy and awareness. You're in the Matrix.

You've moved beyond physical form, because online relationships exist outside the physical dimension. You are essentially going into astral space and making connections with people. This is why virtual relationships with healers, coaches, and mentors can be so powerful and effective and why I often work with people virtually, even if they live within driving distance. I have found that the nature of this connection enhances the intuitive/empathic link while decreasing any static or distraction caused by our physical presence. This is one of the things that can make being part of a healthy group really wonderful but can make being part of a dysfunctional group simply horrid. Remember, one of the most basic things to keep in mind as an empath is: "Buyer Beware!" The online world, where people can hide in anonymity behind a fake profile or avatar, is the wild wild west. As empaths, we must remain mindful of our needs, boundaries, and limitations. We need to take care of ourselves and to step away from any communities or pages which do not nourish and support us.

The Power of Recognition

The reason I begin the entire Empathic Mastery System with *Recognize* is because if you don't know what you're dealing with, it's kind of hard to deal with it. It doesn't work to slap on a bandaid if you can't locate the wound. That's why I feel so strongly about taking the time to look at things and doing the work to recognize what's going on. For example, if an environmental allergy is causing your wacky moods, it's really helpful to ascertain that it is, in fact, the allergy that's the source of your problem. Maybe it's the fact that you have a neighbor who's suffering from major depression and, every night as they watch reality TV, you're picking up on their sour mood. Once you recognize the source, you can create both strategic and energetic solutions. I strongly believe that we are best served when we acknowledge what we're dealing with and take some time to honor it *before* we try to surround ourselves with a ball of light and think happy thoughts. The beauty is, the more we work with mindfulness and recognition, the more comfortable it gets. Being calm becomes easier and more habitual.

I use a body scanning technique, which you'll find in the next section, to listen, pay attention, and tune into what's really going on. This allows me to go deeper into the questions, "How am I feeling? What's going on? What do I get from doing this?" EFT can be used for further clarification, particularly when you don't know what you're feeling. Journaling is also very helpful -- write all your thoughts and feelings down so you can sort them out. These three excellent tools can help you to get clearer about the basic questions, "Is this my shit? Is it somebody else's? Where is it coming from? What is it about? What do I want to do about it?"

Taking the time to *Recognize* and acknowledge what is really going on for you is exactly what you need to move to the next step of the Empathic Mastery System. Once you know, you can start to *Release* that which no longer serves you.

RECOGNIZE: The Body Scan

The body scan meditation is an especially effective tool when you get a feeling but you're not sure what it is or where it's coming from. It allows you to scan your body in order to tune in to what's going on, how you're feeling, and who, what, where, or when your feeling stems from. You can read this exercise to yourself or have someone read it to you. You can also record and listen to it, or access my audio recording and listen along when you visit EmpathicSafety.com.

Please find a space where you can get comfortable and avoid inter-ruption for the next 20 minutes or so. Grab a pen and journal (or other writing device) so you can make notes after you've completed the exercise.

Take a deep breath. Notice how you feel as you breathe in. Pay atten-tion to the sensation of your breath, then exhale. Notice how it feels as you continue to breathe in and breathe out.

Gently notice how your breath moves in and out of your body. Does it flow freely and easily? Are there places where your breath gets caught or stuck? Are there places where it can only expand so far? How deeply and fully can you breathe? Don't force it. Just notice what it feels like as you breathe in and then breathe out.

Now, inhale as deeply as you can and count in your mind to see how many seconds it takes to breathe in completely. Hold for a beat or two. As you exhale, count and determine how many seconds it takes to breathe out. Breathe in. Breathe out. There's no wrong way to do this. This is just information to give you a sense of what's going on, what your lung capacity is right now, and how your breath is being affected by your feelings, your body, and your thoughts.

Now let's scan to find out what's happening. Continue gently breath-ing in and out. Notice how it feels to be in your body, sitting or lying where you are. Notice where you feel any sensation in your body, con-tinuing to breathe as you notice.

How do you feel in your space? What's the temperature like around you? How are you feeling in your body? What's your level of relax-ation? How do your muscles and joints feel? Continue to notice how you're feeling in your body. Are you hungry? Are you full? Are you tired? Are you experiencing any kind of discomfort or pain? If so, is it sharp? Dull? Persistent? Intermittent? Is it strong or mild? Notice what you're feeling and where you're feeling it.

Starting with your feet, notice the sensations in your toes. Notice if there's anything unusual. Tune in and see if you sense any colors, emotions, or feelings that you might associate with sensation in your toes.

Moving further into the joints of your feet, feel into your arches and across the tops of your feet. Notice what's going on in your feet. Moving into your heels and your ankles, become aware of any sensations. If you have not yet closed your eyes, try closing them now. See if any colors, thoughts, or images cross your mind as you pay attention to your feet and ankles.

Moving up into your shins and calves, breathe in and notice any sensations in your lower legs. What kind of energy do you sense in your legs? Just notice. Are there any colors? Do any images come up for you? Take a moment to scan and notice any emotions, thoughts, or associations. Tune in to your sense of the energy, movement, and solidity of your lower legs.

Move your awareness up to your knees. Notice the front of your knees, your kneecaps, and the backs of your knees. Tune into the entire knee joint. Notice any sensation you're feeling in your knees. Eyes closed, tuning in, see if there are any colors. Pick up what's going on and note whatever you're observing.

Move your attention up to your thighs, through their backs and fronts, through the inner and outer thighs. Up into your hip joints and your buttocks. Just noticing. What are you sensing? Moving into your groin, just paying attention, what kinds of sensations do you feel? What colors do you see? What images, if any, are you aware of? What are your thoughts and feelings as you pay attention to your hips, your buttocks, and your groin?

Move up into your pelvis and lower belly. Feel into your upper hips. Moving through your gut, your belly and your lower back, just notice any sensations. Are there any thoughts, ideas, or images coming to you? Just paying attention, tune in and notice.

Moving up to your waist, tune into your lower torso, especially around your belly button and across your back. Notice any sensations, any images, emotions, thoughts, or colors in this area. Gently tune into all of it, using your breath to deepen awareness as you breathe into your lower torso. Notice what it feels like. Breathe into your core and notice what you're sensing.

Continuing to breathe, move your awareness into your solar plexus, ribs, liver, stomach, middle back, and spine. Extend your awareness into your lungs and upper torso. As you breathe into your torso, pay attention to your chest and upper back. Notice the colors. Notice any images. Notice any feelings or thoughts that come up for you.

Moving further up your body, notice the sensations in your shoulders and shoulder blades, the spaces between your shoulders, across your chest and sternum, and across your upper back. Note any colors, images, thoughts, or feelings and continue to breathe as you scan your body.

Now extend your awareness down your arms, into your elbows, forearms, hands, and fingers. Gently note what you're feeling. Notice any colors, thoughts, or emotions, what you're feeling and where you're feeling it.

As you just breathe into your body, be conscious of how it feels to be in your body right now, in this moment. When you're ready, move awareness into your neck. You may want to move your head or neck. Just observe. How does your neck feel? Breathing in and out, notice any colors, images, thoughts, or feelings coming to you. Pay attention, if you move, to how easily, smoothly, or not-so-smoothly your neck is moving.

Finally, move your awareness to your head. Note what's going on in your jaw and mouth, especially if there's any tension in your jaw. Tune into any thoughts or feelings that come up for you. Notice any sensation in your ears, as well as your upper jaw. Tune into the back of your skull. How does it feel at base of your skull? Continue to breathe in and out.

Send your awareness into your face, noticing how you feel. Breathe in through your nostrils, notice how your nose feels, and tune into your sinuses. Notice any colors, images, or thoughts that come to mind. As you continue to pay attention and breathe, notice your eyes. How do your eyelids feel? What colors do you see when you relax your eyes and look inside the lids? Make note of the energy or tension you are holding in your eyes, eyelids, forehead, and brow. How do they feel? What are you seeing, if anything?

Move your awareness up past your eyes, through your forehead, right up into the crown of your head and through the top of your skull. Notice how it feels. What kinds of sensations you are experiencing, what colors, what images come to mind? What emotions might be connected to your head right now? Just breathe in and out, simply paying attention.

Now that you've scanned your entire body, take time to make note of whatever you're feeling right now. Particularly note any persistent thoughts or images that have gone through your mind as you've read or listened to this meditation. Make note of the things that kept jumping into your consciousness. Now is the time to simply acknowledge these thoughts, feelings, images, awareness, or sensations. Allow space for anything coming up for you in this moment. Take time to notice.

On a physical level, are you hungry? Tired? How are you feeling in your body? What's your energy level?

Emotionally, are you feeling fairly even or are you experiencing strong emotions? Take a moment to rate your emotions from zero to ten, with zero being completely calm and neutral and ten being absolutely off the charts. Where would you rate the intensity of your feelings right now?

Perhaps you're feeling numb right now. If so, how strong is that numbness? Numbness is not the same as neutrality. If you're feeling numbness -- or shock -- you can gauge how strong that is, as well. Scanning yourself, ask: "How am I feeling right now? Am I content and happy? Am I hopeful? Am I grateful? Am I feeling sad right now? Am I grieving? Am I feeling disappointment? Am I feeling sympathy or compassion? Am I worrying about someone or something? Am I concerned? Am I feeling fear or anxiety, or something even more intense? Am I feeling irritated or angry? Annoyed? Frustrated? Judgmental? What kind of emotions are coming up for me? And what kinds of thoughts are coming up?"

Where are you in time? Are you here with me now, reading this page or listening to the audio and present in your body? Or are you remembering things -- images, feelings, or sensations from the past? If that's the case, when was it? Where was it? Who were you with? What was going on? Just take note of this.

Perhaps you're projecting into the future. Are you imagining things that have not yet happened? Are you thinking about things that might happen? Are you imagining that you're in a different place, a different time? Are you thinking about people you're not with at this moment?

Notice whether you're in the past, the here and now, or somewhere in the future. Notice any images, thoughts, ideas, or persistent messages you're picking up. Notice what you're hearing, either in your head or in the space around you. What is crossing your mind? Take this time to breathe in and notice all of it.

When you're ready, I invite you to come back. If your eyes are closed, gently begin to open them. Continue to breathe into your body. Notice how it feels to breathe in. As you exhale, notice again how it feels to breathe out. As you breathe out, imagine you're letting go of anything you're ready to release. Breathe your awareness back into the here and now. When you're ready, take your notebook or device and do some journaling. Write about what you've realized, what you've discovered is going on for you right now.

After you work your way through this chapter and have learned to RECOGNIZE what's yours and what isn't the next step is all about letting it go. Knowing what you are carrying around is the first step. RELEASING it is the next.

Chapter 5

Release

"Let it go!" I can't begin to count the times I've heard this, long before the movie *Frozen* came out. Any time I was distressed, anxious, or overwhelmed, some well-intentioned person would tell me that I just needed to "let it go." I wanted to, but truth be told I was baffled as to how. If unclenching the psychic grip was easy then we'd all be doing it. Maybe "let it go" works for some folks, but for me and many of the people I've worked with, it oversimplifies a complex problem. When we've absorbed empathic distress so deeply, we have to recognize what we need to release before we can even begin to surrender it. Effective methods to release the stuff that no longer serves us include visualization, reframing, gratitude, movement, flower essences, and essential oils.

We just spent the last chapter examining the nuances of how to *Recognize* what's going on, whether it's ours or someone else's, and where it came from. Now we can decide how we want to address it. Armed with this knowledge, we can begin the work of *Releasing* what no longer serves us.

We'll discuss a number of tools and techniques in this chapter. We'll explore the physical aspect of *Release*, starting at a cellular level and moving through the whole physical body. This includes detoxing (discharging the gunk we're carrying around in our body), then extends outward to making physical changes in our environment to support our wellbeing. There are aspects of *Release* that address the inner work of mind and heart: mindset, beliefs, thoughts, ideas, and emotions, and how we approach and perceive the different areas of our lives. Finally, we'll address taking action and making behavioral changes to successfully achieve *Release*.

RELEASE: Emotional Freedom Techniques: Tapping Basics

As you'll have noticed by now, I'm a very big fan of EFT. I've already mentioned it in previous chapters, but I'll go into it in greater depth in this one. Simply put, EFT, or tapping, is a form of emotional/mental acupuncture. Instead of using needles, we use our fingertips to tap or put light pressure on specific points on our body. In the same way that acupuncture can shift imbalances in our energy field and release congestion or blockages in our system, tapping can be used to clear and reset our mental, emotional, physical, and energetic systems. One of the cool things about this is, not only do all the points correlate with various organs and acupuncture meridians, the tips of the fingers do as well. So as we tap, we not only stimulate the energy systems connected to the points, we also activate the systems that terminate in our fingertips. In addition, the process of tapping resets the amygdala, the part of our brain that controls our fight, flight, or freeze mechanism. There's a lot of great scientific research about EFT written by experts in this field, so I'm not going to inundate you with a bunch of facts and figures here. Look in the back of the book for more resources if you're interested.

Whether or not you prefer to have a scientific understanding, EFT *works*. I believe it's one of the most effective tools available to move us beyond our limitations and heal our wounds. One of the best things about tapping is that with only a little bit of instruction you can do it yourself and experience the benefits first-hand. Throughout my years of working with energy healing I've explored and integrated many techniques into my practice. While I've witnessed powerful results with each healing modality I studied, I've never experienced anything as simple, elegant, and effective as Emotional Freedom Techniques. I love that EFT is both efficient and quick. I used to work primarily with breath. It would often take fifteen, twenty, or even thirty minutes of nonstop circular breathing to begin reaching a breakthrough. With EFT, it often takes only a few tapping rounds to make serious headway. Sometimes a profound shift can occur in as little as three to five minutes.

I first discovered EFT in late 2006. I experimented with founder Gary Craig's original recipe but, to be honest, tapping did not initially grab me. I actually thought it was pretty weird and awkward. I found Gary's formula confusing and convoluted. I picked up tapping and put it down again many times. This changed shortly after Gary introduced a simplified form of the recipe and I found myself in the passenger seat of a car driving through an ice storm. As a survivor of multiple car accidents, I'd already tried many things to alleviate my stress and anxiety. Even after numerous sessions with other healing modalities (including some major soul retrieval work), I'd still shoot from a three to a nine on the fear scale any time I felt triggered by drivers, bad weather, or anything out of the ordinary. I'd almost given up hope that I could move past my driving distress, but in my desperation, I decided to tap as we navigated the treacherous road conditions. I began tapping on the side of my hand, saying, "Even though we're driving through an ice storm and I'm really scared, I choose to relax and I deeply and completely love and accept myself." I then proceeded to tap through the points while I acknowledged my fear.

Miraculously, I went from a white-knuckled ten down to a relaxed zero after only three rounds. I still knew the roads were dangerous and that it was entirely possible we'd have an accident, but I was able to take it in stride and accept that we'd deal with whatever happened if and when it happened. This experience showed me how truly effective EFT can be. This was the moment I knew I had to learn more. Fast forward to many years later: not only am I writing this book, which shares EFT extensively, I've also jumped through all the hoops to become an accredited trainer because I believe so deeply and completely in the power of this technique.

As we move further into this chapter, I invite you to experiment with EFT along with other tools I share. They may seem awkward or unfamiliar at first. You may not experience the results you are hoping for immediately. Nonetheless, I encourage you to persist. Just as we didn't master riding a bike or pitching a ball on our first attempt, these techniques also take practice. If you're like me, you'll find that the proof is in the pudding. I hope that after using EFT a few times, you'll become as much of an enthusiast as I am.

I share more about EFT in the bonus material I offer through EmpathicSafety.com. This includes a thorough video tutorial that explains the basic recipe, along with links to many tap-along videos I've recorded over the last few years. Also, in case you find you love it as much as I do and decide you want to become an EFT practitioner, I provide information about how to train and become certified in this modality.

Once you have a clear sense of what's getting in your way, you can use EFT to release it. In cases where you don't know what's going on, you can actually tap on the lack of knowledge and see what's revealed as you talk through what you do know. For now, I'm going to focus on tapping for issues we are aware of.

I'm going to illustrate how you can frame a tapping sequence, using the example of tapping on a limiting belief. Say you've uncovered that you feel unworthy of accepting more wealth and abundance in your life. Using the affirmation, "I deserve abundant success and wealth in my life," you notice instant resistance. I invite you to try this right now. Repeat after me, "I deserve abundant success and wealth in my life." How does it feel to say this? What, if any, objections immediately come up? What's the belief that contradicts this affirmation? What came to my mind as I said this was a little voice whispering, "I'm not ready!" Let's use this as an example of how to tap.

Before you begin, identify the underlying issue (e.g., feeling unworthy of wealth and success). Next, evaluate the intensity of the emotional charge or conviction of your belief on a scale of zero to ten. Are you feeling a lot of intensity? Are you feeling a lot of resistance? If zero is no feeling at all and ten is completely over the top, what degree of emotion are you experiencing? Note your numbers; if you can, write them down.

The next step is called the "set-up." The set-up is a phrase designed to acknowledge the complexity (sometimes even the contradiction) of our issue. It often begins with the words "even though," which create space for any resistance or ambivalence, making the issue easier to shift.

A wonderful thing about tapping is that you can tap with other people and experience what are called "borrowed benefits." Even if my story is not quite the same as yours, or I use words that are slightly different than your own, you can declare the intention that this tapping will apply to you as well. You can change the words to work for you and say them aloud, switch them out in your mind, or simply set the intention that your issue will be addressed regardless of the language. Let's try my "I'm not ready" example.

If you're in a place where you can speak aloud, I encourage you do so; if this is not an option, just imagine speaking the words in your mind. Using your first three fingers -- the index, middle, and ring fingers -- tap (or use gentle pressure) on the side of your other hand. While tapping, begin with the set-up phrase, "*Even though* there is a part of me that thinks I'm not ready to accept more wealth and abundance into my life," then choose a positive turn-around statement to reframe this, such as, "I welcome money and success anyway." If you find yourself reacting to your turnaround in an uncomfortable or negative way, drop it and find words you can accept and agree with. "I welcome money and success anyway" might create some pushback because it defies the underlying issue. Perhaps "I'm open to the possibility that I'm more ready than I think I am" could work better, because it offers a new perspective while also honoring the resistance. You can always turn to the classic, "I deeply and completely love and accept myself," as long as this feels aligned for you.

State the set-up phrase three times while tapping on the side of the hand (SH). I like to switch hands, going back and forth; that way, I can make sure that I've done it three times and haven't gotten lost in a set-up tangent. I also like switching for the bilateral benefits -- stimulating both sides of the nervous system and the right and left hemispheres of the brain.

To begin, with your right fingers tapping the side of your left hand, say, "Even though there's a part of me that believes I'm just not ready, I'm open to the possibility that I'm more ready than I think I am."

Switching hands, with your left fingers tapping on the side of your right hand, "Even though there's a part of me that believes I'm just not ready, I'm open to the possibility that I'm more ready than I think I am."

Switching back for the third repetition, with your right fingers again tapping on the side of your left hand, "Even though the truth is, I'm just not ready, I'm open to the possibility that I'm more ready than I think I am."

These words are just an example. You get to choose whatever words work best for you: "Even though I feel completely over-whelmed because I don't have the first clue about how to manage more money than I have now, I am open to the possibility that I can learn how to handle this and I can get help."

As you tap, you get to identify and name your own stuff as it comes up. "Even though part of me doesn't feel like I'm worthy," may shift to, "Part of me thinks that I need to be working harder on this," then, "Part of me thinks that this is just too hard," and, "Part of me doesn't want to do this at all." Just continue to tap on whatever feelings arise, then use a turnaround statement you can agree with, one that has your buy-in from the start.

Following the three set-up declarations, we now go through a full round of tapping on all the different points, focusing on the key issue. It helps to use a short reminder phrase to focus on the issue at hand. For this example, it could be, "This part of me that thinks I'm not ready," or simply, "I'm not ready." Or, "This fear.

This unworthiness. This sadness." It helps to be specific. With emotions, it can be more effective to say, "This sadness about..." With a belief, you can tie in the emotion: "This fear that I am not worthy," or you can stay focused on the belief alone: "This idea that I don't deserve this." Phrase it so that you're naming your issue precisely and succinctly.

There's a sensation almost like a magnet clicking into place when you find your actual tapping points. You may need to tap around a little until you find your sweet spots. When I started doing this on a regular basis, certain points felt so good that my body began to relax in ways it probably never had before.

The first point to tap is at the top of your head, the place known as the crown chakra (TH). As you tap, repeat your reminder phrase -- the wording that really lets you tune into the feeling, situation, sensation, and/or belief you're working on: "This fear," "This unworthiness," "This overwhelm," "I'm not ready." *Continue to repeat your reminder phrase at each tapping point.*

Declare the reminder phrase while tapping on the eyebrow points, just above your nose at the beginning of your eyebrows (EB).

Repeat your reminder as you tap on your temples -- the place beside your eyes next to where the upper and lower lids meet (SE).

Repeating the reminder, tap under your eyes, right at the lower edge of your eye socket (UE).

Tap beneath your nose, on the groove above your upper lip called the Cupid's Bow (UN).

Tap beneath your lower lip, in the space between your lower lip and chin (CP).

Move to your collarbones, about an inch or so down from your throat and following directly below the sides of your neck (CB).

Finally, tap below your armpit, parallel to your breasts on your ribcage (UA). Then return to tap on the top of your head. Stop tapping and take a deep breath. This is one complete round of the basic EFT recipe.

You may feel more relaxed. Some other issue or related belief may be revealed. Perhaps you've gained clarity about a situation in your life. At the end of each round, evaluate. Ask yourself, "How am I feeling? Has my energy/emotion calmed down? Do I feel calmer? Do I feel more grounded? Do I notice any changes in my body? Have I realized something new?" If the issue still feels charged, tap through another round or two until it has settled down.

As mentioned above, EFT is most effective when we are precise and target our issue as specifically as possible. We get much better results when we break it down into small components. Complex projects work best when we follow the step-by-step instructions methodically rather than, say, dumping all the parts of the IKEA dresser on the floor and expecting to put it together in a flash. Sometimes this means experimenting with language to discover what gets you best dialed in to your issue.

Here are some examples:

"Part of me believes . . ."

"This feeling about . . ."

"This belief that . . ."

"And as I tap it makes me feel . . ."

"And I feel so . . ."

"This belief that I . . ."

"Which brings up . . ."

EFT Tapping Points

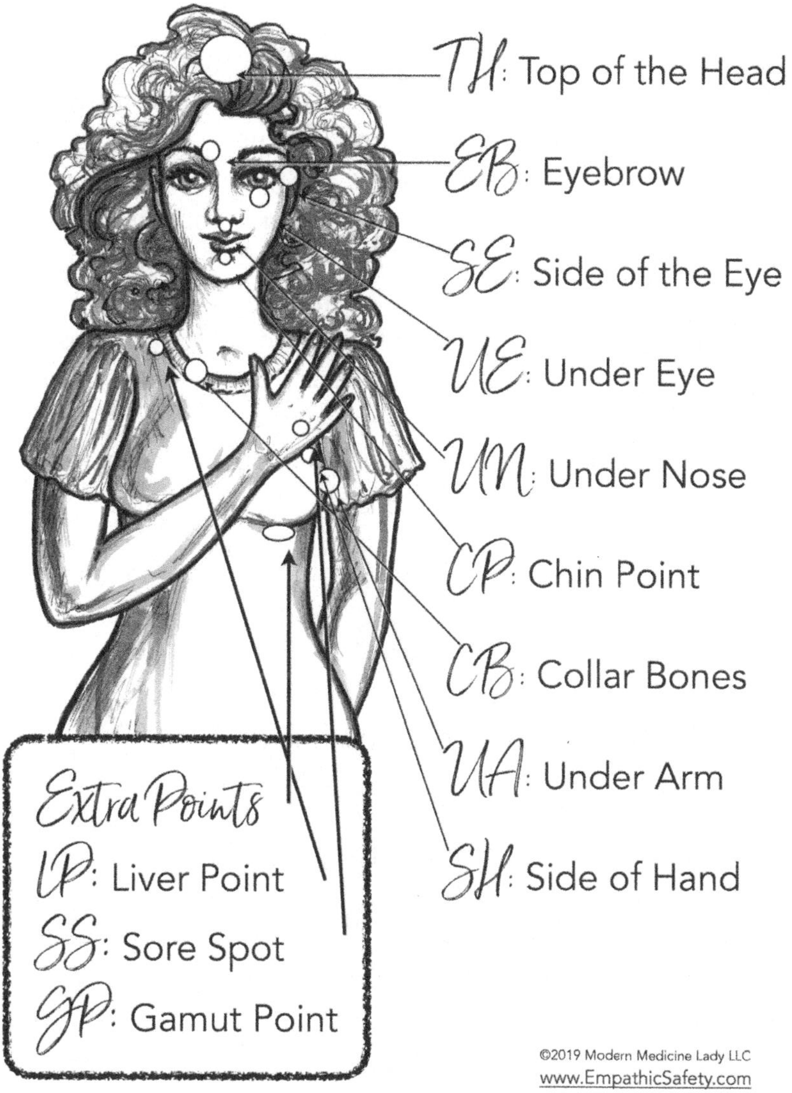

TH: Top of the Head

EB: Eyebrow

SE: Side of the Eye

UE: Under Eye

UN: Under Nose

CP: Chin Point

CB: Collar Bones

UA: Under Arm

SH: Side of Hand

Extra Points
LP: Liver Point
SS: Sore Spot
GP: Gamut Point

Now that you understand the basic recipe, let's talk about the rhythm for most tapping sessions. They generally have three phases: *Acknowledgement*, *Integration*, and *Affirmation*.

In the *Acknowledgement* phase, we address the issue and give voice to the conflict or challenge we're dealing with. We tap through as many rounds as necessary to take the charge down.

In the *Integration* phase, we start to find new perspective and understanding, often finding our own reframes and ownership of pieces of the story that may actually serve us.

Finally, in the *Affirmation* phase, we anchor our new perspective, empower our new choices, and claim the direction we're choosing to go. Sometimes (say, in the case of a physical ache or a reaction to a food or chemical sensitivity) all you need to do is a few rounds of basic tapping and you'll be golden. In most cases, though, the *Affirmation* phase is where we truly move from negativity to acceptance, and then to positivity.

Here are some examples of positive affirmations you can use in those final rounds:

"I'm open to the possibility that..."

"Now that I understand..., I choose..."

"I'm ready to..."

"I claim my..."

"I deserve..."

Over the years as I've facilitated EFT sessions, I've created a series of anchoring statements that can be used at the end of tapping sessions, as well as for daily affirmations to reinforce new, more positive ways of being. I've created an oracle deck based on these affirmations. You'll find a link to view the digital version and information for ordering your own physical deck in the Resources section.

To review:

1. Identify the issue.
2. Evaluate the intensity from 0-10 (aka SUDS: Subjective Unit of Distress Scale or VOC: Validity of Cognition).
3. Repeat the set-up statement three times while tapping on side of the hand: "Even though (issue), I (turnaround)."
4. Reminder phrase while tapping through the points. "This (issue)."
5. Deep breath and re-evaluate SUDS/VOC.
6. Rinse and repeat, moving from *Acknowledgement* through *Integration* to *Affirmation*.

I hope that by experimenting with tapping you've gotten a sense of how quickly and easily you can shift your feelings, sensations, and beliefs. What I've offered is just a small taste of what is possible with EFT. I really want to stress that, while this technique is remarkably simple in its most basic form, it is also incredibly versatile and nuanced. It's important to emphasize that much of the content you may encounter online comes in the form of generic scripts and tap-along videos.

The challenge with most of these is that they are necessarily pre-defined by their content creator. While these approaches can certainly take the edge off, they don't always get to the roots of an issue. Well-practiced, individually focused, and directed tapping allows us to go much further and deeper; we can keep peeling away layers until we get to the core of an issue to transform it. Knowing what is possible by experimenting with a five- to fifteen-minute round of tapping, just imagine what you can do in a dedicated session of an hour or 90 minutes, where you can keep digging up and pulling out the roots as they appear.

RELEASE: Tapping for Memories

Targeting a specific event and tapping on small segments of time within it is one of the best ways to hit pay-dirt. Often, tapping on the initial issue (whether it be physical pain or emotional ache) will lead you back to a moment in the past that seems somewhat random at first glance. When a memory comes to mind, it's most effective to tune in to a brief segment rather than the entire event. The idea is to find individual moments of emotional crescendo and tap them down one at a time. This yields better and more lasting results than keeping it general and/or trying to tackle a whole day, week, or year at a time.

For example, the other day I was working on a memory from when I first apprenticed to become a tattoo artist. I accompanied one of my teachers to a biker festival, where he had a tattooing booth for the weekend. To say that this event was *wild* is an understatement. There were a number of moments when I felt overwhelmed, anxious, and started to question what the hell I had gotten myself into. When my memories about this event started to surface, I certainly could have tapped on the anxiety and over-whelm surrounding the entire event.

However, as a seasoned EFT practitioner, I know it's more effective to tune in to the specific moments of distress and to address each one of them individually. It became apparent to me that two moments really stood out from all the others.

The first was when an extremely drunk, rather crusty and bel-ligerent old biker came up to my drawing table and started to mess with me. I had to stand up for myself (and my table covered with papers) and to tell him in no uncertain terms to "get your f-ing beer off my drawing table!" As I tapped on this narrow window of time, I recalled several other aspects of this story and was able to soothe my naive and rather anxious inner child, as I also recognized how effectively I had handled the situation.

The second emotional crescendo involved the "Port-a-Potties." Without going into too much detail, let's just say that the term "shit-faced" takes on whole new meaning when you have a bunch of bikers three days into a bender. The thing I specifically needed to tap on was the moment I opened the door to the filthy stall and realized just how disgusting and unsanitary it was. Aside from the overall *ick* factor, the real core was my fear that I'd gotten myself in *way* over my head. By tapping down these two major crescendos, I released a set of beliefs about working in the tattoo industry that I'd carried for over 20 years and recognized the sense of struggle and tenacity that had been ignited within me over that weekend.

RELEASE: Decluttering and Detoxing

You've probably heard the saying, "As above, so below." Another way to say it could be, "As within, so without." Both indicate that what we alter in Spirit, our inner world, will be reflected in mate-rial form in our outer world. This goes in both directions, so to release effectively, it's important that we address both our inner and outer worlds. It can be easier to start with outer shifts, because if we don't address physical and environmental factors, they will continue to impact our mood and energy. However, adjustments to our material world will often provoke the need to address corresponding inner issues.

It's extremely difficult to do deep healing, mindset, or energy work when something you're eating, breathing, or being exposed to is interfering with your body's equilibrium. Decluttering and detoxing are effective ways to begin releasing things that do not serve you.

Decluttering is not just about cleaning up your messy room or overhauling that closet storing fifteen years of clothing in multiples sizes. Decluttering is about eliminating the extraneous junk taking up valuable physical, mental, or emotional space in your life.

Decluttering is crucial for empaths because every single object you come in contact with has an energetic signature. It has a story and a vibration. You experience a positive, neutral, or negative association with it. Even if you don't consciously recall details, each time you encounter an object you're influenced by the emotions, memories, and thoughts connected to it. Every time your eye scans a space, these associations can be triggered. A lot of mental, emotional, and psychic energy gets expended trying to process all of this.

As you look around your space and your eyes scan the room, notice if you find yourself having any unpleasant emotional reactions. If you do, in my opinion you have two solutions. If something is problematic and it's not particularly valuable to you, toss it. Get rid of it. Donate it. Gift it. But don't keep it around. If, on the other hand, it's really valuable or significant and you need to keep it around, then it's time to get to the core of why it's causing this kind of emotional distress and tap it out. That way, it's not taxing your energy every time you're near it.

Keep only things which generate positive or neutral responses and pass along or eliminate everything else possible. Not only do we have our own stories attached to objects, the items themselves contain energy signatures we can sense, either through direct contact or simply by being in their vicinity. Each category of things can influence corresponding attitudes, beliefs, and feelings.

For example, on the Mental level, stress is exacerbated by full inboxes, cluttered desktops (both virtual and real), too many newsletter subscriptions, and simply *too much information*. To help de-stress and bring ease to your beliefs and thought processes, delete or archive messages in your inbox and texts on your phone. Unsubscribe from newsletters that no longer serve you and sort through all your media -- books, music, DVDs, magazines, etc.

Ask yourself:

⚜ What beliefs and attitudes do I want to cultivate?

⚜ Which ideas, philosophies, or perceptions have I outgrown?

⚜ What am I holding onto that reinforces an outdated lifestyle or mindset?

On the Emotional level, empathic relief can be expedited by sifting through old letters, photos, and gifts from others. Most of these kinds of objects are loaded with stories, experiences, and powerful emotional connections. Of all the things you have surrounding you, these personal items hold the some of the biggest charge, so you get some of the biggest "bang for your buck" by addressing them.

⚜ Are you holding on to objects from relationships or experiences that you have outgrown?

⚜ Are there objects that trigger memories or feelings every time you touch or view them?

⚜ What things immediately come to your mind as you read this?

Spiritually speaking, your environment, particularly your walls, your decor, and all the knick-knacks and curios you surround yourself with can enhance or detract from your spiritual focus and connection with the Divine. Look at your space and ask yourself:

- ❀ Does this space reflect what I want to reinforce?
- ❀ Does this space mirror my desired intentions?
- ❀ When I scan my space, how do I feel?

In terms of personal identity, sorting through clothing is a great way to redefine your image and how you present yourself in the world. Clothing can be particularly loaded for women, especially when something doesn't fit and/or you had unpleasant experiences while wearing it.

As you hold a garment in your hands, ask yourself these questions:

- ❀ Does this article represent the person I want to be?
- ❀ Does it truly reflect me?
- ❀ Is it comfortable?
- ❀ Does it fit well?
- ❀ Do I feel confident and empowered when I wear this?

Bonus Exercise: Write a description of your Superhero Self. Note the kind of styles, colors, and accessories that best reinforce that ideal self.

Decluttering is a process that works differently for different people. I like Marie Kondo's approach, which tackles categories instead of spaces. Her charming book, *The Magical Art of Tidying Up*, has some really useful suggestions for ways to go about decluttering. I wouldn't say you have to follow her to the letter, but if you're looking for support, she's got some really useful suggestions to offer. What works well for me is to decide what particular category I want to address and schedule a limited chunk of time to work on it over the course of a few days or weeks. Work to time, not to task. Be sure to stop when you planned to and take breaks after each 30-45 minute slot if you're working for more than a total of 45 minutes. Most of us will be better off breaking this down into manageable, bite-sized tasks instead of overdoing it and burning out. This is a marathon, not a sprint. Persistent action over time will yield greater rewards.

The following questions will help you tackle decluttering your physical environment without feeling too overwhelmed:

- ❀ When you consider your own tidying habits over the years, what has worked best for you?

- ❀ What leaves you with a sinking feeling even thinking about it?

- ❀ What area do you want to tackle first?

- ❀ When will you create time in your schedule to do this?

Finally, as previously mentioned, we can be affected by all kinds of physical things -- foods, environmental factors, mold, fragrance, etc. Sensitivities and/or allergies can provoke intense emotional and mental responses. It's crucial to combine physical decluttering with an overhaul of your diet if you suspect less-than-ideal food choices are affecting you. These physical shifts will lead you to the emotional work. Many of us were taught to use food for comfort and self-soothing. When we implement changes to a food plan, it's very common to experience cravings and heightened emotions as we surrender the things that helped us to stay numb and comfortable. We need to do the inner work to be willing to comfortably release our former coping mechanisms. You can't do only the inner work or the outer work; the two are like a pair of hands with interlocking fingers. Ideally, we work to release on all levels simultaneously.

RELEASE: Food and Detoxing

Food is an especially important thing to consider as an empath. Eating a clean, healthy diet allows us to feel calmer and more grounded. Eating a diet loaded with junk like sugar, highly processed and genetically-modified foods sets us up to feel lousy. I wouldn't say that good food alone facilitates release as much as bad food prevents it. Eliminating crap from our diet will initiate physical, mental, and emotional detoxes.

I was 19 the first time I recognized the impact of sugar. I was babysitting a 4-year-old. I was her weekday nanny while her mom was at work. We were hanging out on Halloween, so we broke into the Halloween candy and ate a bunch of it. An hour later, she was pounding her little fists all over me. As this child stood on top of me, trying to beat me up, I thought, "Oh, so it's true -- sugar really does affect us!" It was one of those illuminating moments. With children the effect is often clear, but with adults, although it's more subtle, we're still affected.

Reducing (if not entirely eliminating) starchier carbohydrates and processed sugar from our diet makes a major difference in our physical, mental, emotional, and empathic wellbeing. Eating good food makes releasing work easier. Eating a cleaner diet and drinking lots of water is not only good for the body, but for our energy as well. Getting the toxic sludge out of our system enables easier emotional release as well.

Perhaps you've heard about the gut/brain connection before. Essentially, the health of our gut is linked to our physical, mental, and emotional health. Our intestines are like a garden inside our bodies. There's favorable flora we can cultivate or unfavorable bacteria which causes gut dysbiosis. Candida (aka yeast) and other nasty bugs can grow like invasive weeds through our entire digestive system. These unfavorable gut bugs are fed by starchy carbohydrates which include all grains, pasta, bread, even fruit but especially simple sugars like candies, cakes, cookies, ice cream and the like. The more of these starchy carbohydrates and sugary foods we consume, the more we crave them, which results in even more overgrowth. The problem is that not only do the bad bugs crowd out the good ones, they also cause damage to our intestinal lining. This ultimately causes a condition called "leaky gut." Leaky gut not only contributes to systemic inflammation throughout our body, but is linked to food sensitivities, brain fog, mood swings, depleted energy, vulnerability to infections and germs, and eventually autoimmune issues.

Kicking processed sugar and other starchy carbohydrates isn't just about losing a few pounds, it's about sanity, vitality, wellbeing, and empathic resilience. There's a direct connection between the health and integrity of your intestines and the strength and resilience of your psychic filters. Think of them as two sides of the same coin. Maybe a better way to describe it is like a huge donut or inner tube. Your digestive tract from mouth to rectum is the inside of the hole and your skin and the auric filters which extend beyond it are the outside. The thing is, it's all connected. So when our gut is compromised by a diet that feeds bacterial overgrowth and gut dysbiosis our aura gets weakened too. As above, so below. As within, so without. Our entire digestive tract is the other side of our etheric shields. Therefore strengthening and nourishing your gut supports empathic resilience. This is the biggest reason I remain so outspoken about eliminating sugar from our diet. It affects us on all levels!

A word of warning about fasting and doing extreme cleanses. When you move drastically from one kind of diet to another in an attempt to clean up everything all at once, your vibration is raised very rapidly. This will escalate your sensitivity. It will make you more emotionally open and increase your empathy, intuition, and awareness. If you choose to do a fast or cleanse, it's very important to be mindful of how you're going to protect yourself while eating foods that will lighten you up and provoke a detox (in the next chapter you'll find many tools for self-protection).

Weight loss is another powerful way to release old stuff. We are literally letting go of cells, flesh, and parts of ourselves we've been carrying in our body for God only knows how long. When we start eliminating weight, shit tends to come up. This is because we're letting go of the issues, emotions, and energy that we started carrying when the weight went on in the first place.

I believe that each body has its own truth about what it wants to weigh, which may not match what society thinks we should weigh. Sometimes, we hit a glass floor -- not because we are hitting an emotional limitation, but because we're hitting an energetic limitation. For example, I have a sturdy body. I've come to believe that my body is like this is because I run so much current through my system all the time that I need a certain amount of insulation and density in order to accommodate all that energy and remain safely embodied. Regardless of caloric intake, my body has maintained a set point for years that defies the rules of conventional nutrition.

If this wasn't the case, I might be vulnerable to the kind of nervous system fritz-outs I've witnessed in other energy healers. I can't wear watches on my wrist because they cease to be accurate within hours. A friend of mine destroyed three computers in one week. If our bodies can do that to a mechanical device, imagine what too much energy can do to our own electrical systems. Unless you can modify the way energy moves through your body, you will remain at a certain weight in order to function effectively.

As empaths, rarely can we afford to eat the way ordinary people do. We can't afford to drink alcohol the way ordinary people do. We also can't afford to do recreational drugs the way they do. We need to be more self-aware and take responsibility for our own vulnerabilities. Instead of trying to deny our limitations and subsequently deal with the consequences, it's crucial that we accept them and act accordingly. I'm not going to tell you what works for your body; all I can tell you is what I've discovered with mine and witnessed with many clients I have worked with over the years. Every single body is different, and often the same body needs different things at different times. We need to remain conscious around our consumption of these impactful substances, quieting our minds, sending our awareness deeper into our bodies, and ascertaining what's really going on within us.

RELEASE: Tracking Your Triggers

Once we start recognizing the things that affect us on a physical level, it's helpful to create tracking systems so we're not taken by surprise. It took me fifteen years before I became savvy enough to recognize I was struggling with PMS before I got my period. It never failed: during the week prior to my period I would be in a horrible state, then I'd start to flow and think, "Oh, that's why!" For this particular system, it doesn't take rocket science. I was fortunate to be quite regular, so it wouldn't have been difficult if I'd just marked my calendar in advance and let myself know that my mood was going to be heightened for a few days.

Eventually I established a digital calendar so I knew when to expect PMS. I also use a lunar app on my phone with moon signs and phases. These two records allow me to anticipate dips in my energy and mood so I can schedule the rest of my life accordingly. Whether it's to follow physical changes or emotional responses, it's especially useful to create thorough records so you can recognize shifts. Setting up tracking systems helps to reveal patterns of reactivity as well as giving you cues to anticipate how you'll feel in the midst of hormonal, seasonal and lunar cycles. In addition to following menstrual cycles you might consider tracking: food, mood, dreams, inner dialogue, energy, physical sensations/pain, health, as well as your connection/awareness of global events.

Here's an example.

Date	Reactions, Sensations, Thoughts & Feelings	Regarding or Caused by	Additional Observations
Thurs 3/28	Uncomfortable, restless, insomnia, night sweats, fitful repetitive dreams, irritation & difficulty breathing	Noticeably moldy hotel room. Distinctive mildew odor & funky congested vibe	Used essential oils in diffuser to mitigate the visible mold in ceiling, so felt okay the following day despite lack of sleep
Fri 4/19	Anxiousness, unexplainable sadness, overwhelm, fear & agitation. Sense of foreboding and something coming.	Bombings of churches in Sri Lanka 2 days later on Easter Sunday	With empathic friend who had the same feelings, took flower essences which settled things down.
Mon 4/22	Fatigued, logy, congested sinuses, brain fog & headache	Can of tuna	10 minutes after eating tuna I went from sharp and energetic to exhausted and dull.

Sometimes you'll experience a trigger that you don't recognize. You don't necessarily need to know where it's coming from in order to begin releasing it. You can simply know that *something* is going on and you're not feeling comfortable.

Tapping is a great way to get clear about what's happening and why. You can start by just tapping on what you *do* know. Imagine you have some kind of physical sensation in your body.

First, tune in and rate the intensity from zero to ten. Then, tapping on the side of your hand, "Even though I feel (for example) this dull churning in my gut, tightness in my jaw, and band of tension across my head, I'm just looking at it. I'm just acknowledging it. I'm loving myself anyway." Whatever you use as your positive turnaround is fine.

Then move through all of the tapping points and specifically describe what you know ("this band of tension," "this stress," etc.). That will usually open things up to give you more clarity.

From there, if you don't already know, you'll get a sense of whether it's yours or not. You could even tap with the question, "Is this mine or somebody else's?" If you sense it's about someone other than you, "I wonder who this could be. I wonder what this is about." You'll continue to get more information.

As you become clearer and can identify the topic, you can tap on that precise nugget. Following classic, old-school EFT, use the word "this" and then one or two words to describe the issue you're tapping on: "This tension. This pain. This discomfort."

As you continue to tap, you'll begin to decompress and feel the intensity subside. The energetic congestion will start to release. In the future, you'll be more likely to recognize and release this trigger before it has a chance to set you off.

RELEASE: Getting Support with Letting Go

Some people believe that energy can be added to them or sub-tracted from them. My understanding is that energy is constant; nothing is ever added or subtracted. It is the vibration that trans-forms. As Albert Einstein said, "Energy cannot be created or destroyed; it can only be changed from one form to another." We do not actually absorb someone else's energy or have extra energy added to our own. The other person's energy influences the vibra-tion of our field and creates a new pattern in our own system. It's as if you've received a digital download or a malware virus. You've absorbed the message, the recording, and now you're playing a tape loop in your system. It isn't your message, but it's taking up a lot of bandwidth.

The key is to shift the vibration back to something that feels resonant with you. It's not about extracting or removing some-thing as much as it's about altering your thoughts, feelings, and sensations so they're back in flow with your own truth, not some-body else's. When we're around people who trigger our memories or have such powerful broadcasting systems that we can't ignore their signal, they can alter our tape. When we learn how to sit with our feelings and become fully present with ourselves, it becomes much easier to distinguish what's ours and what's not. The para-dox is, in order to find our own answers in solitude, we often need help from someone else.

RELEASE: The Work of Forgiveness

Another significant key for *Releasing* is forgiveness. While there's a lot of great material about forgiveness, there's also a lot of resis-tance to it. I think that the concept of forgiveness is often mis-understood; indeed, at times it is even maligned. People mistake forgiveness for either complacency or acquiescence, for letting somebody off the hook. When someone has done something heinous and inexcusable, the idea of forgiveness can seem like a denial of the atrocities they committed. But forgiveness is as much about freeing ourselves from the pain of resentment as it is about forgiving the perpetrator.

Forgiveness is not about forgetting.

It's not about letting somebody off the hook. It's not about saying, "You are no longer accountable for your bad choices and your bad actions." It's about having the willingness to accept that something painful has happened and that "it is what it is." It's about letting go of the resentment, the emotional charge, and the intensity. Forgiveness allows us to surrender our attachment to our sense of being wronged, to relinquish the emotional turmoil that keeps us stuck repeating the same negative story ad nauseum. We are not excusing bad behavior. We're letting it go so we don't have to carry it around for the rest of our life.

Eventually, forgiveness can lead to compassion. We may come to the understanding that, even though somebody made a terrible choice or decision, perhaps it was the best they could do at the time. This may sound impossible. Sometimes bare acceptance is about as far as we can go. But in my experience, forgiveness work isn't about freeing the others involved. It's about freeing ourselves, and with that freedom we often gain new perspective and even appreciation for who we have become as a result of the challenges we've endured.

When anger and frustration are deeply entrenched, I recommend a technique I learned from tapping expert Gene Monterastelli. This "Talk About, Talk To, Talk As If" approach was originally developed by EFT Master Gwyneth Moss. This technique is a 3-stage exercise for reconciling situations with other people.

The first step is to tap while you *describe the situation* between you and the other person (or people). Go into detail about what happened, and how you're feeling about it.

Air all of your grievances. Tap on the issue as it is, describe it, and vent. No holds barred. No protecting the innocent. Tell it like it is and express what's going on for you.

Once you've taken down the emotional charge, the second step is to do another round (or series of rounds) of tapping as you say what you need to say *as if speaking directly to the person.* Express your feelings as if they're right there in the room with you. I believe it's most effective to speak from an "I" statement and own your feelings. So instead of, "You're being a total asshole!" try phrases like, "I feel really hurt that you did _____. It reminded me of _____. I felt betrayed. I felt hurt. I felt scared. When you do _____, it scares me because I'm afraid that _____ is going to happen." Own your feelings. Tap and express your truth.

The third step can seem challenging, but it's extremely powerful. Once you've expressed everything you need to express to this person, tap to *explain why they did it.* For example, "After tapping through this, I now understand that this person did this because _____." I want to add a caveat: in cases where you are dealing with an abusive and/or narcissistic person who blames everything on something outside of themselves, this round of explanations is not about letting them off the hook or excusing their bad behavior. It's designed to give you insight so that you can release your own emotional baggage around it and heal.

I've chosen to take this idea one step further: instead of explaining in your own voice why you think they did it, you can *speak as if you are them.* Tune in to your inner version of this person and notice their response. Then answer on their behalf by imagining that you're speaking from their Higher Self. You'll be amazed -- first, by how much you can let go, and second, by how much this can shift a relationship dynamic. You are much more likely to understand what's going on in a relationship after you've done this 3-stage tapping variation.

To sum up: first, describe and vent; second, say what you need to say; and third, explain why they did what they did. Vent and describe, express, and explain.

From there, ideally, you will be ready to embrace and express forgiveness. I especially like to recite the Hawaiian prayer of forgiveness: Ho'oponopono.

Very simply put, it's a four-part prayer:

I'm sorry. Please forgive me. Thank you. I love you.

The order of this prayer is not set in stone; if you search around you'll find variations. Now, because I always like to add a little bit of spice, along with "Please forgive me," I add in, "I forgive you." I find it really helps to have the forgiveness going both ways. More often than not, I am not only seeking forgiveness, but I *totally* need to offer it as well. So my version is:

I love you. I forgive you. I'm sorry.
Please forgive me. Thank you.

I often recite Ho'oponopono while tapping. I start with one line and move through the points, tapping and reciting this prayer until my heart cracks open. I keep repeating it until I feel that the energy has shifted, my emotional charge has released, and I've let go of the situation.

If contemplating doing Ho'oponopono triggers you, I can assure you that you're not alone. If someone has been a total jerk and has hurt you badly, simply coming to acceptance can be a major shift. Having to say, "I'm sorry, please forgive me," can feel like adding insult to injury. In many cases, you really did nothing wrong; it's all about their actions and not yours. For example, no matter how a toddler behaves, they do not owe an abusive parent an apology -- it will always be the adult who is accountable. So if asking for forgiveness only feels like opening up an old wound, please honor your truth, work with your forgiveness for them alone, and only when you are truly ready.

Forgiveness work often leads to the realization that, in order to effectively release something, we need to make amends of our own. Take some time to examine whether you're holding onto any guilt. Guilt often contributes to energetic static. Doing release work with our own residual guilt is very powerful.

As empaths, we can get so bowled over by the magnitude of other people's energy and behaviors that our own choices and behaviors are obscured. Having the willingness to look at our own part with unflinching honesty is an essential step to standing fully in our power.

Denial of our own shadow and overlooking the ways we participated in a difficult situation robs us of our mastery. When we ignore the parts of ourselves clinging to a particular identity (like "vulnerable empath who became the victim of a narcissist"), we relinquish our power to change or control those parts.

Take a personal inventory. Examine the less-than-stellar things you've done. Evaluate and assess whether there's anything hanging over your head, making it hard to let stuff go. Then think it through and determine what kind of amends, if any, need to be made. It could be something as simple as realizing that you've been holding onto somebody's book for six years and it's time to go to the post office and mail it back to them. Maybe you still have somebody's favorite sweater. Perhaps you had a conversation that didn't quite land right. Get in touch and acknowledge it: "You know, I realize that maybe what I said didn't come across the way I meant it. I just wanted to check in with you and see if we're okay. It wasn't my intention to cause you any pain."

When using visualization, I find it especially helpful to tap on the collarbone. As you tap, imagine yourself going into virtual space. Go to your happy place. Envision yourself and the situation or person with whom you wish to reconcile. Then envision yourself having a conversation and imagine what happens. I find it very helpful to ask that part of ourselves, or the person or situation, "What is it that you need me to know? What is it that you need from me?"

In those cases where something really difficult has happened, sometimes you need to shoot fireballs at them in your imagination. Or turn them into frogs. Sometimes you need to dump green slime on them (which tends to be my favorite blasting technique). Sometimes you really need to let someone have it with both barrels before you can change your perspective and take that next step to reconciliation.

RELEASE: Stopping the Train of Thought

This next section on *Releasing* may seem a bit harder. It takes a little more effort, so this can come after you've been doing the previous forms of release work for a while. This step is about quieting your inner five-year-old and getting your adult self back in the driver's seat. Sometimes you need to calm your inner child's hissy fit in order to get the adult back in control. I call this "stopping the train of thought."

Perhaps you suddenly notice that you're careening down the wrong track at 100 mph, heading for a collision with fear. Your mind is just starting to spiral out. Put the kibosh on this the moment you recognize it's happening! There are a couple of different ways to apply the brakes, so you'll have to figure out what works best for you. The most effective way to stop negativity in its tracks is to do what's called a "pattern interrupt." I find that being really firm with myself and saying "Cut the shit, now! Just stop it!" is just what I need to stop going down the road to Awful Town.

There are times when I can recognize that my mind wants to take a Debbie Downer detour, and I need to say "Unh-unh, we're not doing this. Don't go there, li'l buckaroo!" Being firm with your monkey mind is like dealing with a toddler. When you see a toddler starting to go into a place they don't belong, you don't reason with them. You don't explain to them why they can't do it. You get up, run after them, and pick them up before they knock something over or run into oncoming traffic.

If you're dealing with a part of yourself that's already extremely stressed out, frightened, and anxious, sometimes you have to self-soothe to stop the train. Take that scared, young part of yourself and find a safe place to put her, to soothe and comfort her. You can try putting your hand over your heart, skin-to-skin, taking a deep breath, and telling yourself, "I'm sure you're feeling really scared, sweetheart. I'm the one who's in charge right now. You don't have to be the one who's running this train. Let's not go there. Let's just slow down."

Flash floods hit Portland a few years ago. I was driving home from work in some of the most intense rain I'd ever experienced. I was already quite distressed, so although I noticed the cars ahead of me, I didn't register that we were all driving into two-and-a-half feet of rushing water. I kept moving forward, and when the car in front me suddenly stopped, I stopped as well. I could now feel my feet getting wet because the water was rapidly seeping into the car. I was panicking. Fortunately, I was on the phone with my husband. In response to my terrified, "Oh, my God. Oh, my God. The car is flooding. Oh, my God," he calmly asked, "Is there anybody behind you?" When I answered, "No," he replied, "Back up."

This is such a great metaphor for what happens when our minds are rushing in the wrong direction. Once we start driving into the flood zone, we forget that we have the choice to back up. We assume that we must keep driving into the flood. I had already begun to imagine the worst possible outcome: everything was going to hell, I was going to be stuck in the puddle, I would have to have my car towed, the police would have to come and rescue me and my car would be totaled. In about 30 seconds I had barreled all the way down the track. But my husband, who was not distressed, simply said "No, put your car in reverse, back up and get out of there." So I put my car in reverse, backed up, and got out of there. Although I ended up having about $3,000 worth of damage (fortunately covered by insurance), there was no lasting harm and I was able to get to safety. With my husband's help, I recognized that even though I was in trouble, I had options. Remembering that *we can back up* is key when we notice our thoughts taking us down a dangerous road.

RELEASE: Ritual, Prayer, and Spirituality

Wherever you fall on the religious or spiritual spectrum, from my perspective, there's no better way to do the sacred work of releasing than with Divine Source. Your relationship with a power greater than yourself is *your* relationship. While I'm speaking in spiritual terms, I invite you to do what works best for you. Most of what we're talking about is technology that can be used whether you believe in a Divine Presence or not. Whether you feel comfortable with God, Goddess, the Universe, the Force, Higher Power, etc., or you think it's all total hooey, you get to choose what works for you.

What is your truth? What do you want to believe? What makes sense or feels best to you? You can work with these techniques regardless of how you define a power greater than yourself.

Ritual, ceremony, and prayer, however you define them, can be used very effectively for releasing. Rituals can be incredibly complex or extremely simple. A ritual is the container in which our request or our agenda is presented. Some rituals are for purification. Some rituals are for gratitude. Some are for requests. Some are entirely for praise and appreciation. And some rituals are for celebration, to make offerings, and to express joy and delight.

Rituals and ceremonies occur in all cultures and in many forms. From the simplest prayers of grace at a meal to ornately formal observances like weddings, funerals, graduations, and inaugurations, rituals have a special place in our world. They honor and support our growth and transformation.

The power of ritual often lies in our conscious effort to create a separate, sacred space beyond the hectic bustle of mundane life, where our actions focus exclusively on our intention. A ritual can be used to acknowledge achievements and changes that have already occurred, or it can be used as a way to herald changes and new ways.

Ritual has impact for the participants on three basic levels. The first is the personal message we give ourselves by taking symbolic action to show both our conscious and subconscious mind that we are willing and committed to our process. I think that a personal ritual is a way of saying to our innermost self, "Yes, I really mean it!" We often find it easier to take subsequent action, to grow, and to change our behaviors after we've declared our goals in the ceremony.

The second level is the message we give to our community when we ask our friends and family to participate and bear witness to our intentions. Commitments made before others are not only validated from an internal source, but are also recognized and given weight by the community. When community participates in personal ritual, we acknowledge our connections to each other and accept accountability for our witnessed actions.

The third level is our act of faith in creating sacred space for Deity to witness our prayers and actions, and to support our process. Creating ceremony is a way to show intention to self, to community, and to the Universe/Divine Presence. When we become capable of knowing and clarifying our goals, we have taken the most important step toward reaching them. Our hopes and dreams are the seeds to the fruits we manifest in reality. As above, so below.

The intention of ritual or ceremony is to create a safe, sacred space where our intentions can be expressed with room to unfold. Rituals of *Release* may include chanting, toning, dancing, praying, speaking, lighting candles, rinsing or bathing, smudging, and many other ways of symbolically expressing your intentions and desires. You can find or create chants, songs, and prayers that are meaningful to you. You can light a candle and let it burn away what you wish to release.

Prayer for releasing can work like 3-stage tapping:

1. Tell it like it is and acknowledge what's actually happening for you.
2. Ask for what you need and express your desire to release whatever is holding you back.
3. Express gratitude for the things that are already working in your life and for the blessings on their way.

Here's an example:

"Mother-Father God,

I struggle with this pain.

Please relieve me of the bondage of my own fear and worry.

Please lift my concerns and give me the strength to endure the trials before me.

Thank you for the blessings you bestow upon my life today.

Thank you for my breath,

Thank you for this body that carries me,

Thank you for my ability to persevere even on difficult days like this.

Thank you for taking these burdens from my hands.

I turn this over to you and surrender the outcome for the highest and greatest good.

Amen."

Another version of prayer that can be quite powerful is to turn all your distress around by moving it to gratitude and praise. Here is an example of a prayer I wrote during a particularly difficult day of hormonal hell 20-plus years ago:

Oh Beloved God,

You who encompass the vastness of my soul,

I honor You with praise in this time of longing.

My heart pines for You

As beloved,

As friend,

On days when the warmth and beauty of the sunlight playing on my skin is more a reminder of my hunger than a comforter of my grief.

And so because I know of nothing better to do, I will say thank you.

Thank you for my aching heart, for it is my capacity to love which allows it to ache so.

Thank you for my premenstrual emotions, for it is my fruitfulness which creates this intensity.

Thank you for my exhaustion, for it is an abundance of experience in my life for which I am tired.

Thank you for my excruciating thirst, for as it is quenched I may truly appreciate fulfillment.

Thank you for all the aching, longing, itchy, pining, lonely, whining, grieving, sighing, cranky, hopeful hopelessness of my aliveness.

And today as the sun shines brightly, the snow melts while rhododendron leaves uncurl from the once relentless cold.

What a glorious day You, as earth, sea, and sky, have become!

And in exchange for all of this, today I give you offerings to take as smelt for the furnace.

So as I am of You, I forge myself anew.

Saint Brigid, Triple Goddess of this harshest season,

Keeper of the flame begetting transformation,

You who are midwife of my soul,

I know by Your strength and the unyielding, penetrating heat of your forge, You can bear my misery.

I offer my doubt as material for inquisition.

I offer my fear as fuel for action.

I offer my worry as rasp for serenity.

I offer my grief as food for love.

I offer my confusion as catalyst for faith.

I offer my anger as incentive for peace.

I offer my loneliness as seeds for compassion.

Naked I enter the lodge.

In sweat, breath, and silence I am transmuted.

In Your flowing stillness I can know peace.

I am willing to be willing to open my heart, my mind, my body, my spirit to your divine grace.

God, as I am of You, so may I know Your infinite ways.

As You are Strength, so do I claim the strength within me.

As You are Health, so do I own my health.

As You are Truth, so do I welcome truth revealed.

As You are Love, so too am I love.

As You are Grace, so is grace ever present within me.

Beloved God! Thank You for Your blessings.

In You I am whole and complete.

May this truth remain eternally known.

Amen.

RELEASE: The Hidden Benefits of a Challenge

Prayer and meditation is great, but there are times when no matter how much positivity and visualization you throw at it, the issue persists. When it comes to healing and letting things go, one of the reasons people tend to hang on to painful or unhealthy behaviors is that they provide hidden benefits. You may not see the reasons for someone's attachment, but when you get down to it, you'll find there are hidden rewards.

Take, for example, someone with chronic health issues. Perhaps their mother never paid attention to them. When they got sick, suddenly Mom paid attention. One of the hidden rewards of this illness was that it created a way for them to feel loved and noticed. There's a certain part of them that will have difficulty letting go of this condition because it means potentially losing the care they so desperately want and need. Recognizing your own hidden agendas and not-so-obvious benefits is really important when it comes to letting go.

Focusing on these questions can help you shift the energy:

❀ How does this benefit me?

❀ What is it that I'm *actually* getting from this?

❀ What am I learning from this experience?

❀ How is this changing me and helping me to grow?

You can use gratitude on a situation or energy you want to release. Look at it and say to yourself something like, "Okay, so _____ and _____ totally sucks about this situation, but I'm grateful for the _____ and the _____ I've been getting from this experience."

It's not always the case, but often if you ask yourself, "Is there something about this situation that I can be grateful for?" you may uncover a lot more information about why part of you didn't want to let it go.

Additional Tools for Release

You can also use mindful movement, which means deliberately moving your body in order to facilitate release. You can use breath, movement, and intention to discharge through your body. Every time you breathe in while moving, you shift your body's energy. As you breathe out, use your movement as well as your breath to create even greater release.

Using breath and movement simultaneously can be a very powerful way to let things go. I recommend using movement and self-massage to notice where in the body you're holding things. Deliver love to those places. Offer yourself love and support. Go for walks and use the breath to release things as a moving meditation. Walk, breathe, and release. Dancing also works well, as do other forms of exercise paired with the intention to release.

Other powerful tools are flower essences and essential oils. Aromatherapy and fragrances can be helpful for triggering associations and memories. Scent – not synthetic fragrances, but high-quality essential oils – can really facilitate release. You can use essential oils to shift your brain patterns, and thus shift your experience.

Flower essences are energetic medicines that use the vibration of flowers to transmute and shift energy and consciousness. It is a vibrational healing modality that doesn't have a scent, but works with the energetic qualities of flowers. Flower essences are incredibly effective, and throughout more than 30 years of working with them I've seen remarkable results. Flower essences serve as auric healers. They help transmute negativity and patterns of imbalance. They work very gently to transform and transmute our thoughts, feelings, physical sensations, beliefs, behaviors, and patterns. In my humble opinion, every empath should have Yarrow (for shielding) and Rescue Remedy (for trauma) readily available at all times.

What is especially wonderful about flower essences is that there are hundreds (if not thousands) of different essences available worldwide. Not only can you purchase commercially available essences, but with some care and consideration you can even make your own from fresh blossoms growing near you. When you've done your diagnostic work and gotten clear about what's going on, you can dial in very specifically on which flower essences to use and receive very precise support on any issue. I cannot speak highly enough about the efficacy of flower essences. When used properly, they are miraculous.

Fresh flowers are wonderful, too. I almost always have flowers in my videos and photographs. Flowers emit an incredibly high vibration; they enhance the vibration of everything in their vicinity and transmute negativity and static. A simple bouquet from the grocery store or wildflowers from your yard can uplift and support you. For the rewards they give you, fresh flowers offer great bang for the buck. I highly recommend keeping a fresh bouquet in your space. Change it regularly. Unless you have to decide between baby food and flowers, go for the flowers. If you have to decide between going out to see a silly movie and buying flowers, I say buy the flowers. Flowers will last much longer than a 2-hour movie and lousy popcorn, and they will clarify, purify, and enhance the vibration of your space. Flowers act as a beacon for positive, beautiful energy and dissipate and dispel negativity.

Chapter 6

Protect

Protection is strengthened when you create filters and shields to form energetic armor around yourself. The challenge is that when you've already absorbed a lot of negativity and fear, that crap will remain until you do something to shift it. A new shield can prevent more stuff from coming in, but you still have to deal with two challenges: a) it's hard to feel better when you're still carrying the old negativity, and b) trapped negativity will compromise the integrity of your emotional and energetic shields. Until you learn how to *Recognize, Release,* and ground, it will be difficult to avoid further negativity. You'll continue to feel uncomfortable despite the sparkly new bubble of light surrounding you. This is why it's imperative that *Recognizing* and *Releasing* work come before *Protection* work.

The longer you do the work to develop your energy body and create your protective shields, the better you're able to recognize your limitations. It stops feeling like hard work and becomes an established system; you become so used to working with it that it's no longer a big deal. What I wish for every empath reading this book is that you reach the point where you can accept that this is simply what you do. It ceases to be a chore, a burden, or extra homework and it becomes effortless, even fun.

There was a time when all of this felt awkward and forced for me. I'd try things and then forget them. I'd climb up on the wagon and then fall back off. It took me time and the reward of experiencing relief to stay the distance. I won't lie and say I do this perfectly all the time. Some days I still forget to tune in to Source. I forget to reinforce my filters and shields. I decide that I'd rather binge-watch a whole TV series than spend a few hours grounding in nature.

Yet the benefits of adopting these concepts and philosophies and working with these tools and techniques are cumulative. In the beginning, missing a day or slipping on my food plan had nearly instant (and often dire) consequences, but now I've created enough of a buffer that I actually have some wiggle room. While I still have limited respite from this practice, it feels good to be able to coast once in a while without finding myself back in the empathic abyss.

I recognize this may be a new way of approaching your life. At first it won't be a habit. It will likely feel like an artificial imposition as you work to establish a new routine and whole new way of being. Rarely are we offered any of this in the muggle world. It's up to us to find others like us, to commit to our self-care and our personal development, to take our sensitivity seriously even when others dismiss or insult it.

When we are criticized for being "too sensitive," we can turn it around and say: "You're right. I am *highly* sensitive. I'm feeling something really intense right now so I'm gonna take care of myself."

In this chapter we'll examine what it takes to establish sustainable energetic and emotional protection.

Here's the thing: I can't promise you that doing these exercises will always keep you out of harm's way. But what I can say is that when you remember to do them, a) intuition is more accessible, so you are frequently able to detour dangerous situations, and b) you are better prepared for whatever comes, so you can remain calm and focused even in the midst of great turbulence. Here are a few things I have come to believe:

1. This entire planet is in a state of transition. We are in the process of evolving spiritually. Many spiritual teachers explain that we are shifting from the limitations of the fourth dimension of time and space to something that expands far beyond it. As we shift into the fifth dimension,

or "Age of Aquarius," many things are unraveling. What we thought we knew to be true is coming into question, our identities are being shaken, and many people are intensely uncomfortable. My sense is that we are in the early stages of hard labor, giving birth to a new world and a new way of existing. Like actual childbirth, this can be agonizing. The pain comes in waves. We expand and contact as we wait for the head of this new world to crown. We are simultaneously the baby being born, the mother birthing her, and the mid-wife holding space for this birth to happen. We might wish to choose medication and numbness, hoping to wake up on the other side holding a sweet new baby in our collective arms, but for many of us this metaphoric epidural is simply not an option. What this leaves is the choice between react-ing and responding, between running from the pain or lean-ing in and loving ourselves through it. I sincerely believe that remaining calm is one of the most important means of getting through this process. When we choose to keep breathing through it, we are better equipped to endure these contractions of change.

2. Death is inevitable. We will all shed this mortal coil at some point. Trying to fight against this truth is futile; when we live our lives trying to stay safe, we often keep ourselves from joy, connection, and our higher purpose. Relaxation comes from the acceptance of this truth. From this comes the calm and focus we need to navigate turbulence with grace.

3. Fear is a normal part of the human condition. The primal part of our brain is wired to fight, flee, or freeze. It acts as both an emergency brake and an accelerator, designed to keep us safe. Its default is stop/run! However, just because we feel fear doesn't mean we should avoid taking bold leaps. Living an amazing life often means overriding our

lizard brain instincts and taking action despite all our negative thoughts and feelings.

4. Protective filters and shields only work if you use them. Often, when we become overwhelmed or depleted we forget to reinforce personal protection. I cannot begin to count the number of times I have repeated this lesson. I've had to recognize that every single time I've been fed on by psychic vampires, given away too much of my time and energy, and/or expended my resources, I did so because I forgot to fortify my shields and filters. I walked into a situation with my spiritual guard down, oblivious to what was happening until I reflected back later.

5. Distraction and overwhelm are the enemy of safety and ease. Nothing can get you into trouble faster than a system on overload. The irony is that when you hit these depleted resource states, the last thing you remember to do is ground, center, and reinforce your protective filters and shields. The good news is that the more you work with these tools, the more fortified your energetic protection becomes, so you become less vulnerable than you once were. But even with your new tools, please be aware that few things can wear down your protection faster than stress. Anytime life gets especially challenging, doubling down on all of the Empathic Mastery steps can make the difference between smooth sailing and treading water.

6. Embracing protection means that we will be different than we were before. At first it can feel strange not being in a state of perpetual agitation and heightened emotion. Life may even feel flat or devoid of emotion when we start to dial back the drama and intensity we've been accustomed to. Living in this new way means we must let go of the identity attached to being sensitive to the point of debilitation. We may have experienced unconscious or hidden rewards

that come with being so empathic that we are limited in how we engage with the world. Being perceived as special, vulnerable, sensitive, unusual, weird, or different garners attention from others. It may be a bittersweet pill to relinquish that attention. In order to commit to protection we must acknowledge how it changes our life as we know it.

Protection starts with finding balance emotionally, energetically, and physically. Using *Recognize* and *Release* lets us acknowledge how we feel and allows us to soothe ourselves to equilibrium. Once we've done this work, creating strong filters, shields, and energetic supports becomes the foundation of Empathic Mastery.

I don't start with *Protection* because if you don't *Recognize* what's actually going on and *Release* all the stuff that isn't yours (as well as your own distress and pain), then no amount of protection is going to make things significantly better for you.

You must first be able to discern what's yours and what isn't, and whether triggers from the past are sending you down the rabbit hole.

Before you can establish sustainable protection you need to clean house and let go of everything you don't need to carry. If this stuff still feels like it's driving your bus, please go back to the previous chapters and review and practice the exercises that will help you let it go.

PROTECT: Beyond Fight or Flight

There are multiple levels to protecting ourselves as empathic people. It's important to evaluate the situation when we sense we're in danger. We can learn to stop and assess whether we are experiencing a mental or emotional reaction, or if we're actually in real, physical danger.

As human beings we're wired to respond to fear. We're wired to respond to danger, which activates the fight-or-flight mechanism in our brain and body. This response evolved to protect our primordial ancestors. They had instincts which compelled them to run, fight, or freeze. With all their day-to-day caveman dangers, our predecessors needed to either get the hell out of Dodge as quickly as possible or deal directly with the threat if they couldn't escape. Human beings experience a cascade of physiological responses when they prepare to deal with stress and danger. Unfortunately, one of the things this does is create tunnel vision, wherein all of our brain power is diverted to fighting or fleeing, shutting down our capacity to see alternate routes.

It's essential to discern whether or not you feel fear because you need to protect yourself from physical harm and to act accordingly. In the case of an actual threat, getting yourself to safety and/or confronting the challenge is essential. When it's an intellectual or emotional fear, you can work with it using tapping or another mental/emotional technique to clear it.

The first step in protection lies in identifying whether this an intellectual fear or a genuine physical danger. One of the ways to determine this is to ask, "What's the worst thing that can happen?"

I find that this question can ripple out further and further until we've exhausted all the possibilities. Now, if you are prone to "awfulizing," asking this question must not be considered a carte blanche invitation to an all-expense paid shopping spree at the Mall of Disaster.

That said, in a situation where you're feeling fear, ask yourself, "What's the worst thing that can happen?" You might answer, "Well, so-and-so won't like me," "I'll get fired," or whatever else you come up with. You can then keep going: "Well, okay. So if that happens, what's the worst thing that can happen?" This can be a good way to dissipate your fear, particularly if it's intellectual. I've run this question in my head many times, to the point where I get back to the bottom line, which is: "I could die."

This always brings me back to the awareness that once I reach that final destination, everything else will cease to matter. For me, it all boils down to love and Divine Source. It's all the incarnational in-between stuff that gets my panties in a wad. When I return to God/dess, all will be well.

Fear can be mind-numbing, brain-fogging, and option-blocking. To move forward we must soothe our reactivity. I sincerely believe that energy healing techniques are some the swiftest and best ways to calm ourselves down. The fight-or-flight mechanism in our brain gets the cascade of cortisol (the adrenal response) just racing through our bodies, so we become drunk on a cocktail of stress hormones. Resetting the amygdala is the key to moving our bodies out of that fight-or-flight mode. This is one of the most important things we can do to establish modern day safety and protection. More often than not, we are better served by being calm and responsive than by being in a hyper, intensified state of fight-or-flight. Recognizing that we are *not* in actual danger, that we do not actually need to fight or flee, allows us to calm down and reconsider our options. We're then able to look at things in a whole new way. The *Touch and Breathe* technique is my go-to for sudden stress relief.

Touch and Breathe: Inhale slowly and then hold your breath while gently massaging or putting light pressure on a tapping point. Exhale while still holding that point. Move through all the points as you continue to breathe, hold, and release. Even after just one full round of tapping, you should begin to experience a shift.

The Three Facets of Physical Protection: Avoiding, Leaving, Dealing

There are actions you can take to feel safer and more protected. Some may seem like basic common sense, but at the risk of being obvious I'm going to talk about them anyway. From the standpoint of physical protection, there are three stages to be aware of:

The first stage is avoiding harm. This involves sensing when something doesn't feel right and simply avoiding it. For instance, you have a strong gut instinct that you should not be getting in your car and driving somewhere. Hopefully, you follow your gut. You may learn that there was an accident exactly where you were going to go. Or, maybe you do what I've done (as mentioned earlier) -- you don't listen to your instinct and end up in a car accident. Listening to that gut instinct combined with using your common sense, reasoning, and logic helps you avoid putting yourself in harm's way.

Part of this avoidance involves identifying and recognizing potentially harmful behaviors. A lot of us have habits and personal behaviors that don't necessarily serve us well. You can start being mindful of your consumption of alcohol, foods, and other substances that don't serve you. Pay attention to the things that compromise your clarity and put you in a vulnerable position. Recognize the ways in which these things can influence or affect your focus.

This can be something as simple as deciding whether or not to do strenuous physical exercise when you're already tired and overextended. Evaluate your resource state. Determine how rested, healthy, or strong you're feeling. Then, before engaging in the activity, ask yourself, "Is this something that's going to support me? Is this something that's going to nurture and nourish me? Or is this something that could potentially tax my resources, draw energy away from me, or put me in a state where I could be compromised?" The most basic level of harm avoidance is simply recognizing that it's not a swift idea and telling yourself, "Don't go there, little buckaroo!"

I encourage you to be utterly truthful as you determine whether something will be safe or harmful for you to do. Denial can be a powerful deterrent to personal safety. This can be especially true when a part of us wants to engage in self-medicating or other risky choices that may feel good in the short term. If simply admitting something is potentially hazardous means we must abstain from it, then we'll be prone to ignoring the truth to excuse our choice. I believe we are more empowered when we recognize the impact of a choice and deliberately do it despite the risk, instead of simply pretending it's harmless. As an old timer in AA once told my friend Christine, "If you're going to use, use the good stuff."

The second stage occurs when you sense harm in your immediate environment. Say, for example, you're at a party. Something starts to feel uncomfortable, or you're around people who are being rowdy or obnoxious. There's nothing wrong with fleeing harm! Make the decision to get out of there. *Give yourself permission to walk away from things when they don't feel safe.*

I think this is an incredibly important thing to do. For so many of us (especially women), the urge to people-please is a major challenge. We frequently stay in harmful situations because we don't want to hurt somebody else's feelings. We often know that something feels wrong, but we don't listen to our own warnings. We worry that we might be coming across as judgmental or bitchy or selfish. Bottom line: if we simply give ourselves permission to leave when we know it's time to go, we'll manage to keep ourselves out of a lot of trouble.

Thinking through an exit strategy in advance will allow us to be prepared instead of leaving everything up to chance and luck. I learned this lesson the hard way when I was in college and decided to go to a party in a far-off neighborhood. I'll chalk it up to being young and naive, but it didn't even occur to me that I needed to figure out how to get home at the end of the night. I found myself drunk and stranded at a party with limited options for places to crash. I was too broke to call a cab, too proud to call my parents, and too buzzed to leave and catch the subway on time. Because

I felt I had backed myself into a corner, I ended up ambivalently hooking up with one of the guys who lived there. Fortunately, I suffered no real harm and I learned a powerful lesson: not planning ahead, drinking too much, and low self-esteem create the perfect storm for a compromising situation.

In case you're wondering, in all the years since that night I've never regarded this man as a perpetrator or myself as a victim. If anything, I regard myself as 80% responsible and him as 20% opportunistic. The situation was complicated, my signals were vague, and I acquiesced to sex that I would have avoided if I'd been more prepared and mindful. In the #MeToo era, where many sexual predators in positions of power are being exposed, this admission is a bittersweet pill to swallow. It's bitter because it's embarrassing to admit that my own stupid choices put me in a compromising position. It's bitter because my self-esteem was so low at that point in my life that I believed that I owed a sexual favor in exchange for a safe place to sleep. It's bitter because I spent many years living with the shame and blame for this choice. It's sweet because, in truth, it was a confluence of circumstances that led to an experience with little consequence. I was a fatally hip, terminally cool art chick who used a jaded facade to disguise my innocence. This fills me with compassion for the young woman I was, and it allows me to acknowledge that I was doing the best I could at the time. It's sweet because, ultimately, there was no harm and no foul. I learned a valuable lesson for a fairly low price. In hindsight, I can see we were all young, drunk, inexperienced 20-somethings who honestly didn't see any alternatives. The moral of this story is:

1. Young, drunk, and empathic is a vulnerable combination,

2. If you leave things to chance (especially when intoxicated), you may find yourself in the back seat instead of in front of the steering wheel, and

3. Anticipating the need to leave and planning ahead is a far better approach than the alternative.

The third facet of the physical level of protection is when something happens that you can't avoid. When you can't escape, you must fight, freeze, or surrender to it. The choice to fight or surrender is deeply personal. Sometimes yielding means surviving to fight another day. There's a saying: "You can save your face or you can save your ass, but you can't save both at the same time." When it comes to fighting vs. surrendering, the question to ask is: "Am I fighting for my ego or my life?" Thankfully, in most cases fighting harm means standing up for yourself verbally. It rarely means that you need to get into a fistfight, carry firearms, or be a martial artist. Most of the time, defending yourself is about saying, "I'm uncomfortable when you do this, it's not acceptable, and I will not tolerate it. This needs to stop." Most of the time fighting harm is more about intellectual fear and verbal protection than physical acts of self-protection. In modern culture, we aren't generally in physical harm's way.

Sadly though, domestic violence and #MeToo incidents are all too pervasive. If you find yourself in a volatile environment where there is real potential for danger, just saying, "You hurt my feelings" isn't going to cut it. Sometimes learning self-defense techniques may be a good choice for you. Sometimes filing a restraining order and/or talking to a lawyer is necessary. Sometimes taking your kids and fleeing to safety while an abuser is away is the best choice. I'm hoping that for most of the people reading this book, physical self-defense isn't something that needs to be addressed.

I've lived in several urban areas and have always found that alertness, intuition, and making calculated choices about where and when I go walking alone have kept me out of trouble. I've also had a sense of being protected by Divine Source and the trust that, while I might hit bumps in the road (or even drive head on into a flood), I will come through unscathed and wiser for the experience. I choose to live in El Mundo Bueno; in this world I am divinely protected and guided.

PROTECT: External Tools for Protection

There are numerous physical tools available to enhance protection. They generally work best as a supplement to mental, emotional, and energetic management. Used without the inner work, they'll only take you so far. Sometimes though, picking up one (or several) of these tools will take enough of the edge off that you can rally and do the necessary inner work. I have used many tools to support me: stones and crystals; flower essences; clothing and accessories; amulets and talismans; jewelry; statuary; medicine pouches; herbs; essential oils; tattoos; makeup and body art; spoken chants and prayers; orgonite and other EMF protection devices; rattles, drums, bells, singing bowls and other instruments; salt (alone or mixed with water); smoke from sacred herbs such as sage or palo santo, etc.

This is by no means a comprehensive list, but it covers my go-to supports and is offered to give you a sense of what is possible. In working with these tools, I've found they fall into several basic functional categories:

* Calm and soothe
* Ground and release
* Purify
* Balance and stabilize
* Clarify and enhance focus and insight
* Repel negativity
* Fortify, strengthen, and serve as a replenishing tonic

Managing Your Energy Resources

How you cultivate your own energy, how you walk into a given situation, impacts both the way in which things come to you and the way you experience them. The calmer you are, the more you become a beacon for calm. As you become an anchor for serenity, serenity extends and ripples out beyond you. This alone can be a very powerful means of protection.

There are multiple ways to receive information and multiple ways to take an energetic hit. It's fairly easy to deal with something coming straight at you -- when you see it coming, you can put up your shields, deflect it, and affirm, "This is going to be fine." It's the stuff that comes in sideways that gets us. When we're in a state of depleted resources and already tired and overextended, we're far more likely to be caught off guard by an energetic disruption. It's less likely to happen when we're grounded, stable, and balanced. Your level of vitality, focus, and resilience really impacts the dance of avoiding, fleeing, or fighting harm.

As empaths, it's essential that we be honest with ourselves about our level of energy and mental bandwidth. Be clear about what you're capable of handling in a given day. If you're like me, you may have a tendency to bite off more than you can chew. When I overextend myself, I'm much less able to go with the flow than when I'm centered, refreshed, and feeling grounded. In an ideal world we'd always be functioning from a grounded, optimally resourced state. But in this day and age that's not always the case, so we need to create layers of energetic insulation to protect us at the onset of intensity. If something then comes at us sideways, it will glance off the perimeter of our energy body instead of penetrating our core.

Overwhelm and distraction are two important conditions to watch for. Both of these states can prevent you from noticing something is awry until much later. I'm not really joking when I refer to 2013 as "The Year o' Death."

From Halloween of 2012 through Yule of 2013, I experienced nine deaths, including five family members and four others who were friends, clients, or beloved family members of dear friends. By that August, when a friend died unexpectedly from a rare brain disease, part of me became untethered from my body. As someone with a capacity to connect with souls who've crossed over, I had a taste of heavenly bliss which was more ecstatic and glorious than anything I'd ever experienced before. A piece of me had drifted from the physical world and was surfing the radiant sweetness of the other side. Consequently, I didn't notice when a minuscule deer tick burrowed into me. I came down with pneumonia in late October and was knocked on my ass for two solid months, then struggled for six more months after a conclusive Lyme diagnosis. This was a wake-up call for me. I knew that my emotional overwhelm, grief, and openness had all contributed to my vulnerability. In hindsight, I recognize that nearly every crisis I've ever experienced was due to being overextended, overwrought, distracted, and/or discontented with my life while being unwilling to admit it or take action to change.

At the very core of safety is *truth*. When we cannot consciously acknowledge and change what isn't working in our lives, our minds and bodies will often force the issue. We manifest wake-up calls and crises to provoke change when things become too difficult to bear any longer. In order to protect ourselves from subconscious attempts to find relief, mindfulness and honest assessment of where we're really at are imperative.

PROTECT: Emotional Protection: Boundaries & Degrees of Awareness

In terms of emotional *Protection*, the first degree of awareness is *anticipation* (which does not mean awfulizing in advance!). If you can realistically anticipate what might happen and be preemptive, you can often keep yourself out of harm's way.

For example, perhaps you're planning to attend a family gathering. If you think about the familiar cast of characters and imagine who you're going to be dealing with and how they're likely to behave, you can anticipate quite a bit and ascertain who to be mindful of so you're not surprised or caught off guard. You're now better prepared should something occur.

Obviously this works best when you already know the lay of the land and have engaged with everyone involved before. But even if you're walking into a new situation, you can still run through possible scenarios and consider how you might set boundaries and limits in advance.

For most of our day-to-day life, however, we're walking into situations we can anticipate and can take time to prepare for. When you actually walk into a place, scan the room. Check out the space and the people and tell yourself what you've noticed. You may say something like, "It seems like the behavior and energy in this space looks okay. But *that* person appears to be a bit off the wall. Duly noted. I'll need to pay attention, give them a wide berth, and protect myself from their wackiness."

The second level of emotional *Protection* involves *boundaries*. I'm not referring here to energetic boundaries, but to basic behavioral boundaries. This kind of boundary work concerns what you will and will not accept.

When somebody asks you for something you're not comfortable with, the answer can be as simple as "no." If someone tries to impose upon you in a way that is not acceptable, say "no."

The challenge is that most women are taught that it is rude and inconsiderate to be so abrupt and blunt. "Just say no!" might sound easy, but most of us are taught very early to manage other people's feelings and to let them down gently. This often means we acquiesce when we don't really want to. When we do screw up the courage to say "no," we often pad it with excuses and apologies. This does not serve us and it doesn't serve anyone else. Others may feel disappointed or annoyed when they don't get their way, but when you go ahead and do something you really don't want to do, it doesn't flow.

Setting boundaries is something we stretch into. At first it can feel terrifying as we anticipate another's reaction. It often takes saying several "no's" before we realize the sky won't fall and some of our anxiety lifts. Boundary setting is usually incremental. Start with the simple "no's" and get used to claiming them. As those get easier to set, move onto the higher-value ones.

Over the years I've learned the following things about boundaries:

- ❋ There is often a cycle with boundary setting. First it's uncomfortable and we must overcome fear, feelings of unworthiness, and the desire to please others. Then, as we timidly begin to set limits, we wait for the other shoe to drop. It's not uncommon to go through a phase of righteousness, indignation, and even anger as we start flexing our "no." This is especially true when we are setting limits for the first time in our lives.

- ❋ We teach people how we are willing to be treated. The best approach is to get clear about what we want and start there.

- ❋ Anytime we uplevel our lives, we must uplevel our boundaries too. Just because it got easy to say "no" to a previous issue doesn't mean we won't have to stretch outside our comfort zone when it's time to set new limits.

- ❋ It's easier to establish ground rules and define terms of agreement in advance than to correct a situation later.

- ❋ Saying "no" and setting limits takes practice. The more you do it, the more you'll trust the process and yourself.

- ❋ Now, there are times when we attempt to set boundaries but end up dealing with people who do not respect our "no." A short, sweet-but-firm "no" generally works far better with bullies than excuses, apologies, or attempts to negotiate a compromise. Most of these people will test your resolve by challenging it, but when you make it very clear that you refuse to play, they give up.

Once you recognize that someone is a bully, you can choose to acknowledge that they simply don't have the capacity to respect your boundaries. You can make the decision to pull away from this connection, because no matter how hard you try, it won't be a healthy relationship.

The suggestions I share are geared towards relationships with rational, non-violent people. *By no means am I suggesting that if you are in an abusive relationship you can just start saying "no" and suddenly everything will turn around. This oversimplifies a complex situation which can take time and planning to leave safely. Disengaging from a bully or an abuser can be really scary, even dangerous, particularly if they're someone you've become intimately involved with.*

Bullying is often learned at an early age as an attempt to get attention. Acting out and aggression are warped ways of getting emotional needs met; it's more harmful to the human psyche to be ignored and abandoned than to receive negative attention. Children who are neglected will often act out to provoke some kind of reaction. Ironically, at the very core of bullying behavior is an extreme fear of abandonment and rejection. In some cases, when you stop engaging with their drama, they will attempt to turn up the volume to keep you sucked in.

Sometimes you have to just cut your losses and give them a "yes" to stay safe until you find the best way to protect yourself and change your life. You know best what this person is capable of. Use your survival instincts and intuition to guide you. Fortunately, there are some great resources to help women leave abusive situations. If you are reading this and recognize your own situation, please know that you are not alone. There is help available and there are solutions. I've included a link in the Resources section with a list of national resources and support.

The next layer of emotional *Protection* is *clarification*. It starts with defining your personal boundaries and limits. Strategic mental boundaries can be discovered by asking clarifying questions such as:

- ⊛ What are my terms?
- ⊛ What am I willing to accept?
- ⊛ What am I *not* willing to tolerate?
- ⊛ What are my personal limitations?
- ⊛ What am I comfortable with?
- ⊛ What am I not comfortable with?

I invite you to consider a situation in your life and use the questions above to do some journaling to clarify your boundaries. Think of a relationship where you feel your boundaries are being imposed upon. Clarify what really matters to you in terms of negotiables and non-negotiables. It's key to get really clear. I first sense boundary violations in my gut; I feel an instant tension in my solar plexus when someone is not respecting me or my space. One common boundary violation occurs with "close talkers." You know when somebody has stepped through your outer shield and into your personal bubble. It's palpable. It's physical. Remember that sensation of intrusion -- you will experience a similar sensation when someone's behavior pushes up against your psychic boundaries.

A caveat here: there can be a funny line when it comes to our imagination -- the stories we tell ourselves -- versus the reality of a situation. Sometimes when we feel unsafe or sense that an emotional situation is escalating, it's actually our old triggers and previous experiences casting their shadow over something quite benign. Therefore, it's useful to ask clarifying questions. One of my favorite techniques is to ask, "I am imagining that you are feeling (fill in the blank); *is this true?*" Usually, that blank will be some variant of "angry with me," or "disappointed about xyz." As long as I'm dealing with people I can trust to respond honestly, this approach diffuses many conflicts before they have a chance to begin. This technique requires emotional mindfulness on your part. You must accept that it's entirely possible that you are projecting something onto the situation. It also requires the willingness to be vulnerable and share that you're anticipating some kind of negative emotion, which may or may not be real for the other person. One of the shadow sides of being an empath is the conviction that because we feel something, we know what it means and can therefore use it to validate what we perceive as truth. Just because we can sense things that remain unspoken or pick up suppressed emotions, it doesn't mean we can rely on this ability to confirm our suspicions 100% of the time. It's astonishing how often what we imagine does not match the other person's reality.

Seeking clarification is vital. It gives us the ability to dial back and recognize that the reaction we're having (and the accompanying sense of danger) is not actually about the present moment. It's about the inflection of someone's voice, the words they used, or a behavior that triggered a reaction rooted in a different experience. When we are able to clarify that our response is not to something happening here and now, we have the ability to address the original trigger. When we believe that we're protecting ourselves from something currently in progress while in fact, we're actually being provoked by the past, no amount of self-defense or protection is going to make it better. If anything, our reaction will only escalate the situation because the other person will experience our reaction and respond accordingly. Being open to the possibility that there's more to the story than we know (and more than one way to look at it) allows for precious wiggle room in the dance of relationship.

The fourth level of *Protection* is *emotional self-defense*. This involves recognizing when it's time to defend ourselves, to stick up for ourselves and say, "This is not acceptable. This is not okay. This needs to stop." Emotional self-defense can sometimes involve simply realizing that you're uncomfortable and excusing yourself to go out for a brief walk or a bathroom break. Going to the bathroom is remarkably effective. Stand at the sink, turn on the water, and wash your hands until you feel you've siphoned off your reactivity and washed it down the drain. If you have time, do a round or two of tapping to give yourself a sense of protection and acceptance for what is. Taking the time to recognize that you're uncomfortable and removing yourself for a few minutes can make a real difference. Even if you're in a situation where you can't leave the room, you can always check out for a second. Pause and deliberately go to your happy place. Unless you're engaged in a lively conversation or delivering a speech and suddenly stop talking, nobody will know you've taken a break.

Going to your happy place is different than dissociating. Dissociating happens when you leave your body unconsciously. Going to your happy place is a deliberate choice. You can decide, "I need a break. I'm gonna put myself on autopilot while this person just keeps talking. I can still say things like, 'Oh wow, sounds really difficult. I'm so sorry you had to go through that.' But I don't have to get sucked in." Disengage from emotional involvement. Allow yourself to detach and just go through the motions. Dial back your engagement and give yourself permission to be less than 100% present.

Sometimes, if you're in an intimate, deeply connected relationship, you may suddenly find yourself defending or protecting yourself. You can breathe through it and simply notice that you're feeling uncomfortable. If it's a situation where you recognize that you actually do need self-protection, sometimes just disengaging, pulling back, and not being 100% involved is a great practice. Emotional distance is something we must practice as empaths. It comes naturally to empathize and tune into the other person's story. It may feel inauthentic and/or foreign to detach and not to engage so deeply. The truth is, we only have so much mental and emotional bandwidth on any given day. It is not our responsibility to be fully present and emotionally available for every single encounter we experience throughout the day. It's really okay to choose when and where to put the effort into giving our all. We are allowed to decide that right now it's an unnecessary expense.

PROTECT: Energetic Protection

Energetic protection is one of my favorite aspects of this work. When our energy is aligned and fortified, we are able to manage the physical and emotional with greater ease and efficiency. For over thirty years I've worked with a meditation I developed called the Earth-Sky Meditation. The full text of this guided meditation can be found later in this chapter. This meditation helps to shift your perception of yourself as an isolated, individual unit, free-floating on the Earth to that of a connected part of the planet, plugged in and supported.

One of the major problems with Western culture is that we currently operate as if we all run on battery packs. We've been encouraged to believe that we are self-sufficient, self-sustaining beings running on our own limited, self-generated power. In reality, we are substantially more empowered than this. We have a much easier time managing life when we learn to ground and connect, relying on energy sources far greater than our own. We must remember to both receive and give, to accept and release energy, so that we are in a perpetual circuit.

We've all heard the term "grounding." People talk about it all the time. From my perspective, there are two components to grounding. It's not simply a connection to the Earth; rather, it's an energetic circuit that connects us to both Earth and Sky, allowing us to become a center point between them. We create a figure eight of energy in which *we* become the axis point, filled with light, intention, and energy. We receive light from the Sky and warmth and support from the Earth. This figure eight of energy is constantly moving through us. It comes up from the Earth, meets in the body at our heart, our core, then moves up to the Sky to draw down energy, support, and divine guidance. It then brings all that energy back down through us and into the Earth, draining off any excess.

When this circuit is working properly, we are constantly recycling, replenishing, and moving energy through us as part of a greater system. We send our intentions, prayers, and thoughts upwards while releasing our excess energy back down into the Earth. We're like a fountain -- the water is constantly recirculated and refreshed by the movement. It doesn't stagnate. It doesn't get stuck. It is replenished and cleansed as it flows, transmuted by both Earth and Sky. We are supported by the energy as it cycles above and below us.

When we forget to ground for any significant period, our energy can begin to stagnate and eventually dissipate. Ironically, the longer we practice our Earth-Sky grounding, the greater our energy reserves become, so we may not notice at first that we've become disconnected. We may sustain our energy center initially, but if it's not circulating properly over time, we're more likely to get sick or have a meltdown. Signs that this is happening include feeling overwhelmed, exhausted, emotionally drained, overwrought, depleted, put upon, hopeless, anxious, fearful, triggered, or distracted, to name but a few. We also become more vulnerable to taking an energetic hit; when our energy isn't flowing and moving, we aren't keeping ourselves protected as well as we could. When we become depleted by challenging circumstances or a prolonged hiatus from this exercise, we may need to put more effort into reestablishing and reinforcing our filters and shields.

I cannot stress how worthwhile this practice is for our wellbeing and empathic protection. You may have to work to establish your shields at first, but it will become easier as you continue. Eventually you'll be able to activate the whole circuit with just a few intentional breaths. When we deliberately cultivate this Earth-self-Sky circuit, building up our figure eight with the energies of Earth and Sky, we create a protective aura around our body. The more we practice this exercise, the stronger our filters and shields become and the easier it gets to sustain them with minimal effort. I experience these shields as three layers.

The first layer is our inner core of light -- our prana/chi/orgone/vital life force. When we accept energy from Earth and Sky, this core of life force is supported and enhanced. We become stronger, healthier, and calmer, simultaneously energized and inspired. In its healthiest state, our inner core is like a star of light that originates in our heart and expands to fill our entire body. By the time we reach late childhood this light is often diminished. When a body ceases to be filled with its own energy, a vacuum is created, pulling in all kinds of other material to fill it. This material can include other people's physical, mental, and emotional pain; old memories or traumatic experiences that stay locked like holograms in our system; chronic illnesses, tumors, growths, bacterial, viral and fungal loads; even spirits and other entities. Learning how to claim and support a light body that fills our entire physical body is vital for our wellbeing and longevity.

Beyond the core of light, there is a second layer within our primary filter. This layer processes the energy that we absorb and protects us psychically and emotionally. This layer can have varying degrees of porousness, thickness, density, and elasticity, which are all affected by trauma, distress, overexertion, and emotional intensity, as well as physical exposure to toxins such as mold, chemicals, and smoke. The degree of porousness ranges from completely smooth to threadbare and shot with gaping holes. The density and range of thickness goes from robust and sturdy to practically imperceptible, again depending on vitality and stress. Elasticity is impacted by defensiveness, mental and emotional rigidity, and unforgiven resentment and anger that calcifies as we hold onto it.

Whenever I practice the Earth-Sky exercise, I imagine creating a thick, cotton-candy-like sheath that envelops my core of light and forms the shape of an egg surrounding my physical body. A healthy middle layer is smooth, vibrant, and flexible. It's dense enough to filter negativity but not so dense that it blocks love and emotional connection. It extends as a luminous ball of light around us and allows us to take in what we need to know while protecting us from negativity and information overload.

Beyond this layer, there's an outer shield which covers both the middle filter and inner core of light. This shield is thin and flexible. It serves as a protective membrane. In a healthy state it's a strong, elastic, translucent or transparent sheath that coats the surface of the filter. It protects us by deflecting negativity and preventing energy from penetrating the middle filter, instead allowing it to slide or bounce off.

Imagine these three layers as an egg: our inner core of light is the yolk, the filter is the albumen (white) that surrounds it, and the outer shield is the shell, which protects the inner layers from harm. Just as an egg can still take in the oxygen it needs through its shell, our energetic egg can absorb what it needs while repelling the rest. The challenge is that, just like Humpty Dumpty, our energetic eggs can be vulnerable.

Having worked with numerous empaths, I've noticed that many have compromised filters. They have big spongy holes, the layers are extremely thin, or they suffer from both conditions. The outer sheath has been penetrated, shattered, eroded, or never developed correctly in the first place. As a result, everything has a tendency to come flooding in. As discussed in earlier chapters, there are several reasons for this: some of us are born with weaker filters than others, and trauma, challenges, and difficulties wear down even healthy filters. Being sensitive and empathic can be a double whammy: not only do we tend to start with less robust systems than others, but those systems are further compromised by the distress and pain we absorb from the world around us. The intense energy coming at us is abrasive; like sandpaper, it wears away our already minimal filters.

In order to turn things around, we must learn to consciously build up these filters so we can protect ourselves. The good news is, once we start building up these filters and shields, we don't have to be bombarded by stuff 24/7. I can tell you from personal experience, in terms of being able to function effectively in the world, this is the difference between night and day. Plus, because we've lived with empathic abilities, we can then deliberately choose when and where we wish to open our channels to receive information.

If you want some extra protection, it's possible to adjust your outer shield by throwing what I call a "Cloak of Invisibility" over your entire energetic egg to move through a space or situation without attracting attention. You can also calibrate your shield so it has a particular energetic signature or a specific design, so that it invites and welcomes only the people and situations you wish to deal with and diverts the rest. The symbol or design acts as a keyhole, so only the people who have the key are able to get through. It doesn't block energy coming to us, but filters it so that we receive only what we need and the rest just bounces off. Having a shield of energy that is calibrated to call in our intentions and desires is an incredibly effective way to start living the life we want to live.

Earth Sky Connection

1. Send awareness down to the Heart of the Earth
2. Check in
3. Ask for what you need
4. Inhale and draw the energy up
5. Exhale and send it up to the Sky
6. Check in
7. Ask for what you need
8. Inhale Divine Light down
9. Exhale it to the Earth
10. Keep breathing
11. Create a figure 8 with you as the center point
12. Fill your body with Light/Energy
13. Exhale the extra energy around you as a ball of light and safety

Feel your connection to the Earth and Sky. Let yourself be supported and nourished. Envision the radiant ball of light surrounding you & relax into it.

Heavenly Source

Heart of the Earth

©2019 Modern Medicine Lady LLC
www.EmpathicSafety.com

PROTECT: The Earth-Sky Meditation

I've developed and worked with this meditation for over 30 years. It is my primary exercise for strengthening filters and shields. Once you become proficient with the Earth-Sky meditation you'll be able to establish it very quickly. Doing this exercise frequently reinforces its protective power. You can read it to yourself, have someone read it to you, record and listen to it, or check the Resources section for a link to access my audio recording. I suggest you read through the entire meditation first, then proceed whichever way works best for you.

Earth-Sky Meditation

Get comfortable. Begin by breathing in calmness and relaxation and breathing out any distractions or concerns. Inhale ease. Exhale stress.

As you continue to breathe calm and presence into your body, become aware of the power of the Earth below you. Feel your body firmly supported as you sit or lie comfortably. Send your awareness through the floor, down into the ground, further and further down, until you reach the very heart of the Earth. Keep breathing.

Take a few moments to check in with the heart of the Earth. Let the Earth know what's going on for you and, when you're ready, ask for the support you need.

Begin to draw that support to you by inhaling and drawing the energy up to you. Breathe it up from the very heart of the Earth. Breathe it up through the ground. Breathe it up through the floor. Breathe it up through your feet, through your ankles, your shins, and your calves. Continue to breathe it into your knees and through your thighs, into your buttocks and hips, up through your root and into your belly and lower back. Let the energy of the Earth travel up your spine, through your trunk, your chest, lungs, and heart. Breathe it into your arms and hands. Breathe it up through your shoulders, into your neck and your throat, through your face and your head.

As you continue to breathe, send the energy of the Earth out your crown and through the space above you. Send it out through the roof, through the sky above and beyond you, past the atmosphere of our planet. Send it up and out to the stars, all the way out to the very Source, the Divine brilliance, intelligence, and wisdom of the All. Keep breathing.

Take a few moments to check in with the Divine wisdom of Sky. Let Source know what's going on for you and, when you're ready, ask for what you need.

Begin to breathe it down to you. Inhale and draw the energy of Source down past the stars, to our planet, through the sky, through the clouds, through the roof above you, into your space. Breathe the light and energy down through the crown of your head, so bright that you can see it travelling past your eyes, your face, your neck, and your throat. Continue to breathe, letting it shower down through your chest and lungs, your belly and lower back, down through your hips, buttocks, and thighs. Let it pour down through your arms and hands. Let it fill your thighs, knees, shins, and calves, down into your ankles, your feet. Continue to breathe, sending the energy of Sky down through the floor and into the ground, traveling into the very heart of the Earth.

Feel the energy of Earth rising up through you and extending to the Sky. Feel the energy of the Sky pouring down through you to the very core of the Earth. *You are the center of a perfect circuit.* The energy of the Earth rises up through you and touches the Sky, and the energy of the Sky pours down through you and touches the Earth. Breathe this energy into your very core and, as you exhale, let it expand to fill your entire body. Breathe in this energy and support, and let it fill your heart with light. Let this light radiate from your heart in all directions. Let it expand until you are a radiant star, centered between Earth and Sky.

As you continue to breathe, radiating Earth-Sky energy in all directions, envision yourself enveloped in a cocoon of light, a dense, sparkling filter of energy and safety. Inhale to fill yourself with light, then exhale and strengthen this sphere of safe, sacred space, this solidly fortified filter of energy all around you.

Use your breath to surround your newly fortified filter, now strengthening and reinforcing your outermost shield with smooth, flexible, protective energy. This powerful bubble of light and safety allows you to attract what you want and need and to deflect the rest.

Consider what you want your shield to welcome in at this time. Consider the qualities you wish to live with right now. Imagine a word or symbol that represents those qualities. Create the intention that your shield attracts and accepts only your highest and greatest good from now on. Know that your shield is now calibrated to attract and accept only the energy you truly need and desire.

The energy of the Earth supports and nourishes you. The light of the Sky guides and protects you. Anything that does not serve you simply flows around you. Inhale the energy of support and wisdom, light and guidance. Exhale and reinforce the filters and shields around you.

From now on, whenever you need support, you need only think of your connection to the Earth and breathe it up and into you. Whenever you need divine guidance, breathe the light down and into you. *It is as simple as one breath.* Breathe in to receive the support you need. Breathe out to fortify the filter and shield around you.

Add-ons:

- ✹ In addition to the bubble of light formed in the meditation above, you can also create a layer of mirror to cover the surface of your shield, so whatever comes at you will be deflected. I imagine it like the Batmobile: a set of mirrored scales that act like armor and snap into place all around me, a shiny set of mirrors deflecting all negativity. You can also imagine it as a smooth, highly reflective skin coating the surface of your protective egg. As always, use whatever image works best for you.

- ✹ You can also drop a cloak of invisibility over yourself, but the cloak of invisibility isn't really effective if you haven't built up your shields or developed strong filters. You might wear a cloak of invisibility, but you'll still be receiving and absorbing everything around you.

- ✹ Visualize a sign or pattern on your energy shield so the people you wish to recognize you will be attracted to you. That way, your tribe can still find you and identify you as kin.

PROTECT: The Rock in the Stream

I call this technique "the Rock in the Stream." As we establish our energy body and replenish our core of light and the protective filter and shield around it, we can imagine we are like a rock in a stream. Just as water simply flows around a rock, we can allow energy to simply flow around us. As something comes towards us, we can take note and envision diverting it to either side. I first discovered this tool thanks to a friend who was experimenting with techniques for the spiritual warrior. He taught me how to assume horse stance and to use my breath and intention to deflect negativity being directed at me. In his class we'd practice "shooting" balls of energy at each other and, as the blast came toward us, using our hands and arms to deflect it. I realized a few things from this. First, I could actually sense what was coming towards me. Second, even if I moved slowly, I could deflect it. Third, staying relaxed and calm was the key to navigating this.

There's something quite powerful about recognizing you're in a chaotic situation, taking a moment to breathe, and then reinforcing your filters and shields to strengthen your feeling of protection. As you breathe and imagine everything rolling off you, you can declare, "I am a Being of Light. I am safe and protected. This chaos simply flows around me." You can then ask yourself, "Do I really need to be here? Do I really want to be here? Is this any reason I'm obliged to stay here and keep doing this?" At the core of martial arts teaching is the concept that it's better to avoid an actual fight in the first place.

Once you recognize that you're in a turbulent environment, you can choose to just get the hell out of there at any time. If it's happening in your own space, consider what you need to do to turn down the volume. Ask yourself, "Am I doing anything to contribute to this situation? How is this pushing my buttons? Is this really worth my time and energy?" Certainly there will be times when other people are responsible for creating the drama and you're powerless to change their behavior. Walking away is frequently the most effective line of defense. This could mean literally exiting the space or simply disengaging mentally and emotionally.

Now, I will add one caveat: this is NOT about conflict avoidance. Detaching from drama and negativity and/or cutting it off at the pass is different from acquiescing or remaining silent instead of sticking up for yourself, setting boundaries, and standing firm in your truth. There will be times when the best resort is calmly pushing back. So in any challenging situation, consider, "Is this fight worth it? Is this a hill I am prepared to die on?" Fighting back is always the choice of last resort. Again, as the martial arts teach us, the best protection lies in our ability not to engage in the first place. A variation of this is preemptive protection.

I love the scene in *Star Wars IV*, the first *Star Wars* episode, when Obi-Wan Kenobi and Luke Skywalker are stopped by Stormtroopers. Obi-Wan looks directly at the guards and informs them, "These aren't the droids you're looking for." He instructs the Stormtroopers exactly how to respond. Like the Jedi Master, you can meet a situation with the clear intention of letting people know, "This is the way it is." You have the ability to protect yourself by defining your terms and holding true to them. This approach works best when delivered from a place of calm, assertive confidence and ease. There is no strain, no concern. Part of your mind is already on the other side of the resolved situation.

When we have learned how to cultivate calm within ourselves, when we don't lose our head or go into a fight-or-flight panic, we have the ability to flow with what comes at us. As we continue to release emotional triggers and strengthen our light, we can take things that might have devastated us in the past in our stride. Our capacity to manage stress correlates directly with our ability to avoid being triggered by it. As the saying goes: "Don't sweat the small stuff. . . *and it's all small stuff.*"

Rock in The Stream

1. Ground & Center
2. Inhale Earth Connection Up
3. Exhale to Sky
4. Inhale Sky Connection Down
5. Exhale to Earth
6. Exhale Ball of Light
7. Exhale Smooth Crystaline Shield
8. Let Everything Flow Around You

Heavenly Source

Negativity & Other People's Stuff

Energy of the Earth

PROTECT: Using an Anchor Phrase

Back in the early '90s, I watched an American variation of the French film *La Femme Nikita* called *Point of No Return*, starring Bridget Fonda and Anne Bancroft. One particular scene has stuck with me all these years. When Bancroft's character meets Fonda's, she teaches her to use a casual phrase during times of great stress: "I never did mind about the little things..." This statement becomes an anchor phrase for Fonda. Anytime she encounters a stressful situation, she says these words to defuse her anxiety and take a moment to hit reset.

One of my mentors later taught me how to use anchor phrases for negotiations and stressful conversations. Whenever it felt like I was drifting away from calmness and clarity, I could use an anchoring statement that fit the situation. This allowed me to collect my thoughts and remember what was really important. Using an anchor phrase is great any time you need to regroup. It can be as simple as declaring to yourself that whenever you say X (your phrase), you are directing your mind, body, and heart to relax and release the stress.

Here are some examples of anchor phrases:

- "I never sweat the small stuff."
- "I never did mind about the little things."
- "It's no big deal."
- "Whatever."
- "It's all good."
- "I'm sure there's a perfectly good reason for this."
- "Not my circus, not my monkeys."
- "Fuck it."
- "Don't give up before the miracle happens."

- ✹ "I'm sure there's an even better solution."
- ✹ "I'm open to finding something that works for all of us."
- ✹ "I'm ready to see this from a new perspective."
- ✹ "Someday I'll understand this in a whole new way."
- ✹ "I trust the Universe is unfolding as it should."
- ✹ "I've got this."
- ✹ "Breathe."
- ✹ "It's okay, I'm okay."
- ✹ "Relax."
- ✹ "This too shall pass."

You can use any grounding and calming phrase that works for you. An even more effective way to lock in this program is by tapping while you say the following to yourself:

Side of the Hand: "Even though there may be times when I feel stressed or anxious, I'm okay. From now on, whenever I say (your chosen anchor phrase) I'm signaling my mind, my body, my nervous system, my emotions, and my soul to relax and release any worry or stress I've taken on, and to focus on what really matters to me, which is: (positive quality such as love, kindness, compassion, calmness, understanding, tolerance, etc.). (Anchor phrase) reminds me that I'm a beloved child of this Universe and (positive quality) is the real truth." *Repeat 3 times.*

Top of the Head: "From now on when I say (anchor phrase), I give myself permission to release any anxiety, concerns, or stress and replace it with (positive quality)."

Eyebrow: "Anytime I say or even think (anchor phrase), it's safe for me to relax and return to (positive quality)."

Side of the Eye: "When I notice I'm feeling stressed, anxious, distracted, or out of sorts in any way, I can simply think or say (anchor phrase) to release and shift to (positive quality)."

Under Eye: "I now direct my subconscious mind to respond whenever I say (anchor phrase) and clear and heal any negativity or patterns of imbalance that would keep me from my best and highest self."

Under Nose: "From this day forward, each and every time I think or say (anchor phrase) I give myself permission to relax, to breathe, and to let go of any tension or worry and return to a state of (positive quality)."

Chin Point: "(Anchor phrase) will now direct my Higher Self to restore my awareness of (positive quality) and fill me with (positive quality)."

Collar Bone: "Every time I say (anchor phrase), I relax and return to (positive quality)."

Under Arm: "I simply think or say (anchor phrase) and my body, mind, heart, and soul return to (positive quality)."

TH: "(Anchor phrase) mirrors the truth that I'm a beloved child of this Universe and that (positive quality) is the thing that really matters."

Deep breath.

Another deep breath. "And SO it is!"

What phrase will you choose? What positive quality to you want to welcome in place of stress?

PROTECT: Spiritual Protection

The final level of *Protection* is spiritual protection. This is about inviting in Divine Presence, angels, ancestors, spirit guides, animal totems, Elementals of Earth, Air, Fire, and Water, and other beneficent helpers. There are additional beings such as devas (spirits of the plant and mineral kingdoms), fairies, mermaids, dragons and other mythical creatures. Spiritual protection can come from any energetic or spiritual force that you wish to call on for extraordinary support and help. This aid will act as an additional layer of protection beyond your own energy system. If you're feeling the need for extra protection, you might invite and envision dragons or angels to surround you and keep you safe and out of harm's way. Now, I need to mention that whenever you invite anything other than Divine Presence itself -- such as ancestors or spirit guides -- it's important to hold the intention that everyone and everything may only come for the highest good. *Insist that all who enter must come good and clean.*

This level of spiritual protection works as a barrier and/or guardian to prevent negativity from reaching us. It keeps us on the path of sweetness and grace. It prevents us from slipping into areas of trouble and misalignment. In the next chapter we'll explore a level of protection that goes beyond even this, as we develop and strengthen our connection with the Divine both within and without us. Eventually we can become so filled with Holy Radiance that we maintain a steady alignment with goodness.

PROTECT: Protecting Yourself in Public Places

Aside from just avoiding hectic, crowded, or chaotic places, the best way to protect yourself in a public space is by entering it with your filters and shields reinforced and fully engaged.

Before you decide to go to an event, assess whether you've got the spoons for it. If you're already overly stressed or exhausted, don't go. You have the right to say no. If you find yourself in a social situation you're obligated to attend -- like the graduation of your sister's kid or a family wedding or funeral -- but you're tired and emotionally drained, make time for self-care *in advance*. Tap on any stress you anticipate. Start taking Rescue Remedy a couple of days ahead. Drink lots of water. Wear your superhero outfit. Consider wearing layers of clothing, using the outermost layer as your shield. Put on protective jewelry. Carry protective stones in your pockets or bra. Wear comfortable shoes that feel grounding to you. Wear soothing essential oils. Bring along your Rescue Remedy and/or other appropriate flower essences, drink plenty of water, and have an exit plan. Before you enter the space, do some tapping for calmness and breathe in your connection to Earth, Sky, and Divine support.

Then go into the event with your filters and shields up. Pay attention to how you're feeling and every few minutes pause to evaluate what you need. Take a break every time you start to feel depleted. Leave when you need to.

When you're headed into a crowded area like a convention center, concert venue, or busy city, it's essential to avoid getting energetically overwhelmed. Thoroughly shield *before you arrive* instead of waiting till you get there. This is something that many of us learn the hard way. We show up and then realize we forgot to prepare and we're bowled over by the intensity.

Sometimes we'll remember to put up our shields, but the energy is so high that our normal filters aren't adequate and we have to fortify them. In these cases, the fastest way to shift is to go outside and stand in nature. When you notice the energy is really intense, take a moment or two and separate yourself from it. Go and put your feet firmly on the ground. If you can, go over to a tree, touch it, and let the extra energy you've absorbed drain off through the tree into the ground. If you can't find a suitable tree, simply put your hands on the ground and let that shit go. Then go into the bathroom. Go to the toilet and siphon off all the extra energy as you urinate. Wash your hands thoroughly and let everything rinse down the drain. Inhale calm and peace, exhale tension and stress. Take the time you need to release what doesn't serve you.

Once you've let the extra stuff go, return to your breath and breathe light into your heart and let it expand to fill your whole body. Breath is the vehicle for controlling and mastering your energy body. Until you learn to breathe consciously, your effectiveness will be limited. Breath is at the core of everything else. Use your exhale to release excess energy when you notice you're feeling overstimulated. Inhale the qualities you need, exhale what does not serve you.

A few years ago I attended a Foo Fighters concert at Fenway Park in Boston. When we arrived, the Mighty Mighty Bosstones (a local ska band with a massive horn section) were playing *really* loudly. I panicked. The sound mix was tinny, distorted, and unbearably noisy. For some reason I'd forgotten to bring my Rescue Remedy or earplugs. On the verge of totally losing it, I sat down in the midst of the chaos and breathed. I froze out the world around me and took a moment to tap. First I acknowledged that I was really, really agitated and uncomfortable. By accepting this, I allowed myself to calm down. I kept breathing and eventually succeeded in reinforcing my shields. Fortunately, we had arrived for the very last song of the opening act and once the Foo Fighters came on the sound was mixed to perfection. This experience reminded me yet again how crucial it is to be prepared. Even when I forget my physical bag of tricks, I can still use tapping and my breath to turn an overwhelming situation around.

All of us occasionally find ourselves in a loud, crowded space where leaving isn't a viable option, times when we're in the thick of it and need to calm and center immediately so we can be 'on' right away. When you need to recalibrate in the midst of a crowd, it can help to return to an anchoring phrase, mantra, or affirmation that helps you to ground and to restore your focus.

My husband and I have a system: he asks me, "What's the bottom line?" and I say, "God." Then he asks, "What do you do?" and I reply, "Breathe." That will usually bring me back. Breathing brings me back.

PROTECT: Sensory Overload

When you're hitting the wall and maxing out, avoiding media, extra noise, and other sources of overstimulation can make a substantial difference. Most people tend to have one or two dominant senses, but empaths can pick up information from multiple senses – even senses that have yet to be defined or quantified by modern science. On top of that, empaths may not only experience information via their own sensory awareness, they may also receive information from the dominant senses of others.

Empaths can get information through whatever sensory system is being triggered by whatever is going on in the world around them. So for example, even if you're primarily a visual person, when you're around an extremely auditory or kinesthetic person, you may get information through their sensory processing systems as well as your own. We do not just imagine or sympathize with what others are feeling -- we experience it. We pick up signals coming from somebody else and transmit them; we are the antenna, the receiver, and the speaker, which is why we tend to become so easily overloaded and prone to sensory processing issues.

Protecting Yourself in Your Own Home

Sometimes you need to protect yourself from discordant energies in your own home. There are a number of factors that can contribute to this:

❀ The physical environment, which includes how your space is organized, all the objects in it, and any pollutants (including chemicals of any sort, dust, mold, or pollen).

❀ The emotional environment, which includes every living being who dwells in or visits your space, the overall mental and emotional state they broadcast, and the interrelations between all inhabitants.

❀ The spiritual environment, including the overall vibration, Divine Presence, and positive guides and spirits, as well as negative entities.

With all of these factors, the first step to a safer, calmer space is to address and eliminate the problems you discover. Of the factors mentioned above, the emotional environment can be the most challenging because you can't just eliminate a family member who is disruptive and chaotic. The only person you can change is yourself and the only way to shift the relationship dynamic is by addressing it within you (other sections of this book are devoted specifically to this issue). Fortunately, when you change a space, it often changes everyone within the space as well.

Purifying and protecting a space has five components:

1. Declutter and eliminate objects that have negative associations for you.
2. Physically tidy and clean your space.
3. Break up and clear congested energy in your space.

4. Invoke protective guardians and place objects that deflect negativity and enhance harmony, peace, and sweetness.

5. Bless and recharge your space with positive intention and energy.

If your physical space is disorganized and cluttered, then decluttering is the place to begin creating balance and safety in your home. Your own comfort-to-discomfort ratio will determine how tidy you need your space to be. Pay attention to anything that nags at you every time you consider it.

Assuming your space is now physically tidy and clean, let's also imagine that you've taken inventory and removed the objects which are no longer serving you. You can probably feel a difference already. However, there can often be some lingering, congested energy from accumulated emotions, thoughts, or even spirits or ghosts.

There are a number of approaches for decongesting a space that is thick with unpleasant energy. You can use:

⊕ Sound

⊕ Scent and smoke

⊕ Movement and air flow

⊕ Water

⊕ Intention and visualization

You can use one method or multiple approaches. It is especially effective to use techniques that involve multiple senses, as any process that integrates different levels of awareness is more deeply experienced and anchored. It's generally considered most effective to move counterclockwise, as this is considered the direction of unwinding, whereas clockwise is associated with winding up and building up energy.

More crucial than your choice of specific cleansing method is your mindset -- your *intention and visualization* of what you are doing as you move through the space. Use your imagination to "see" the icky negative energy and where it is stuck in your space, then imagine it breaking up and moving away.

As you gather the energy, visualize that you are moving it around the room as if it is debris you're sweeping away with a broom. If there is a door leading outside, it's best to actually sweep or fan the energy right out the door and past your entryway. If sending it outside through a door is not possible, then open a window and send it out that way.

After you've taken the time to purify and decongest your space, it's time to install guardians and wards to protect it going forward. For the physical space, I like to place stones and crystals in a grid pattern that incorporates my entire home. I put pieces in every corner of my house, as well as against the shelves and window sills. Imagine that each crystal generates a ball of energy which forms connecting lines with the others. You can also use orgonite and mirrors to help shield and alter the energy of your home.

On the energetic and spiritual level, I invoke and welcome not only the four directions and Elements to protect and bless my space, but also the guardians of the land, benevolent beings of the plant and mineral kingdoms, and forces for good including angels and protective mythological creatures like phoenixes, dragons, and griffins, to name but a few. There is no wrong way to do this! Your intention is the most important part. You can use invocations written by others, you can create your own, or you can be totally spontaneous and just follow your gut. The best way to do this is to simply follow your intuition and imagination. Most of all, have fun!

Once you've invoked spiritual protection for your home, the final step is to bless and sweeten it. This is when you bring out the sweet-sounding singing bowls, the fragrant incenses, sweet water to sprinkle everywhere, colored lights, lovely new decorations, pleasant music, and essential oil blends to contribute to peace and harmony.

PROTECT: Protection from Difficult People

Empaths tend to have their care dials turned up to eleven constantly. Ordinary humans have a greater capacity to detach when a situation doesn't apply to them. While I'm not telling you to become a selfish jerk who doesn't give a damn about anyone but yourself, there's a lot to be said for putting care in the proper perspective. Not all needs or demands for your attention and time are equal.

It helps to distinguish between people who'll puke their emotional vomit anywhere and those sincerely seeking support so they can shift. There's a difference between venting to let something go and chronic complaining. Expressing the hard stuff in order to clear it is an important part of the healing process, but getting stuck in a tape loop of non-stop negativity just digs deeper grooves into neural pathways and reinforces habitual thought patterns.

When I gave my undivided attention to every single person I encountered every single day, I wasted precious resources on circumstances that did not warrant that level of care. Not only did this leave me feeling depleted and emotionally exhausted, it also caused me to be chronically late, putting off my own work and projects to meet the needs of others.

Just as certain people lack empathy to the extent that they're incapable of recognizing extreme pain and suffering in others, empaths often lack modulation or distinction between true crisis, exaggerated drama, and minor distress. When we are constantly bombarded with other people's energy and pain, everything becomes loud and starts to feel like an emergency. Every encounter seems as sincere as the next.

Whether someone just broke their favorite mug or a child died suddenly, empaths will pour their hearts into offering the same degree of comfort. One of our challenges is that caring for others is often deeply rooted in our identity. Changing this behavior means we must become willing to re-evaluate the ways in which unconditional care and consideration actually serve *us* as well as the people we comfort.

I used to feel I owed my genuine focus and time to anyone who struck up a conversation with me. I'd often find myself feeling resentful as I politely listened to someone vent after cornering me at a social event. Giving myself permission to stop caring and not engage has been a game-changer for me. When I realized it was okay to triage my support and save my energy for situations and people who really needed it, I stopped feeling overwhelmed, overbooked, and drained.

At this point, before I engage with anyone I pause to ask myself the questions, "Is this really mine to care for? Do I have the resources to commit to this? Is this really as serious or important as I'm imagining? Has this person actually asked for my help and, if so, am I really the best one to offer it?" I invite you to notice where you are giving away your time and energy.

It's really okay to go through the motions and say, "Isn't that interesting? Wow, that sounds so complicated," while only part of you is the least bit interested. You don't always have to give 100 percent, especially where you know that you don't have an emotional investment. Give yourself permission *not* to give away the farm when you don't owe it.

There's a certain person I know who's a particularly challenging character. You might say they're an energy vampire; definitely a drama queen. They have no ability to read social cues. They're a close talker. They take anyone who'll listen hostage and spend hours sharing inappropriate, intimate details of their life. Not only do they constantly complain about everything, they have no insight about their own part in any of their issues and have no interest in accepting feedback or solutions. Their life remains the same escalating shit show it's been for the last twenty years. While I do not spend a lot of time with them anymore, there are rare occasions when we must attend the same event. Admitting to myself what a drain they are was my first step to establishing distance.

Shortly after this realization, we were both invited to a party. Before the date, I made a bracelet (mala) of rose quartz beads. My intention was to have a talisman to support me while dealing with this person. On the day of the party I wore it on my wrist. When they approached me I discreetly pulled the beads up to my fingers and repeated an anchoring affirmation in my mind as they launched into their drama. Whenever I noticed myself hitting a wall with them or starting to think, "Oh my God, you're driving me frickin' crazy," I just breathed in silence as they went on and on. I held my mala bracelet and worked the beads through my fingers. I repeated prayers, offered blessings to them, and focused on my breath while inhaling peace.

This helped me to create a degree of insulation between us that diminished a long-standing dysfunctional connection. Interestingly, this relationship has changed substantially since I made that bracelet; that event was the last time they cornered me in a conversation. By working my mala bracelet, I changed how I engaged with them. It prevented our customary exchange of energy and provided the wedge I needed to separate empathically. I ceased to be a source of nourishment, so they quickly stopped turning to me as one their go-to people.

When you're dealing with people who are complainers or narcissists, it can be incredibly helpful simply to say things like, "Wow, that really sucks. That sounds so difficult. Gee, that sounds really challenging for you. I can't imagine what I'd do in your situation. I hope you find what you need." You can say such things without being snarky about it. Acknowledge, but do not engage emotionally.

When dealing with someone who never stops talking about how much their life sucks, this detached acknowledgment can be quite effective. Validate their feelings, but do not give them the emotional juice to keep the tape loop running. If someone isn't ready or willing to do anything about their problems, you can acknowledge and validate while simultaneously thinking, "let it go, not my problem, not my job." When you recognize that someone only wants to vent and express their discontent, reaffirm that it's not your job to fix it. Give yourself permission to withdraw your emotional energy from anything in which you have no actual investment.

Empaths have such an incredible sense of responsibility. Most of us have been conditioned to believe it's our responsibility to listen intently. Perhaps you worry that people will notice if you're not giving your all. The truth is, we notice subtleties that other people don't. You can show up with ten percent of you and most people can't tell that you're not 100 percent there. Even if they do, they may not actually care -- often they're just looking for a place to hear themselves speak.

You do not have to pour your heart and soul into helping someone who has no actual desire to change their life. Show up for the people who *deserve* you. Give your 99% to the ones who are giving their 99%. Let the others go.

PROTECT: Keeping It Together in a Crisis

How do you keep it together when someone else is losing their shit? What do you do when you are in the direct, physical vicinity of somebody who's really having a hard time? This is not a time to just "trust the Universe" or rely on the luck of the draw. You must plan ahead. When you'll be going into a setting that has the potential to be emotionally challenging, intense, or volatile, it's vital to prepare yourself. Before you enter such a space, *acknowledge* that it's going to be difficult. Don't trivialize or deny it. Recognize that this emotionally charged situation actually is emotionally charged.

You can acknowledge the other person's pain. You can hold the space for them without trying to fix them or becoming emotionally enmeshed. Hold love, calm, and soothing energy in your heart, mind, and body. Be still and stable. Your role is to detach with compassion so you can serve as a sturdy, solid anchor. As their distress comes toward you, let it deflect off your external shields and envision it sliding down and away from you. If you find yourself absorbing anything, breathe into your core, let yourself pull back emotionally, and then send whatever you've picked up all the way down into the earth beneath you.

Don't hold onto it. Don't process it. You already know what it is -- it's distress. You don't need any more information than that. You can just continue to send that energy down through you and let it release. If you wish, you can open your crown, third eye, and inner ears to your connection with Divine Source to transmit divine love and energy. Accept love and light into your body from your receptors for spirit. Breathe it into your core, into your heart. Radiate this back to the person or people in distress.

When processing information in a stressful situation, it's key to remain mindful of how you're feeling so you can recognize when you've hit your max. Be sure to take regular breaks. Go and use the bathroom. Drink plenty of water so you can flush out anything you've absorbed into your system. If the weather is good and you have the opportunity, go outdoors and take a walk. Check in with a friend. Text or call someone supportive. Step away for a break and notice how you're feeling; this way you can recognize whether you need to take more space or if you're okay to come back to the situation.

Now, in certain intense crisis situations you will have to be "on" for a while. In these cases, call for Divine Support. Invite your Higher Power, guardian angels, guides, or Holy Presence to come to your aid and get you through what you need to endure. Plan to take extra care of yourself when the time of crisis has passed. For the days or weeks after you've been depleted by something really intense, take time to replenish.

After being around others who've been through an ordeal, you may find that the experience triggers a period of your own grieving.

Honor the feelings that surface. When you have space for yourself, use it as an opportunity to do your own healing work and address what came up for you. Give yourself permission to make full use of the tools you now have at your disposal and *take good care of* you.

All the exercises I've discussed in this chapter are powerful and effective. However, if we leave a vacuum after we release the old gunk, we remain vulnerable to reabsorbing negativity. Filling that void with positive energy through a divine connection is the most powerful way to sustain this. This is what we'll address in the next chapter.

Chapter 7

Connect

Back in September of 2008, I was in Sedona, Arizona. The U.S. stock market had just crashed, and it was right before an uncertain presidential election between John McCain and Barack Obama. I was anxious about what might happen next. Before heading back East, we hired a guide to hike Cathedral Rock, which is considered one of Sedona's major energy vortexes. There are several of these sites in Sedona. Each of them is known to amplify the intentions and energy people bring with them. Whatever you're thinking, whatever you're processing, whatever you're doing, it's going to be strongly reinforced, enhanced, and magnified there. If distracted or thinking negative/chaotic thoughts, people can easily get injured or find themselves in strange situations, because the energy of these rock formations mirrors the stuff we carry around inside us like an echo chamber. Whatever is going on in your mind tends to get exaggerated.

I was aware of this effect when I went to the vortex. I thought, "Okay, I'm going to keep my thoughts pure, pure, pure, pure, pure." So as I hiked the red rocks, I prayed. I prayed a lot. I prayed for the best possible outcome for the election. I didn't pray for Obama to win. I didn't pray for McCain to win. I prayed for the best possible outcome for the benefit of the entire planet. I chanted, "Best possible outcome, best possible outcome, best possible outcome." I hiked for half an hour, maybe longer. When I got to the top of the ridge, the heart of the vortex, the locus of wisdom, I put my hands on the big red rocks and in my mind I said: "Hello."

In my mind I clearly heard them reply, "We mean you no disrespect, but please, allow yourself to be insignificant."

Then the Red Rocks showed me the vastness of time. They said, "We are young. We've been here far longer than you have, and we are still young. Look at how long it took us to build this valley. Look how long it took for these canyons to come into existence. Yet we are young.

There are other rocks and places on this Earth that are so much older than we are. We are but a blip in the Universe. Everything on this planet is but a blip in the Universe. Your idea that you are so significant, that everything you do as human beings is going to have so much impact -- we hate to break it to you, honey, but you're not even a split second in eternity. You're a nanosecond in the existence of time. And no matter what stupid shit you guys do, it's going to be okay. Because eternity is so much bigger than anything you can bring to this."

I took a deep breath and thought, "Oh. Okay."

I was able to let go and be. For that moment I could surrender and know, "I am nothing. I am an atom of stardust. I am nothing, and yet, I am everything." I felt such a deep sense of peace in this understanding. Eternity is so much bigger than anything we can conceive of, and no matter what we do, we will continue. Matter will continue. Life will continue. Existence will continue.

It was my capacity to connect with a wisdom and a sentient Presence far greater than myself that allowed me to find comfort and relief during a period when I was particularly concerned. Often to connect with a power greater than ourselves we must be willing to suspend our disbelief and be open to miraculous possibilities.

I'd originally included this story in an earlier chapter of this book, but I realized the idea that red rocks spoke directly to me might seem far-fetched if not utterly preposterous for anyone just starting to grapple with the ramifications of being a highly sensitive empath. I hope that by now you're recognizing the many ways you've been sensing and picking up information from the world around you for most of your life. For empaths few things are silent. When we take the time to pay attention, we receive the messages of Nature and Her wisdom. For me, Divine Connection starts here.

To me, God is all things and no things, within us and without us, no gender and all genders, ageless, timeless, and infinite. I use this and other words to convey a vast, infinite, mysterious, conscious force of which we are but a mere speck.

But beliefs vary widely. They range from Universal Love and the inclusivity of all faiths to This Is the Only Right Way To Do It

And We Have The Market On The One True God. A lot of rules can accompany religions. While such traditions can serve those round pegs who fit into the round holes perfectly, I've witnessed time and time again how hard it is for people who do not fit the parameters of what it means to be a "good (fill in the blank)."

There's a long history of persecution and violence done in the name of God, as well as countless incidents of sexual abuse and violations of power all over the religious world. Between the Inquisition, the Burning Times, the Nazi Holocaust, and the recent scandals in countless churches, temples, and ashrams, feelings of ambivalence, confusion, and doubt are pervasive. As a result, more people have strayed from conventional religions than perhaps ever before. This leaves what people in 12-step programs call a "God-shaped hole."

As a culture we are more distracted, addicted, and overwhelmed than ever before. How to find, much less sustain, a personal connection with the Divine frequently falls to the bottom of our ever-increasing list of priorities. The problem is, when we try to do everything under our *own* power, it's like running around on a battery pack -- there's only so much charge available to us before we run out of juice.

When we remember that we're part of something much greater than ourselves and plug into that sacred source, Earth energy, or however else you prefer to think of it, we have far greater resilience, vitality, and perspective available to us. This chapter serves as an invitation to plug into "something greater" no matter how you personally choose to define it.

I'm sure you've heard the saying, "Nature abhors a vacuum." In order to sustain lasting change, not only do you need to *Recognize, Release,* and *Protect*, you must change the energy and intention you carry within yourself. Instead of waiting passively for more negativity to flood you and sponging up whatever's going on around you in the meantime, you need to cultivate a new, positive vibration. You can start by considering the qualities you want to work with and how you really want to feel. This chapter is about learning to hold a positive intention, anchor a specific vibration, and invite and accept divine support.

You don't need to feel a connection or be aware of Divine Presence to begin asking for intervention and support. As a matter of fact, connection with God often starts by simply asking for help and experiencing ordinary (and not-so-ordinary) miracles as a result. Discovering that our Higher Power is listening and supporting us builds trust in this sacred relationship. Conscious connection with God feels like a direct, one-on-one visit. Prayer often feels one-sided, like sending a letter or leaving a voicemail -- you send your needs and wishes into what may feel like a void, then you wait for a response. Sometimes the answer comes right away, other times it can take a little while to get a reply.

For some of us, merely finding the willingness to pray is a hurdle. Whether you've been raised in a tradition that teaches that the Almighty is judgmental and punitive, or you grew up being told there's no God at all, it can feel pretty vulnerable to approach some new and unfamiliar Benevolent Force to share your hopes and concerns. Perhaps you were conditioned to believe that God has a rigid set of rules that you must obey or there will literally be Hell to pay; perhaps you were told there's no one at all to see or hear you so it's ultimately all up to you. Either way, the fear of being reproached or disappointed is understandable.

No matter your upbringing, I invite you to try asking for support and protection anyway. Just show up and tell it like it is. Try acting as if God/Goddess/The Universe is actually listening and genuinely cares about you. Make your request and then let it go. In the same way you relax once you've hit send, try making your petition and then surrender the outcome. When you pray, always keep your requests open-ended enough that the Universe can provide what is best for you. This may or may not result in receiving the specific details you think you want or need. Anytime I make a request to the Universe I affirm, "I welcome this or *something better*, whatever is perfectly aligned with my highest and greatest good."

Here's a prayer I use:

Mother Father God, Great Spirit, Divine Source,

As You are always of me and with me, it's my awareness of You that I pray for now.

I humbly request Your Divine Help, Guidance and Intervention.

Grant me the Grace to receive your Grace and please show me the Beauty Way.

Grant me the willingness to be willing to walk that way as it is revealed.

Let me be a channel for Your Peace, Your Love and Your Creativity.

Let me be a Source for Your Healing that I may be healed and be a healer.

Allow me to recognize each choice and action that leads me towards the highest & greatest good.

May I accept All Blessings and Help offered with grace.

May I relax knowing Your Holy Presence surrounds me.

Even when I'm distracted or forget this truth, I irrevocably welcome any and all support, healing, protection, and energy You offer, forever more.

For all the blessings I've received, am receiving, and will receive, thank you!

In faith, I am eternally yours.

Amen

Even if the prayer on the previous page is a stretch for you, I encourage you to change them to work for you and try it anyway. Often, shifting to greater faith starts by "acting as if." The bottom line is, there's nothing lost by asking, and you might just be pleasantly surprised when you do.

CONNECT: Your Connection is Unique To You

I'm of the belief that your connection to Spirit is deeply personal and intimate. How you approach your Higher Power is quite individual. You may find yourself comfortable with particular ways of approaching the Divine at different times in your life. As time passes, other paths may call to you. There is no "best" way to do this.

Some methods may seem more effective than others, but the notion that "there is only one right way to do this and if you don't do it this way, you can't be saved" simply isn't true. There are certainly people who will adamantly tell you otherwise, but whether you choose to agree with them or to follow the unique celestial spark within your heart is entirely up to you. I personally choose benevolence over damnation and eternal bliss over fire and brimstone. I believe the Universe is good, loving, and abundant.

If you have difficulty feeling like you're making a connection, then seriously: *fake it 'til you make it!* Pretend. Put the words in your mouth. If you're trying to connect and you can't see, hear, or feel anything, then start by creating answers you'd imagine your Higher Power would give you. Like the popular meme from the '90s, WWJD (What Would Jesus Do?), *make it up.*

Our imagination is often the vehicle through which divine inspiration comes! If we can't access it another way, our imagination can prime the pump and get things moving. Start by "acting as if" to begin forming that connection. From there, the connection will start to flow.

There are a number of ways that we can cultivate sacred connection. I have found that breath is one of the most powerful and consistent ways to fill myself with energy and a Power greater than myself. Conscious breathing enforces and sustains this connection.

You can use the Earth-Sky meditation from the previous chapter as a conscious breathing exercise to connect with God/dess. As you breathe the energy of the Earth up and the energy of the Sky down, there's a point at which you become filled with light. At that point you can begin to reach *beyond* the Earth-Sky connection and welcome Divine Source.

As you breathe, send out your call -- it can be like picking up a phone line to say, "Hey there, Higher Power, I welcome you and ask you to fill me with awareness of your presence and support."

Take this in on all levels. See it, hear it, smell it, taste it, touch it, feel it, move through it, think it. Draw it into yourself even further. Hold it in with your breath. Firm it up, make it strong, whole, and complete. Breathe it all the way in . . . and release it. Send it out to the Universe to be answered. Know that, from this time forward, every breath you take reinforces your wish. You don't even have to be paying attention. Every single time you breathe in, you reinforce the quality you wished for, strengthening and drawing it to you. Every single time you breathe out, it's sent further out into the Universe to be heard and answered. Once you get used to using your breath this way, you can make that divine connection nearly instantly. It gets easier each time you do it.

It's as simple as breathing.

CONNECT: Dealing with Non-Believers & The Righteous

I was really lucky. My mom left the Catholic Church before I was born and my dad was raised in a family of intellectual atheists who'd stepped away from their Southern Protestant heritage long before he was born. I consider myself lucky because I never had to reconcile my personal relationship with God with any conflicting religious laws telling me how I must behave to be considered acceptable in the eyes of the Lord. Ironically though, being raised by atheists has its own set of limitations. Believing in divinity *at all* meant I was jumping the fence and defying their social expectations. I grew up expecting to be challenged anytime I spoke about my paranormal experiences, my sense of wonder and magic in this world, and especially my perceptions of ghosts and the idea of an afterlife. But even as a young child, atheism rubbed me the wrong way. It felt contrary to my innate sense of magic, and of the divine force that surrounded me. I was poised between my own *felt* knowledge of Holy Presence and my extended family's message that everything unseen and unproven is hogwash and that religion is the "opiate of the (uninformed) masses."

For the first 15 years of my dating life I was attracted to atheists. Not only did they disagree with my worldview, they often criticized and ridiculed me for it. I know that this was my way of working out my family of origin issues; I was conditioned to be in relationship with people who denounced faith. I perpetuated this dynamic in my attempt to resolve the conflict within myself. As I grew into my faith and became ever more solid in my conviction, my attraction to such people subsided. I have spent enough time around fundamental atheists to testify that their convictions can be as unyielding and rigid as their evangelical counterparts. It was only when the pain of trying to adhere to their beliefs exceeded my fear of ostracism that I began my spiritual path in earnest.

My friend Alice was raised in a scripture-based, fundamentalist Christian church. As we've shared about our relationship with God, I've noticed that we both had to contend with crossing the rigid barriers of our respective traditions. While Alice had to navigate the message that she'd face eternal damnation should she stray from the righteous path, I faced the doubt, despair, and existential crisis of Infinite Oblivion. For either of us to step away from our family's rules posed the threat of alienation, even total abandonment. One of the hooks that keeps many of us attached to religious systems we don't agree with is our primary human need to belong. To remain a member of the tribe, we must accept the tribal rules and beliefs. Alice and I are not the only humans to struggle with this. What does it mean to outgrow these rules? What does it mean to follow our truth? How can we stand in our faith when facing others who disagree?

I choose to live outside the notions that, on one hand, we exist in a void and when we die we are nothing but dust, while on the other there is only One True Path and I've strayed from it. I figure that if the former is true, there's been nothing lost by living a life filled with joyous wonder and an imagined sense of divine connection, while if the latter is true, there will be plenty of opportunities to be of service in the fiery pits of Hell.

Fortunately, at this point in my life I'm unconcerned with either of these outcomes. I've experienced far too many remarkable and inexplicable things to believe in either Oblivion or Hell. Perhaps it's true that certain Christians go to a special place that excludes the rest of us, but if condemning gay people to Hell and teaching women to remain in abusive marriages is the ticket to this exclusive party, I'll gladly pass, thank you very much. As I sit outside writing, a hummingbird hovers in front of me, the late afternoon sun shines its lemon-yellow light on everything, the bees gather nectar from the budleja, rosa rugosa and hyssop, and I cannot deny my sense that Divine Force weaves this Universe together.

I have chosen to live my life with the core belief that God is Love and the Universe always strives for benevolence and health. Whatever defies this truth is a pattern of imbalance that seeks equilibrium.

I share the above because I know all too well how challenging it is to be around "non-believers." As we attempt to understand and navigate what it means to be an empath, encounters with others who cannot feel what we do -- and who insist that we can't feel that way either -- is especially difficult. We are extremely vulnerable to other people's opinions and judgments while we're still coming to terms with what we are. It really helps to have community and support from other empathic people. Having others who can validate our unusual experiences and normalize the things that set us apart is priceless. It allows us to grow into greater confidence and unflappable assurance in who we are. Eventually, we can simply think to ourselves, "I'm sorry you can't understand what I'm talking about. That's because you lack the abilities I have." It's important that *all* of us give ourselves permission to own who and what we are.

CONNECT: So What Does Connection Actually Feel Like?

A couple of years ago I recorded a *Word of the Day* video with my then nine-year-old fairy godchild. We talked about what it felt like to receive messages and how we knew when we were getting them. She explained that sometimes she suddenly just knew something, and other times she felt a little pinch. I explained that sometimes I, too, just know things, and other times I'll experience shivers running through my whole body. How do you know when you're connected? In the same way that every relationship with Higher Power is personal and unique, the ways in which we experience connection are likely to vary. Your experience will be influenced by your dominant ways of taking in information (whether you're a visual, auditory, or kinesthetic person), as well as your current emotional state (whether you're calm and focused or stressed and distracted).

My first experiences of the extraordinary were very physical. As a young child I'd have feelings of hopeful excitement, of wistful possibility. My awareness of the Force felt like butterflies in my stomach and wonderment in my mind. Images were sharper, sounds were clearer, smells were stronger, and my body felt electric. I experienced a sense of bubbling possibility. Unlike some, I did not see apparitions with my physical eyes, nor did I see colors in my mind as I do now. As an adolescent, my connection became primarily an internal emotional sense of something as yet nameless.

I'd started to explore the paranormal and meditation and really wanted to "see" energy.

I discovered candle gazing and would focus on altering the height and breadth of the flame (sometimes successfully, sometimes not). At this point I'd read enough to know what was possible, but my experiences felt "flat" in comparison to what I imagined could happen. Although I was highly sensitive, it took discipline and training to see and feel energy, to fill with divine presence the way I do today. I believe this was largely because it's easiest to access connection when we are calm and clear, and I was neither at that point in my life.

In my late teens and early twenties I started to explore metaphysics and spirituality in earnest. I remember two particular exercises I'd try with friends. In the first, we'd hover our hands over one another's and try to feel the energy coursing between us. I remember being pretty underwhelmed. I was so bogged down with anxiety and depression that I was too distracted to pick up much of anything. The second exercise proved more effective for me. A friend and I would soften our gazes and stare into each other's faces and as we'd stare, our faces would shift and change. I remember watching a seventeen-year-old girl's face transform into an old crone's and I sensed who she'd been in other lives. I always had an innate awareness that there was more, and even though I couldn't quite access it, I kept searching.

It was only when I began to sit in stillness that I was able to experience being filled with light. Over the years I've taken many workshops and classes, studied a great deal, and explored alone and with others to develop my abilities. Each piece has served as a building block for the next. The journey to awareness has been long and circuitous, with many a detour along the way.

I'm periodically asked, "How can I tell if it's Divine Source or something else? How can I stay safe when I'm inviting communion with Spirit?" For me, true divine presence lacks any static, manipulation, or force. It feels like unconditional, loving wisdom that wants what is best for me. Lesser entities usually have an agenda. They offer temptations and distractions. If you stop to ask whether this is truly for your highest and greatest good, you will know the answer.

Unfavorable spirits are kind of like potato chips -- they might look really yummy, but a part of you knows they just aren't good for you. This is why the previous keys of *Recognize, Release,* and *Protect* are so essential. The more conscious and clear we are, the easier it is to identify when something feels wrong. As you integrate the Earth-Sky meditation, you'll fortify your filters and shields and get in the habit of forming the specific intention to let only goodness in.

When you actively call on Spirit/God/Higher Power, it helps to dial the right number. Get explicit about who and what you want to invite. Make your intentions clear that this, *and only this,* is what you will allow. In addition, request perpetual divine intercession so that the angelic gatekeepers let in only what is best for you and yours.

CONNECT: *Good and Clean*

When it comes to working with spirits, ancestors, and non-divine spiritual helpers, it's important that you declare you'll only accept it if it comes *Good and Clean.* The author Luisah Teish wrote a book called *Jambalaya* in 1988, about the Yoruba Lucumi tradition. Luisah was the first spiritual teacher I ever met to explain that when you invoke Spirit -- even when you invoke the Divine -- it's imperative that you insist it come *Good and Clean.* You have the right to say, "Leave your baggage at the door. I'm only welcoming the good stuff. I welcome you to bring your blessings. I welcome you to bring your wisdom. I welcome you to bring love and kindness. I welcome you to come good and clean."

When I do any kind of deep work, I start with a prayer that any ego, assumptions, or issues that might come between me and Source -- as well as the person I'm working with or serving -- be cleared; that all negativity, distraction, or karmic debts be released, so we may do the work for the highest and greatest good. Then I say a prayer to set the intention to offer myself as a clear, open channel and ask again to release anything that would get in the way of doing this work for the highest and greatest good.

CONNECT: Divine Affirmations

In Chapter 5 I went into detail about how to work with tapping and affirmations. I spoke about how our negative reaction to a positive statement can offer valuable insight into the heart of an issue.

To review:

- ✺ Make an audacious statement.

- ✺ Pay attention to your reaction.

- ✺ Ask yourself: "What am I sensing? What am I feeling? What's happening for me?"

- ✺ Tap on any feelings or limiting beliefs that came up.

- ✺ Tap until you sense a positive statement you can agree with.

- ✺ Create an affirmation as an antidote (turnaround) to your issue.

There are many examples of acceptable affirmations in my Empathic Mastery Oracle. Every single one arrived near the end of a working session, as we reached understanding of a core issue. From that understanding, we created effective new statements to use as positive anchors.

In the beginning was the Word, and the Word was with God, and the Word was God.

—John 1:1

Words can be used to positively entrain our thoughts and feelings. They allow us to tap into the divine wisdom that lies beyond our conscious understanding. Language has the power to shift energy toward ease and health or distress and disease. The New Testament's Book of John literally tells us that "the Word was God." The word "Word" appears 1,123 times in the NRSV (New Revised Standard Version) Bible. More often than not, it refers to the *Word of God* or the *Word of the Lord*.

We humans can access not only spoken language but written words as well. While many other species on the planet have elaborate means of communication, the capacity to take our thoughts and ideas and convert them into symbols lasting well beyond our lifetime is unique to us. This is a powerful gift that we can use to achieve magnificent things, but it can also be used to inflict great harm. We can use our words to bless or to curse.

Don Miguel Ruiz speaks to this in his book, *The Four Agreements*. In the first agreement, "Be impeccable with your word," he explains in depth just how significant our words are and why it is imperative to choose them wisely. Ruiz tells us that what we say can either liberate or imprison us depending on the words we use.

Becoming mindful of your words is a process. This applies not only to the words you speak aloud, but also to the inner dialogues running in your mind, the triggering old tapes that repeat until you turn them off, the conversations you overhear from others, and the near-constant barrage of radio, television, and internet messages assaulting you throughout your waking hours. What if every single one of these words is influencing who and how you are? How many unconscious, random words are you exposed to every day that reinforce negativity and distress instead of goodness and health?

In his book, *The Hidden Messages in Water*, the scientist Masaru Emoto shares years of research showing how specific words and emotions impact the physical structure of water. Positive, life-affirming words generate beautiful, harmonious water crystals, while negative, harmful words distort and compromise their formation. When you consider that an adult human body is composed of roughly 60 percent water, it follows that the words we expose ourselves to either contribute to or diminish our wellbeing.

During the 20-plus years I've worked as a professional tattooer, I've always been extremely mindful about the images I put on people's bodies. I've approached this work as a healing art and offered what I call "tattoo medicine." My tattoo medicine tagline was, "Putting prayers on people's skin. Helping truth and beauty surface." I've been engraving affirmations that last a lifetime. I've witnessed firsthand how well-chosen images and words enhance and support thriving, while poorly placed, negative pieces reinforce discord. Bottom line: words, images, and intention matter. Choose your words with care because they will affect both you and those around you.

In my early years of working with affirmations, I tended to use them constantly. I would pick a series of statements (usually about prosperity) and repeat them over and over as I went for walks, drove my car, bathed or showered, swam laps at the Y, washed dishes, cooked, made art, and nearly everything else that didn't involve other people or words I needed to pay attention to. One of my favorite ways to do this was to sync each affirmation to a rhythm I would move or walk to. "I am safe — loved — and protect-ed in my body," is one that I still use to this day.

There are so many ways to work with affirmations to align with Spirit and improve your attitude. You can write them in a journal, post them on the walls and mirrors around your home, make them into beautiful art, cross stitch and frame them, write them on your body, speak them aloud, imagine them in your mind, sing them, chant them, tap as you repeat them. You can dance, walk, do yoga, or ride a bike as you recite them to yourself. The possibilities are limitless and, as long as the words feel good and aligned to you, there's no wrong way to do this. Here are a few examples of affirmations to prime that Divine Connection pump:

I am a being of light and love.

I am filled with Divine Radiance as I breathe in Holy Presence.

I am a clear channel for divine joy and delight.

I sense God's presence within me and without me.

I am light and joy. I am *Divine.*

I live in alignment with the perfect unfolding of the Universe. I turn my life and will over to the care of my Higher Power.

I am a precious, loving child of God/dess.

I move beyond any illusions or distractions and see the Divine Perfection in everything.

I am a pure channel for Divine Love.

I am an anchor for joy in this world.

I am guided by divine truth and bliss.

I am led on my perfect path every day through Divine Guidance.

I welcome my highest and greatest good.

I am a clean clear open channel of God/dess's abundance.

I live in joyous service to the Divine.

I am open and ready to receive divine support, prosperity and infinite riches now!

I am receiving the help, wealth, and abundance of the Universe today!

CONNECT: Using Your Strengths

As you cultivate connection with your Higher Power, it's helpful to recognize your sensory processing system and the primary ways information and connection tend to come to you. Many people receive information through their sense of smell, our most primal sense. We may not even be aware of all the information we pick up with every inhale. Most are ordinary scents, but we may occasionally experience phantom fragrances which seem to have no logical source; evocative, heavenly fragrances of which we suddenly catch a whiff. Some people are auditory people, whose information comes to them in the form of sounds, words, and language-based thought. Some are visual, experiencing connection through images, pictures, colors, and light, even through visual memories playing back in their minds like movies or flashes of old photographs. Some people are sensory; their experience is deeply embodied. A visceral, physical sensation can feel like surges of energy. Some people process through feelings; they receive information as an emotional quality in their hearts and minds. For people like this, divine connection is a heart-centered experience. Some people receive information through flavor. Some people's connection is kinesthetic, processed through movement. This goes beyond the sensation of touch and expands into their movement through space, the ways their bodies interact and engage with the world around them. We may receive and process information in any of these ways.

Pay attention to the ways you most often express yourself. Listen to your language and see what sensory words you use most often -- "I hear you," "I see you," "I feel," or "I think." I find that most empathic people experience connection through multiple senses. Generally, the more empathic we are, the more developed our senses are across the board. Sensitives pick things up through multiple channels simultaneously, absorbing information from diverse streams, pathways, and experiences. Empaths may also tap into the dominant sensory processes of whomever or whatever is in their proximity; we are such mirrors for other beings that we'll receive information through their dominant sensory awareness instead of our own.

It's important to be aware of this as you start cultivating your connection with the Divine. The way information comes through for you will be affected by your dominant means of receiving. As I've said before, there's no one right way to do this. The way it works for you will more than likely be different from the way it works for me.

CONNECT: Being the Beacon

The more you cultivate divine energy within yourself, the brighter a beacon for the Holy Spark you become. The deeper you anchor these practices within yourself, the greater your ability to shift the vibrations that constantly surround you. Instead of feeling like a perpetual psychic vacuum, you get to change the mechanism. Without tools or support, most empaths live in a state of perpetual absorption, but we can turn this around. Right now, as you read this book and work with this information, you're flipping the switch, becoming a beacon for divine light, radiating positive healing energy, and transmitting kindness, peace, and ease out to the world.

CONNECT: Transitioning to Deeper Breathing

You might not be accustomed to breathing as deeply as I encourage you to do in this work. Most of us learned to hold our breath as a coping mechanism very early in life. When we're scared or threatened, it's instinctive for us to momentarily stop breathing. By restricting our breath, we can dial back the intensity of our experience. This is a way to lock out consciously feeling things. The problem is, this is a really ineffective strategy because when we're not breathing, we freeze the mental and emotional intensity into our bodies. We create blockages in our energy flow which can eventually lead to chronic pain and illness.

I've been working with conscious breathing exercises for nearly half of my life. When I began training to become a transformational breath facilitator, I learned that most people do not know how to breathe correctly. Most of us have restrictive breath patterns of one kind or another. Because the larger culture can be profoundly stressful, nearly all of us have had early experiences that affected the way we breathe. It's absolutely normal to have some kind of restriction or pattern of imbalance with your breath. Unless you were raised by a yoga teacher who taught you how to breathe properly from the time you were an infant, chances are that the breathing modeled around you was restricted, shallow, and intermittent.

When you increase the volume of oxygen in your body, you start to feel more energy moving through your system than you're accustomed to. You may feel floaty and tingly. You may suddenly feel energy coursing through your hands and your feet. You may feel like your body has pins and needles. You may feel like you're made of Holy Fire. When I first started, I found deep, powerful breathwork not only emotionally evocative, but physically energizing. I often felt like I was plugged into an electric socket. I'd spent so much of my earlier life shallow breathing that when I started to breathe deeply and fully, my whole system was activated. Vitality flowed through me in a way I'd never experienced before.

As you work with conscious breath, your body develops greater capacity. When you breathe, you move energy through your body. As you begin exploring your breath, you'll discover how profound and remarkable something as simple as breathing can be. However, like any other new thing, it may feel odd or foreign at first. If you notice that things feel more intense than you are ready to deal with, slow your breathing and try massaging one of your favorite tapping points. You might use some tapping to help yourself ease into breathwork: "Even though it feels really intense to breathe this way, I am okay. I am safe. I'm all right."

As you begin breathing more deeply and consciously, it can feel as if things are starting to thaw and melt. Because it can feel so heady and intoxicating, people sometimes feel afraid they're going to pass out when they experience more oxygen than they're used to. It's similar to eating a rich dessert after living on bread and water -- it can be shocking to the system. The good news is that this too shall pass. The more you develop your capacity to breathe freely and deeply, the easier it gets.

As you continue to breathe into your connection with Divine Source, using this system gets easier and more automatic. In the same way riding a bicycle or driving a car becomes second nature, there comes a point when being in contact with your Higher Power simply is. At first the steps of *Recognize, Release, Protect and Connect* all require deliberate and conscious effort on your part. You must work on each concept and this can feel awkward or strained. Where initially you may spend hours, days or even weeks working with each individual key, over time this process becomes seamlessly integrated. This is when we get to take everything to the next level, where we not only achieve empathic safety, but also start using our abilities to create a life we love. Taking action is the key and that is where we're going with the next and final chapter.

Chapter 8

In Conclusion: Act

"Words without Works is Dead."

— Just Dave,
my first magical teacher.

Ideas are great, but without sustained *Action* they wither on the vine. To maintain our sense of protection while functioning in the world as responsible empaths, we must adopt ethics and responsible ways of being.

We've spent the last seven chapters exploring the ramifications of being empathic and have learned to stop just trying to get by. We've gained tools and techniques to control our sensitivities and to become anchors for calm and healing instead.

I led you through the initial four-step process to achieve empathic safety. First, we learned to *Recognize* and discern what's going on. Second, we worked with *Releasing* and letting go of our internal refuse. After we cleared the channels so we weren't simply shellacking our old crap inside ourselves, we started building up filters and shields by practicing the Earth-Sky mediation. Once we balanced our energy and installed *Protection*, it was time to develop even stronger *Connections* with the Divine. We understood that when we fill ourselves with positivity, no room remains for the old negativity. We became more aware of how to connect with our Higher Power. We experienced what it's like to breathe into and become more aware of Spirit. We've covered a lot of material!

Hopefully, you've noticed shifts and experienced benefits from the work you've been doing. Now that you've learned this system, the question is, *how will you sustain it?* Now it's time to commit to doing what it takes to keep moving towards health and growth. This starts with intention.

You've reached the next step in achieving Empathic Mastery. As you continue to evolve in your relationship with yourself as an empath, I invite you to return to sections of this book as you need them. Keep a journal, review the questions, experiment with the tapping sequences, take notes, and try tapping for yourself. Keep returning to *Recognize, Release, Protect, Connect* & *Act*.

ACT: Empaths and Old Patterns

Most humans are programmed to react with fear, anger, and defensiveness. A lot of people function this way all the time. This means they say things that can push our buttons and trigger reactions in us. Ingrained behaviors can cause backslides. When we fall back into some of these old reactions, our reserves are weakened. All the work we've done to be safe and protected erodes. We find ourselves falling backwards into old behavior patterns such as people-pleasing, taking on other people's burdens, trying to fix things when no one has asked for our help, and feeling responsible for the pain and suffering around us. Preventing empathic spin-outs takes deliberate commitment to acting in a new way, changing how we engage with the world around us, and agreeing to live by a code of ethics that holds us accountable and responsible for our choices and actions.

After many years of trial and error, hitting numerous walls, and supporting my clients as they navigated their own journeys, I created The Responsible Empath's Code of Ethics. Assuming you've worked through the previous chapters, you now have tools to support and protect you as you move forward. The Code is about the lifestyle shifts that are necessary to sustain and support this new way of being. Whenever you notice yourself slipping or falling off the wagon, consider it an opportunity to review the basics in depth. Do whatever it takes to *Recognize, Release, Protect*, and then *Connect*.

Once you feel grounded and centered again, it's time to ask, "What do I need to notice about my choices and actions regarding this situation? Is there anything I could be doing in a better, healthier way?"

ACT: Living in a Safe Universe

What does living in this new way mean for us as empaths? I sincerely believe that our world is poised at a tipping point for global healing. Environmental, political, and social climates are heating up. Our literal and emotional glaciers are melting at breakneck speed. Each time it seems like we've seen the worst expression of human greed and cruelty, someone comes along and ups the ante. It can be hard to trust that the Universe is unfolding exactly as it should when there is so much pain, suffering, and distress swirling around us.

At this period in our planet's evolution there are undeniable atrocities, illnesses, and imbalances occurring everywhere. This leaves many of us contending with triggers, limiting beliefs, and ancestral legacies of pain and dysfunction. Such distress manifests as physical pain, illness, stress, feelings of overwhelm and anxiety, self-sabotaging behaviors, addiction, and procrastination, and that's just the tip of the iceberg. Without effective tools, we find ourselves spinning our wheels in the muck. I believe that the system I share in this book offers potent, practical tools to help transform emotional hot messes into calm, collected anchors for hope and wellbeing.

In order to sustain this sense of grace and ease, we need to remember the big picture and pull away from the petty details our ego wants us to focus on. Some days it's easier than others to remember this. When I get sucked into the flurry of social media distress and start reading everyone else's opinions about the most recent political controversy, it's easy for me to sink into doubt and despair. That's when I remember what the red rocks told me in Sedona: "We mean you no disrespect, but please allow yourself to be insignificant."

Instead of regarding myself as a separate being with a finite beginning and end, I recall that I am but one tiny cell in the body of the Universe and that my soul is but a drop in the Ocean of Consciousness. I can then relax into the infinite vastness of it all. I can remember that even if things do not go as I hope, even if there is pain and suffering, even if we are still unraveling generations of abuse, racism, sexism, oppression, and violence, that there is a fundamental urge to exist, to grow and thrive.

There is a primal force threaded through the fabric of all life. When I cultivate my relationship with the Divine and spend more time in conscious connection, praying, meditating, and being in this awareness, it is easier for me to trust that we live in a beneficent world that wants the best for all. When I drop my personal practice for too many days, watch too much television, or read too many angry, fearful, conflicting opinions, I'm vulnerable to slipping away from love and trust and plummeting into fear and doubt. It's both a choice and a discipline to regard the Universe as inherently good. It takes the willingness to do the personal work to stay in balance and to restore equilibrium when I do -- inevitably -- get thrown off-center. It takes cultivating the trust that, even when I fall, even when I forget, even when I doubt, even when I take the wrong path, in the grand scheme of Infinity, Life is resilient. Life is adaptable and Life prevails.

Now, while I sincerely believe that the Universe is on an inevitable trajectory towards love and wellness, we *can* influence the timeline. If we want to steer this planet in the right direction sooner rather than later, we need to take action now. It's *all hands on deck* for everyone ready and willing to show up and love this world better. I believe it comes down to this: when empaths are unprotected and overwhelmed, we amplify the pain and negativity we absorb. We can either be part of the problem, contributing to the chaos and stress in the world by making choices that keep us vulnerable, depleted, and excessively open, or we can be part of the solution. The good news is, when we commit to the work of staying calm and grounded, our energy weighs in on the healthy side of the scale. We become the anchors for peace and healing the Earth needs right now. We become beacons for light and love. We become clear channels for Divine Source. This means that we must live differently than we have before.

I believe that people like you and me are needed on this planet more than ever before. Because of our unique ability to sense and feel what others are experiencing, we can learn to use our gifts to diagnose and help others. We can become so finely tuned that our accuracy and effectiveness allow us to be magnificent healers, teachers, mentors, guides, leaders, collaborators, and makers. We can offer this planet gifts beyond quantifiable value. Imagine how it will feel to offer effective help in times of distress and suffering. Imagine creating deep and lasting shifts for yourself and those who seek your support. Imagine taking your work even further and developing skills that make you knowledgeable and effective for the mission you are called to serve. Imagine how committing to the techniques and concepts in this book will build your confidence, improve your life, and open opportunities, both personally and professionally.

In this book I have offered you principles, exercises, and tools I've honed over decades. I believe that mastering *Recognize, Release, Protect, Connect,* and *Act* is what it takes to live a safe, joyous, and satisfying life. As you continue to develop your empathic chops and this system becomes nearly effortless, the next volume awaits. Who do you want to be? How will you make a difference?

In case you are wondering where to go from here, I'd love to invite you to join me in taking the next step. We all know information is essential. However, with millions of videos uploaded online every day, and countless articles, blog posts and books providing more than we could digest in ten lifetimes, it's guidance and implementation we need for sustained, effective transformation. Therefore, to support empaths who want to take this work to the next level, I've created the Empathic Mastery Academy. You can learn more at EmpathicMasteryAcademy.com and sign up to be notified next time enrollment opens. The Academy offers interactive engagement, community, valuable tools and exercises all designed to help you integrate the material that we've gone over in this book AND to move beyond it.

ACT: The Responsible Empath's Code of Ethics

The following is a list of 20 principles and ethical agreements to let us live as responsible empaths instead of vulnerable empaths. When we agree to adhere to this code of ethics and behave accordingly, it helps us to maintain our sanity and perspective. These principles support our serenity and our ability to function more peacefully in the world. This is my personal code of ethics. I share it with you because it works for me. This is what I have hammered out of my personal experience. It's what I've come to believe. The ideas, opinions, and wording are strictly mine -- *take what you like and leave the rest.* I invite you to try it out for at least 30 days and see if it resonates for you.

Responsibility: Responsibility involves the agreement that every one of us has free will. Each of us is responsible for our own choices and actions. The only exception is that we may, under certain conditions, rescue or intervene on behalf of those who do not have free will or agency to act on their own behalf. This includes young children and, if we're first responders, people who are incapacitated by violence, accident, or disability. But for any freestanding adult, the bottom line is that *they* decide whether they're going to get with the program or not. It is not our job to fix them. It is not our job to repair them. We can offer support, but we cannot rescue them.

The Agreement: I acknowledge that every one of us has free will and is 100 percent responsible for their own choices and actions. Just as my own true growth only comes when I accept my responsibility for it, I support others in their own choices to grow. I can give love and energy, share my perspective, offer guidance, and then let go of the outcome. I rescue or intervene only for those who have no free will or agency to act on their own behalf.

Impeccability: If you've read *The Four Agreements* by Don Miguel Ruiz, you know that the first agreement is: "Be impeccable with your word." Don Miguel explains that to be impeccable with your word is about being clear and mindful with your intentions, energy and how you conduct yourself in all aspects of life. Ultimately it is the choice to persistently dwell in love and truth to the best of your ability. The way I look at it, when you make a decision, when you claim something, you must recognize your choice and own it completely. This is something of a growing process. There are times we are better able to recognize the full ramifications of our words and choices than others. Impeccability is about keeping our side of the street as clean as we possibly can; doing everything possible to stay as clear, as focused and as mindful of the purity of our actions and intentions as we can.

The Agreement: I engage in persistent vigilance of my thoughts, actions, and integrity. I uphold my clearest intention for the highest and greatest good. I choose to be impeccable with my words, goals, and deeds. I recognize that there is great power in my abilities and it is my duty to act with impeccability at all times.

Sobriety: I'm not talking about AA sobriety here, although that can be a part of this. I'm talking about the sobriety of a mind free from the intoxication of negativity, fear, or judgment, free from engagement with the things that throw us off. Maintaining sobriety includes the ability to recognize when we're intoxicated, identifying the things that take us out of centered clarity, and doing everything we can to shield ourselves from those things. Be rigorously honest with yourself about when you are not clear; when you have gone over the edge and fallen into mental, emotional, or spiritual intoxication. If you choose to party on any level -- if you choose to indulge in something that may affect your clarity -- do not attempt to do strategic, energetic, or intuitive work with others during that time.

The Agreement: I strive for purity of mind, body and spirit. I will remain vigilant for anything that causes physical, mental, emotional, or spiritual intoxication and I will avoid and abstain from it, unless I am truly "off duty." If or when I find myself under the influence, I agree to relinquish all responsibilities that would be affected by my state of being.

Health: Wellbeing starts with you. It starts with your ability to focus on your own health and on clearing up your own piece of the street. From there, you can help other people.

The Agreement: My own physical, mental, emotional, spiritual, karmic, and epigenetic health and recovery are the first priority for my soul. Only through willingness to do my own work, and through the rewards I gain through that work, am I truly able to serve anything or anyone else.

Permission: Use your abilities only when you have permission to use them. I regard this as a fundamental rule when working as an empath. We are allowed to be of service or to intervene only when we have acquired permission to do so. Again, the exceptions are children under the age of consent and adults who are incapable of responding. If you see a small child chasing a ball into the path of an oncoming truck, the Universe gives you permission to rescue that child. You don't need to hesitate; the Universe gives you permission to *Do The Right Thing.* But when it comes adults with free will, doing work on their behalf always begins with their consent.

The Agreement: I use my abilities, offer service, and intercede in situations only with explicit permission. *Just because I can* does not *mean I should.* I honor other people's privacy and mind my own business unless I am asked to do otherwise and/or my offer of help is accepted. Even though I may be able to examine others' thoughts and feelings, and even influence or control them mentally or emotionally, it is not appropriate for me to this without their permission.

Discernment: We have a natural tendency to respond to other people's discomfort. We've been taught not to let people cry or be upset, to try to ease their pain and, on occasion, to go so far as to stop them from feeling their feelings. When we sense that others are in pain, it sometimes triggers our own internal pain. Therefore, it's really important to check our true motivation for helping when someone else is in a state of distress. It's important to discern whether we're interceding not because the other person needs our help, but to soothe our own discomfort.

Part of discernment is knowing when a situation actually needs immediate action (once again, action is imperative when an innocent being without free agency needs intervention). If needed, take action and sort out the details later. If someone has just been wounded in a drive-by shooting, it is not appropriate to wonder, "Hmm, why were you just shot? Do you think it was something that happened to you when you were five?'" No. You put pressure on the wound to stop the bleeding, call 911, and get them to the hospital ASAP. If you do have the luxury of time, tune in, pray, and really ask yourself what your motives are. Check in with your Higher Power and ask, "What's my job here? What am I supposed to do?"

The Agreement: I will seek clarity and discernment before I act. I will always strive to determine what motivates my impulse. I will ask myself, "Am I responding from my own ego, emotional triggers, and/or desire to avoid discomfort and pain or am I responding for the Highest and Greatest Good?"

Purpose: It's okay to do your job and let others do theirs. You are not the only person doing this work. There will be somebody else to take up the slack when you need to stop. Trust that you are part of a great colony of others who are doing this work.

The Agreement: I accept my purpose and mission for this life. I agree to pursue the obligations and lessons on my soul's journey and do the work that is mine to do. I understand that I serve this planet best when I do my job exclusively. I acknowledge that if I try to assume anyone else's assignment unsolicited, I hinder another's purpose and I tamper with Divine Order. I choose to trust that there will always be another who can take up the slack when I have completed my tasks and need to pause and recharge.

Respect: Even when you don't think a person is where they ought to be on their path, as a responsible empath you must respect and honor wherever they are and have the willingness to let your opinion go. Have the humility to admit that, as a human being, you are limited. You don't know all the answers. There is a lot of information you simply don't have. It's entirely possible that whatever you think is the best possible outcome, isn't. Maybe there's something even better. It's really important to sit in the willingness to accept that you just don't know.

The Agreement: I respect every person's freedom of choice and personal will. Regardless of where someone is on their journey, I choose to accept them as they are and to remember that they are a child of this Universe worthy of respect and dignity. I respect their limitations, boundaries, and privacy, and will only go where I am invited and welcome.

Privacy: Empaths may know intimate details about other people's lives. *This is a privilege.* What you know should be regarded as sacred. Unless you have explicit permission to share a story, it's your job to protect it by keeping your silence.

The Agreement: I honor the privacy of every story or secret with which I have been entrusted. I recognize that it's a sacred privilege to be trusted and it is my responsibility to uphold this confidence. While I may mindfully share my own experience and any feelings that arise for me, I understand that it's imperative for me to protect all details and information which might compromise someone else's anonymity unless they have explicitly stated what can be revealed.

Acceptance: Acceptance does not mean acquiescence. It does not mean complacency, surrender, or just giving up. It means that we acknowledge what *is*. It is less effective to resist than to acknowledge what is and move forward.

The Agreement: I accept things as they are, even if I don't like them. I can acknowledge what is and accept that it is true for now. I recognize that my resistance to accepting what simply is only drains me and costs vital energy that I could be using to address and change it.

Consent: Just because somebody once told you that they were willing to let you work with them does not mean you have permission to do it in perpetuity. It's always about checking in and asking, "Does this feel comfortable to you? Can I work with you in this way? How is this for you?"

The Agreement: I will always seek consent before I probe, sense, explore, detect, serve, help, heal, support, touch, or intervene with anyone. I understand that consent is an ever-evolving process. I recognize that consent is only effective through continuous clarification and explicit agreement. I will establish a contract of ongoing communication with everyone I engage with. I will confirm their assent before I proceed with any additional actions.

Caution: This means going in confidently but carefully, with the awareness that you may need to adjust your course. Go in with the humility of knowing you might not be right. You may need to shift gears. Be mindful that if you offer information and somebody tells you that you're off, you need to adjust accordingly. You need to pay very close attention and listen for feedback so that if, for some reason, something is not as you expected it to be, you can adjust and work appropriately.

The Agreement: I will approach all encounters with caution and mindfulness. I will remain attentive to the impact of each action I take, pace myself, and correct my course accordingly as I proceed.

Care: As my friend Chase (founder of the Mommy Rebellion) always says, "Put your own fucking oxygen mask on first." We must take care of ourselves and be sure that we have sufficient fuel for this journey. We need to evaluate what we've got in the tank and work from a surplus. There will be emergency situations, times we need to tune in and ask God for *a lot* of help because we're comin' in on a wing and a prayer. This is inevitable over the course of a lifetime. Most of the time, however, there are enough other people around us to help out and pick up the slack. It's not our responsibility to sort out details when we're running on nothing but fumes.

*The Agreement:*I will uphold self-care to the highest standard. I will offer care from my surplus, after my own needs have been fulfilled. I will strive to recognize when I am depleted and to ask for help. I agree to step away from caregiving and let others take over until I have restored my own reserves.

Clarification: I have heard so many stories about people working with psychics, healers, tattoo artists, and other practitioners, in which the client says, "This is my truth, this is my experience, this is what's going on for me," and the "professional" looks at them and says, "Oh no. That's not true. That's not what you're really experiencing. I know what you're really experiencing, and this is what it is." Personally, I feel that that is the biggest load of shit. It also demonstrates incredible hubris. Never, ever say to anyone, "I'm right and you're wrong. I know your life experience better than you do." This work is about service and being in alignment with the highest and greatest good. It is not about proving that you can do some kind of parlor trick. Asking questions and clarifying whether you're on target is essential. It's a sign of your integrity and your willingness to be of service, not a sign of weakness. Clarify continuously.

The Agreement: I recognize that even though I have empathic abilities, I cannot know everything. Even when I think I know, it's best to clarify and confirm that what I suspect is accurate and true. I understand that anytime agreement is not found, it's best to adapt my approach rather than attempt to convince someone that I know best.

Curiosity: Instead of entering into a dialogue rigidly fixed on your own conclusion, choose to enter every exchange with the willingness to discover something you've never known before. Perhaps you'll have your mind changed or your perspective altered because somebody shares something different than you were expecting. The willingness to change starts with the willingness to be curious.

The Agreement: I choose to approach all situations with curious inquiry. I release judgement and premature conclusions. I recognize that true communion occurs with a willing heart and an open mind. I must be receptive to alternative perspectives if I want others to consider mine.

Surrender: Of all these principles, surrender is perhaps the most emotionally challenging. Instead of trying to micromanage every detail and fret over the "cursed hows," surrendering allows us to "let go and let God." It means we're willing to put our faith and trust ahead of our control and fear.

The Agreement: I surrender my agenda and expectations for myself and others. I acknowledge that this Universe is vaster and more mysterious than I could ever conceive within the limits of my human perception. Though I might desire a particular outcome, I open to possibilities beyond my wildest hopes and imaginings.

Reciprocity: This is a really big one for me personally, because as an empath, I was taught to just give and give and give and give and give. There is an irony in this: when we give and give without allowing others to return the favor, we actually disempower them. When you regard yourself as the only one in a position to offer, you automatically put the other person in the position of being ineffectual and weak. This is extremely invalidating. Holding people to the expectation that they can give something back is profoundly empowering. The ability to receive and to recognize the balance of reciprocity in the Universe is essential to thriving.

The Agreement: I affirm that the Universe is Balance. For every inhale there is an exhale, for every ebb there is a flow. I accept that I can only give as much as I am replenished, and all my exertion must have its corresponding rest. I acknowledge that for any transaction to be complete, there must be give and take. Whenever I give ceaselessly and block my acceptance of reciprocity, I deny the natural order of the Universe and dismiss the capacity of others to appreciate and thank me. In the same way that I am rewarded when another truly accepts and receives my gifts, I profoundly bless others with my grateful receptivity to what they offer me.

Release: This means taking responsibility for healing yourself and owning the continuous nature of your work. When you cook, you understand that just because you've cleaned something up, it doesn't mean that you're all done cleaning for the rest of your life. Life is like cooking. You're going to have to keep cleaning the pots and pans on an ongoing basis. That's just how it works.

The Agreement: I release the things which no longer serve me. Whenever I offer service, care, or engage with others, I will take time to let go of whatever I have taken on or has been triggered within me, that it may be shifted and healed.

Cleanliness: We need to maintain the willingness to purify ourselves on a regular basis. It's a necessity if we're to function well in this world.

The Agreement: I recognize that it is imperative that I maintain physical, mental, emotional, and spiritual hygiene at all times. I understand that as an empath I am vulnerable to picking up energy that affects my clarity. I can only be as effective as I am pure. Therefore, I agree to practice regular cleansing and purifying to be the clearest, most open channel I can be.

Trust: This is about our willingness to accept that Spirit is in charge, even when our minds are trying to tell us otherwise. We can choose to dwell in faith, that state of doing what we can do, taking action when we can, then turning the rest over to our Higher Power and letting go of the outcome.

The Agreement: I believe that I am but one among many who are here to serve our precious planet. I do my share and I let go of the rest. Divine Source is far greater than me, so I choose to surrender control and trust that the Universe is unfolding as it should.

ACT: The 7 Pledges of the Responsible Empath

As we come towards the end of this book, it's time to make some commitments. These are personal agreements designed to guide us to take care of ourselves and to understand what taking right action as an empath can be distilled down to. By committing to the 20 principles above and these seven pledges, we can avoid causing harm or reinforcing negativity and agitation. Instead, we can start focusing on the positive contributions we want to offer this world and be lasting agents for love and healing.

I pledge to make my own care and safety my first priority. I acknowledge that when I am stable and strong, I offer so much more than when I'm in a place of depletion.

As discussed, one of the empath's biggest challenges is that we feel the needs of the world around us. We so deeply sense what's going on inside other people that it's almost unbearable to be around their pain unless we have our filters and shields in place. It's absolutely natural for an empath to want to jump in and rescue others because it's so agonizing to feel their panic and urgency when we have nothing protecting us. Ironically, as long as we're susceptible to their panic, urgency, and pain, we only amplify those energies. If we're stressed while attempting to save others, we become caught in a feedback loop. We can't serve their greatest good because we're seeing things through their filters of fear and desperation. It is essential that we put on our own oxygen mask first if we're going to make a difference.

I pledge to be mindful of my triggers and my mental and emotional reactions. I will make every effort to own my feelings as they arise, and I will pause to explore what they're about before I jump to action or judgement.

Sometimes it's about other people, but sometimes it's really about us. Every so often, something deep in our core is triggered by the way another person is feeling. Like a guitar string resonating to a chord of the same frequency, we resonate to similar feelings within others. We may be entirely unaware of that emotional harmonic within us, but we are triggered nonetheless. When you feel something, it's important to take a moment to pause, breathe into it, and just wait. Take a beat to hold back before jumping into action, judgment, conclusion, or assumption. Sit with it and ask yourself, "What does this remind me of? What is this really about?" Over the course of this book, you've acquired a number of tools to help you do just that.

I pledge to keep the focus on my own work and my own process.

As long as we keep the focus on ourselves and hold our centers, we can support one another to amplify this work and achieve truly incredible growth. When we distract ourselves by turning our focus outside, things quickly become as distorted as a carnival hall of mirrors. As we do this work, it's crucial that we pledge to keep the focus on our own work and our own process. If you find yourself becoming reactive when somebody mentions incidents unfolding in their life, if you feel deep sympathy and just want to jump in and do something about it, then it's time to step back, take some time, and turn the focus back on yourself. Ask yourself, "Why is this yanking my chain? Why am I feeling so strongly about this? What it is about me that's bringing these feelings up?"

I pledge that when I need help, I will ask for it clearly and directly.

This may sound like an easy one, but I can tell you from personal experience that learning how to recognize when we need help can take years. Knowing what we need specifically takes time to figure out. At first, it may simply be, "I need help to figure out what I need." As long as you ask for it as clearly and directly as you're able, that's a great place to start.

I pledge to refrain from intervening with unsolicited help for others. I will always seek consent before I provide any support.

If they haven't given consent, it's none of your business when someone decides they want to go down the rabbit hole. A caveat: if they're going down the rabbit hole and dragging a lot of people with them, there may come a point at which intervention is necessary. In such cases you can say, "Your behavior is unacceptable. I won't tolerate it. There are consequences for what you do," and hold them to those consequences. Aside from such extreme cases, if somebody doesn't want your help, *don't give it*. As empaths, our job is to serve those who are ready and willing to accept our help.

I pledge to honor confidentiality in all my relations. I shall only share another's story with their explicit permission.

As stated in the privacy section above, if it's not your story and you don't have permission to share that story, then you may only share what you've learned from your personal perspective. It is not your right to share anyone else's details. When talking about something that involves someone else's experience, you must get their permission to tell anything other than your own part of the story. This goes back to keeping the focus on yourself and your own work. When you share a story, share it from your own experience. Share it from what you've learned or discovered; *never* share any revealing details.

I pledge to show up to the best of my ability and to do the best I can. I acknowledge that I am accountable to myself, my community, and my Higher Power.

We do the best we can, understanding that we are responsible for our choices, our actions, and their impact upon others. It is not up to anyone else to hold us accountable. It is nobody else's responsibility to call us out on our shit or to track us on our words and actions unless we have specifically requested that they do so. It is up to us to request accountability from others.

Name: _____

Date: _____

Here we are at the end of this book. I'm so glad you've stayed with me to reach these final pages. I hope you are feeling happier, healthier, and lighter. My wish is that you've discovered a greater capacity to shine and to show up for the unique mission you were born to fulfill. If you have found value in this book, please help to spread the word and get this into the hands of the people who need it by posting an open and honest review on Amazon.

This is your life, and you were born this way for a reason. It's my sincerest desire that you leave these pages understanding your empathic nature in a new way.

End

Resources

Additional Support for You *(includes additional bonus content, EFT tutorials, audio recordings and more)* http://EmpathicSafety.com

Al-Anon http://al-anon.org

Alcoholic Anonymous http://www.aa.org

Bach, Richard, *Illusions : The Adventures of a Reluctant Messiah* (Dell, New York, NY; 1989)

Bilazarian, Robin, *Tapping the Mighty Mind: Simple Solutions for Stress, Conflict, and Pain* (CreateSpace Independent Publishing Platform; 2018)

Blakeslee, Sandra, "Cells That Read Minds" January. 10, 2006, https://www.nytimes.com/2006/01/10/science/cells-that-read-minds.html

Boston Fire Historical Society, "The Story of the Cocoanut Grove Fire," https://bostonfirehistory.org/the-story-of-the-cocoanut-grove-fire/

Brown, Brené, *Braving the Wilderness: The Quest for True Belonging and the Courage to Stand Alone* (Random House, New York, NY; 2017)

Brown, Brené, *Netflix Original Brené Brown: The Call To Courage* https://www.netflix.com/title/81010166

Bruner, Pamela & Bullough, John, *EFT and Beyond: Cutting Edge Techniques for Personal Transformation* (Energy Publications Ltd; 2009)

Callaway, Ewen, "Fearful Memories Passed Down to Mouse Descendants," *Scientific American*, December 1, 2013, https://www.scientificamerican.com/article/fearful-memories-passed-down/

Co-dependent's Anonymous http://coda.org

Doyle, Glennon, *Love Warrior: A Memoir* (Flatiron Books, New York, NY; 2017)

Duffield-Thomas, Denise, *Chillpreneur: The New Rules for Creating Success, Freedom, and Abundance on Your Terms* (Hay House UK, London; 2019)

EFT International Trainings, https://eftinternational.org/eft-training/

EFT International, The Science and Research Behind EFT Tapping https://eftinternational.org/discover-eft-tapping/eft-science-research/

Emoto, Masaru, *The Hidden Messages in Water* (Atria Books, New York, NY; 2005)

Ferraro, Kris, *Energy Healing: Simple and Effective Practices to Become Your Own Healer (A Start Here Guide)* St. Martin's Essentials, New York, NY; 2019)

Forleo, Marie *Everything Is Figureoutable* (Portfolio, New York, NY; 2019)

Frankl, Viktor E., *Man's Search for Meaning* (Beacon Press, Boston MA; 2006 *first published 1946)*

Gawain, Shakti, *Creative Visualization: Use the Power of Your Imagination to Create What You Want in Your Life 40th Anniversary Edition* (New World Library, Novato, California; 2016)

Gilbert, Elizabeth, *Big Magic: Creative Living Beyond Fear* (Riverhead Books, New York, NY; 2015)

Go Cognitive, "Giacomo Rizzolatti - Mirror Neurons" http://gocognitive.net/interviews/giacomo-rizzolatti-mirror-neurons

Grout, Pam, *E-Squared: Nine Do-It-Yourself Energy Experiments That Prove Your Thoughts Create Your Reality* (Hay House, Carlsbad, CA; 2013)

Hay, Louise, *You Can Heal Your Life* (Hay House, Carlsbad, CA; 1984)

Heiman, Rev. Terri Ann, *Confessions of a Shower Tapper: The Ultimate Guide to Living Your Purpose with EFT* (Natural Forces Studio, Birmingham, AL; 2015)

Katie, Byron, *Loving What Is: Four Questions That Can Change Your Life* (Three Rivers Press, New York, NY; 2003)

Kingston, Karen, *Creating Sacred Space With Feng Shui: Learn the Art of Space Clearing and Bring New Energy into Your Life* (Harmony, New York, NY; 1997)

Kondo, Marie, *The Life-Changing Magic of Tidying Up: The Japanese Art of Decluttering and Organizing* (Ten Speed Press, Berkeley, CA; 2014)

Little Buddha. Directed by Bernardo Bertolucci. Performances by Keanu Reeves, Bridget Fonda, and Ruocheng Ying. Recorded Picture Company, 1993.

Lynn, Christopher, "Hearth and campfire influences on arterial blood pressure: defraying the costs of the social brain through fireside relaxation," November 11, 2014, https://www.ncbi.nlm.nih.gov/pubmed/25387270

Markova, Dawna, Ph.D, *The Art of the Possible: A Compassionate Approach to Understanding the Way People Think, Learn and Communicate* (Red Wheel/Weiser, Newburyport, MA; 1991)

Maté, Gabor, MD, *In the Realm of Hungry Ghosts: Close Encounters with Addiction* (North Atlantic Books, Berkeley, CA; 2010)

Melody, *Love Is in the Earth: A Kaleidoscope of Crystals: The Reference Book Describing the Metaphysical Properties of the Mineral Kingdom* (Earth Love Publishing House, Wheat Ridge, CO; 3rd edition 1995)

Miserandino, Christine, "The Spoon Theory," https://butyoudontlooksick.com/articles/written-by-christine/the-spoon-theory/

Moore, Jennifer, *Empathic Mastery Oracle Deck*, http://EmpathicMasteryOracle.com

National Domestic Violence Hotline, https://www.thehotline.org

National Suicide Prevention Lifeline, https://suicidepreventionlifeline.org

Ortner, Nick, *The Tapping Solution: A Revolutionary System for Stress-Free Living* (Hay House, Carlsbad, CA; 2014)

Ortner, Nick, *The Tapping Solution for Pain Relief: A Step-by-Step Guide to Reducing and Eliminating Chronic Pain (Hay House, Carlsbad, CA; 2015)*

Overeaters Anonymous https://oa.org

Point of No Return. Directed by John Badham. Performances by Bridget Fonda, Gabriel Byrne, and Dermot Mulroney. Warner Bros, 1993.

Ponder, Catherine, *The Dynamic Laws of Prosperity* (DeVorss & Company, Camarillo, CA; 1985)

Ray, Sondra & Mandel, Bob, *Birth and Relationships: How Your Birth Affects Your Relationships* (Celestial Arts Berkeley, CA; 1987)

Roth, Gabrielle, *Sweat Your Prayers: The Five Rhythms of the Soul - Movement as Spiritual Practice* (TarcherPerigee, New York, NY; 1998)

Roth, Gabrielle and John Loudon, *Maps to Ecstasy: Teachings of an Urban Shaman* (New World Library, Novato, CA; 1989)

Rowling, J.K., *Harry Potter and the Sorcerer's Stone* (Bloomsbury, London, UK; 1997)

Ruiz, Don Miguel, *The Four Agreements: A Practical Guide to Personal Freedom* (Amber-Allen Publishing, San Rafael, CA; 1997)

Shinn, Florence Scovel, *The Game of Life and How to Play It* (CreateSpace, Scotts Valley, CA; 2013)

Silver, Tosha, *It's Not Your Money: How to Live Fully from Divine Abundance* (Hay House, Carlsbad, CA; 2019)

Silver, Tosha, *Change Me Prayers: The Hidden Power of Spiritual Surrender* (Atria Books, New York, NY; 2018)

Stapleton, Peta, *The Science Behind Tapping: A Proven Stress Management Technique for the Mind and Body* (Hay House, Carlsbad, CA; 2019)

Starhawk, *The Fifth Sacred Thing* (Bantam Books, New York, NY; 1993)

Teish, Luisah, *Jambalaya: The Natural Woman's Book of Personal Charms and Practical Rituals* (HarperOne, San Francisco, CA; 1988)

Thomson, Helen, "Study of Holocaust survivors finds trauma passed on to children's genes," The Guardian, August 21, 2015, https://www.theguardian.com/science/2015/aug/21/study-of-holocaust-survivors-finds-trauma-passed-on-to-childrens-genes

The Trevor Project: Saving Young LGBTQ Lives, https://www.thetrevorproject.org

Watson, Lyall, *Lifetide: a Biology of the Unconscious* (Hodder and Stoughton, London, UK; 1979)

Wolynn, Mark, *It Didn't Start with You: How Inherited Family Trauma Shapes Who We Are and How to End the Cycle* (Viking, New York, NY; 2016)

Acknowledgements

How does one even begin to express the gratitude and appreciation for all the hearts, hands, eyes and spirits that help to bring a book into the world? It has definitely taken a village. Words barely convey the fullness of my heart as I write the following acknowledgements. So in no particular order I give

MY BIGGEST THANKS TO:

My husband David for all the love and persistent encouragement, the countless loads of laundry, for participating as one of the few or often the only male in the sacred circle, and for enduring many a late-night conversation well after our brains were toast.

The Empathic Sisterhood for their willingness to sit through many hours of teaching as I spoke the initial content into reality and for all the ongoing conversations (all my love to Andrea P, Arly S, Britt B, Carrie K, Chase Y, Jess A, Kate S, Kim C, Linda H, Marteen S, the Melissas B, C, L & R, Monica Z, Nancy H & Ronit H).

Marteen Santerre for providing the gorgeous workshop space where this book was born. For being one of the first people to grasp and understand my mission and for working tirelessly to spread the message of spiritual healing in this world.

ALL of my students and clients. Over many years I've learned more from their candor, willingness, and trust than any book, course, or retreat could ever teach me. This book could not possibly exist if it weren't for their incredible courage, honesty, and persistence.

All the amazing people who've asked questions, shared their stories, and poured out their hearts via social media. My biggest thanks to those who take their valuable time to watch FB lives, to stay up past their bedtime, and who keep showing up and helping me to spread the word.

Diana M. Needham, my book shepherd, for holding the vision of this book from the start, for helping me to articulate my BIG WHY, and for explaining and managing the million details that went into making this book a reality.

Emily Cooper for transcribing hours of lecture and question & answer sessions into the written words that created the foundation of this book.

Michelle Dionne Thompson for helping me to hammer out the basic flow and initial outline, for being the first one to comb through the transcripts, for all the feedback that helped to make this the book it is today, and for offering clear, doable suggestions as one of my beta readers.

Nikki Starcat Shields, my book midwife, for accepting the Herculean task of content editing and cobbling all the major sections together. Words hardly convey my appreciation for the steady support and consistent check-ins that kept me on track, and my biggest gratitude for the loving hand that pulled me back up when I'd fall off the writing wagon.

Amy Anderson, my grammar surgeon, for following after me and picking up all the extra *thats, ands* and *in my experiences.* My gratitude for making this book unapologetic and clear, and for countless conversations over the years and being the ears when I need to sort nearly anything out.

Arly Scully for holding the vision from the very beginning, for encouraging me to keep going, for being a beta reader, and especially for taking the nearly final draft and chipping off any superfluous, distracting, or irrelevant last bits.

Chase Young, Joshua Brown, Kathy Courchene, Lucretia Hatfield, Maggie Knowles & Melissa Beasley for being my additional beta readers. I can hardly begin to express my gratitude for all the priceless feedback and suggestions that helped to make this book more accessible and understandable.

Shannon Plummer for sharing so much nutritional wisdom and helping me to fine-tune my message about the problem with sugar.

Britt Bolnick for countless conversations, hours of visioning, clarifying and goal setting BUT most of all for loving me and believing in me from the get-go.

Pamela Bruner for the Divine Downloads, the superhero tapping, the strategic wisdom and practical guidance, and for igniting the Empathic Woman spark and drawing out the essence of this work before I even had the words to explain it.

Ingrid Dinter for giving me a solid & detailed EFT foundation, for sharing devotion and love of tapping with our group, for encouraging all of us to tap together even as beginners, and for holding such impeccable standards for certification and mentorship.

Jade Barbee for elevating my understanding of EFT and handing me the map to navigate through the darkest forests, thickest brambles, and deepest emotional depths. For all the generosity and sharing such a gentle approach to tapping, for the hours of mentoring, conversation, education and supervision, for confidence in me as a trainer and enthusiasm in handing me the torch.

Jondi Whitis for the wisdom, generosity, and inspiration, for the chance to witness and learn from such a skilled Master trainer of trainers. For all the selfless devotion to energy healing and EFT, including but not limited to Spring Energy Event. For initiating and nurturing a rich and precious community where the rest of us can flourish.

Gene Monterastelli for all the tapping that got me past the hurdles, beyond my overwhelm, and able to do the next right thing, for all the strategic coaching, tips, tools, and just plain good advice. AND for answering the call to spread the Gospel of Tapping and helping to make EFT more available in this world.

Barbara Belmont for being my tapping partner and for being willing to dive deep into anything I brought to the table, for being game to be my guinea pig for every experiment, new modality or nuanced technique, for all the love, acceptance, and unconditional kindness.

Lucie Monroe for lighting the torch and holding it high here in New England. For the devotion to tapping and growing the Alternative Healing Alliance and for offering a place to experiment, explore, and share what I love with others.

Kris Ferraro, my sister in book birthing, for going ahead of me and giving me the chance to witness and support the birth of a book, and for all the support, faith, and authenticity offered. My biggest love and appreciation for the raw, real, *tell it like it is* badass that you are.

Kari Mitchell for the energy and healing support that kept me aloft through Lyme flare-ups, visibility hangovers, upper-limit emergency brake pulling, and for understanding my work and entrusting me with your dreams and truth as well as nurturing mine.

The Surrogate Sisterhood (Beth S, Cynthia J, Donna M, Kelly R, Kris F, Laura G & Lucie M) for having my back, for all the generous support, and for sharing EFT miracles that strengthen my daily resolve to spread the message about this remarkable technique.

Gillian Windsor for our weekly Monday afternoon calls that kept me on track, for the support to keep my eye on the prize, for sorting through the details and cautioning me when I was biting off more than I could chew.

Melissa Beasley for your candor, for sharing your faith journey with me, and your unflinching devotion to the Holy Spirit. BIG gratitude for witnessing my brain dumps and helping me to make sense of more ideas than I can accomplish in a lifetime.

Elaine Monterastelli for understanding my vision for the Empathic Woman from the get-go, and for all your encouragement and clarity.

Amanda Lopes for your love, support, and always being in my corner. A special shout-out for all of our conversations about systems, delegation, and showing me there's an even better way to run a business. Thank you for sharing your knowledge, for connecting me with the best team members, and for being you.

Chase Young for sharing your platform so generously, for knowing the posts, memes and videos that delight and interest me, for helping me to spread my message in this world and keeping my social media on point.

Lisa Presley for knowing what I need often before I do myself, for juggling all the moving parts and making my life so much easier. Thank you for sharing your magic, helping me to stay in the flow, and for all the love and devotion you bring to the Empathic Empire.

Patrick Landers and the Mindful Building Team for taking my dream and making it a reality. Thank you for building the Ark and offering safe sacred space to carry us through turbulent times. Thank you for creating with such impeccable grace. Thank you for carrying my vision and literally building the place for me to land after taking my greatest leaps of faith.

Shelley Swift for being the GODDESS of decluttering, for showing up exactly when I needed you, and for helping me to uplevel and create the sacred space of my dreams. You meet me in my mess and you guide me through it. For your tireless persistence, humor and willingness to do all the things, THANK YOU

Pam Adams for keeping my world greebly-free and degunkifying the ick, both psychic and pug related.

Jen Dean for literally seeing me and expressing my inner truth with your camera lens. For creating a space where I can be myself and for your support and enthusiasm for Empathic Mastery.

Anna Pereria for your warmth, enthusiasm, and encouragement. My biggest appreciation for the ease you bring to our collaboration and for going above and beyond in helping me to share my message with other Empathic Entrepreneurs. Thank you for all the ways you spread the light and carry the torch for lightworkers, healers, and other sensitive souls.

Nicole Whitney for listening to Spirit and welcoming me into your tribe, for offering a soapbox for my message of Empathic Mastery, and for boosting the signal so it can spread far and wide.

To my beloved soul sister Melissa Landers and her precious family, so much love for being with me through many lifetimes and finding your way to my heart in this one. For all the meals, walks, talks, pilgrimages & adventures and for confirming all the times we receive the same download simultaneously.

And finally my deepest appreciation to AL, AP, AS, BB, BM, CB, CY, DN, ED, GA, GR, JA, JB, JC, JG, JL, KC, KM, KV, LH, MB, ML, MR, MS, MZ, NS, PT, RH, SB, SS, SW, TC, TG & VA.

About the Author

Former Hot Mess and World Class *Awfulizer*, Jennifer Moore is a mentor and teacher for sensitive, intuitive women. Born from long lines of high-strung people, Jen (as her family and friends call her) spent the first thirty years of her life struggling to control fear and emotional overwhelm.

This constant white-knuckling left Jen exhausted, anxious and over-medicated. Out of sheer desperation she surrendered to embracing professional support, self-help programs and personal recovery. The relief Jen felt was life changing. This inspired her to develop her own professional skills and share what she learned with others who suffer too. Today Jen stays (mostly) calm, centered and compassionate even while the chaos and intensity heats up on this planet.

With well over thirty years of professional experience, a Master's degree in Psychology & Religion and the distinct honor of being one of EFT International's 18 accredited Master Trainers in the United States, Jennifer brings depth, compassion and wisdom to her work helping empathic women.

Jennifer lives in coastal Maine surrounded by flowers, herbs and elderberry bushes. She shares this green (though sometimes snow covered) paradise with her husband David, Bob the pug, Lyra the Maine coon cat and George the groundhog who's taken up residence beneath their deck. Find her at www.ModernMedicineLady.com and follow her on Social Media for the latest news.

A Special Gift for You

Now that you've read Empathic Mastery, I imagine you're well on your way to feeling calm, confident and centered, even in the midst of chaos. It's my sincere hope that you've been discovering new ways to understand and utilize your empathic nature so that it can serve you and those you love.

I created an additional gift for you to add to your tool kit. It's the Empathic Safety Kit. It's packed with additional content including audio recordings of the Earth Sky Meditation and the Body Scan, tapping videos and more resources that will support you in taking your work to the next level.

While the Empathic Safety Kit is offered for sale, as a special bonus you can claim it for free at:

EmpathicSafety.com

The sooner you learn to manage your sensitivity, the easier it becomes to be a channel for peace and healing even in the eye of the storm. I'm in your corner. Please feel free to reach out and let me know if I can help further. Here's to your Empathic Mastery!

xoxo Se

With Love and Brightest Blessings,

Made in the USA
Las Vegas, NV
09 September 2022

54997820R00213